W9-BWB-475

FROM LUTHER TO TILLICH

From Luther to Tillich

The Reformers and Their Heirs

WILHELM PAUCK

Edited by Marion Pauck

1817

Harper & Row, Publishers, San Francisco
Cambridge, Hagerstown, New York, Philadelphia
London, Mexico City, São Paulo, Singapore, Sydney

Credits begin on page 216

FIRST EDITION

Designer: Jim Mennick

Library of Congress Cataloging in Publication Data

Pauck, Wilhelm, 1901-1981
  FROM LUTHER TO TILLICH.

  Bibliography: p.
  Includes index.
  1. Theology, Doctrinal—History—Addresses, essays, lectures. 2. Theologians—Addresses, essays, lectures. 3. Pauck, Wilhelm, 1901-1981—Addresses, essays, lectures.
  I. Pauck, Marion. II. Title.
  BT21.2.P35 1984   230'.044'09   84-48229
  ISBN 0-06-066475-4

84 85 86 87 88   10 9 8 7 6 5 4 3 2 1

Contents

History is the legacy of past generations which each new generation must appropriate for itself. This means that we "have" only as much history as we are able to make our own. We possess only as much civilization as we are able to appropriate for ourselves by means of historical decisions.

WILHELM PAUCK, *The Meaning of History*

Preface

This book of enduring essays by the historical theologian Wilhelm Pauck (1901–1981) reflects the wide range of pivotal figures in Protestant thought who claimed his passionate attention and critical interest. In his eloquent introduction, Jaroslav Pelikan delineates the shape of Pauck's scholarly work as that of "an ellipse with one focus in the Reformation and the other in the modern critical temper." The chapters in this book sharpen that double focus.

The fact that Wilhelm Pauck's name was primarily linked with that of Martin Luther and the Reformation is almost a cliché. Innumerable scholars have pointed out that, as mediator of the grand tradition of historical and theological scholarship in which he had been trained in his native Germany, Pauck indelibly shaped Luther studies in this country. What has been less widely recognized and discussed is the fact that he was also a keen analyst of modern thought beginning with the work of Schleiermacher and ending with Barth and Tillich. For this reason we have placed more than equal emphasis on the second half of Pelikan's equation by including four chapters on the Reformers and six on their heirs.

The essays in this book were written over a period of 50 years at different times and for different purposes, yet they form a consistent and unified whole. They demonstrate their author's constant interest in the nature of the Christian faith and its implications for contemporary understanding. They are a blend of historical description, informed criticism, and tender compassion by one whom James Luther Adams has described as an "observer of men and events who possessed a special aptitude for the significant event or the illuminating aphorism."*

In ten portraits drawn with characteristic sparseness of words,

---

*J. L. Adams in his book review of W. Pauck, "Harnack and Troeltsch," in *Union Seminary Quarterly Review,* Vol. XXIII (1968): p. 402.

Pauck takes us from Luther's biblical faith through the entwined lives and ideas of his contemporaries Butzer, Calvin, and Melanchthon. Then, leaping over the Protestant Scholastics, for whom he had little sympathy, he introduces the reader to the heirs of the Reformation, who were forced to come to terms with modern science and the historical method. At the beginning, Luther speaks to us about biblical faith and the terrifying reality of God; at the end, Tillich raises disturbing questions about the Bible and the Christian faith. Throughout this period of 500 years, two major themes—the tensions between biblical Christianity and humanism on the one hand, and between biblical faith and historical criticism on the other—are sounded.

Pauck's unique way of transmitting the history of Christian thought was through discussion not only of the exterior but especially the interior forces of that history. He believed that the historian's craft finally rests upon *Sehnsucht* (yearning or nostalgia) and a peculiar piety toward the dead rather than upon the unearthing of dry facts. He himself relished nothing more than giving speech back to voices fallen silent. Once, after he lectured on Schleiermacher, students in his class were sure that they had been listening to Pauck expound his own position. They applauded and stamped their feet. But as Pauck walked to the door, he put his hand on the knob, waggled his finger at the whole class, and exclaimed, "But it isn't so!"*

In this gallery of portraits so replete with anecdote, Pauck's own voice is heard only contrapuntally. He was a reserved, private man who rarely spoke about his inner life. The attentive reader will hear occasional echoes nonetheless. In the chapters on Ernst Troeltsch and Karl Holl, we meet the two men who exercised the most decisive influence upon Pauck's intellectual development. In these pages, written with affection and criticism, we come face to face with an only slightly veiled *apologia pro vita sua*. Pauck's synthesis of his teachers' legacy to suit the American scene and occasion, might be described as one of his own unique achievements.

Like Ernst Troeltsch, Wilhelm Pauck was both "a skeptic and a

---

*In a letter dated 11 September 1981, Joseph Sittler related this anecdote to me. The chronology of Pauck's life and work at the end of the book will asssist the reader.

believer; simultaneously analytical and constructive; in need of faith and thirsty for life."* These are characteristics which he also shared with his older colleague and friend Paul Tillich, about whom he writes in the final chapter of this book.

A special word about this chapter is in order. It represents the first third of the unfinished second volume of our biography of Paul Tillich on which Pauck was working during the last years of his life. Although this chapter is primarily about the young Tillich, much that Pauck writes here applies also to Tillich in his mature years. It was Pauck's unchanging conviction—one which he held from the 1940s onward—that Tillich formulated his major ideas early in life and that everything following represented development, refinement, elaboration, or even a footnote to the original statement. It was Pauck's intention not merely to summarize Tillich's position as so many others had done, but to analyze the development of his thought. Pauck writes,

I intend to show that Tillich's thinking developed out of the encounter of his extraordinarily sharp, analytic, and constructive mind with the religious and cultural movements of his own time. Throughout, I direct special attention to Tillich's relation with thinkers of the past and present in order to demonstrate how, throughout his career, he held steadfastly to the position he had assumed in dependence upon his Lutheran heritage and his early training in the philosophy of German idealism. Tillich constantly modified and enriched this position through critical analysis of the major movements of his era, namely dialectical theology and existentialist philosophy, Marxian socialism and expressionist art. As a theologian, Tillich inherited the mediating theology of his teacher Martin Kähler and opposed the neo-orthodoxy of Karl Barth. As a philosopher, he is characterized as a congenial and total pupil of F. W. J. Schelling, who, next to Fichte and Hegel, was the most imaginative of the German idealists. As one of the chief advocates of religious socialism, he is described as an ally of Reinhold Niebuhr, and as a spokesman of a theocentric and radical Protestantism. As one of the foremost spokesmen of existentialism, he is aligned with Jaspers and Heidegger and at the same time put in opposition to them. As a Protestant theologian, he resembles Rudolf Bultmann, yet is set apart from him by his advocacy of the deliteralizing rather than the demythologizing of religious-theological language. In connection with these analytical

---

*W. Pauck, *Harnack and Troeltsch: Two Historical Theologians* (New York: Oxford University Press, 1968), p. 50.

comparisons, I attempt to clarify the origin and the development of the philosophical-theological achievements that have come to be most closely identified with Tillich's name: (1) the construction of a Christian theological system by means of "the method of correlation" in which the symbols used in the Christian message answer questions arising from an analysis of the human situation; and (2) the formulation of a "theology of culture" in which religion is interpreted as the substance of culture and culture as the form of religion.*

Pauck's death in 1981 intervened before this grand plan, which might have been an introduction to the history of theology in this century, could be completed. The long chapter published here, as well as extensive notes and outlines representing the arduous labor of many years, survive. Many inner and outer factors joined to prevent the synthesis of Pauck's work. His perfectionism, his systematic, unhurried way of preparing himself, his deliberate, tightly woven writing style (his first draft was always his final draft!), as well as a continuing inner struggle with Tillich's point of view, converged at a time when illness and old age were taking their toll. Pauck's admiration for Tillich's creative genius and his serious reservations about Tillich's philosophical theology (Tillich's obscure language and his reliance on Schelling gave Pauck pause) had been part and parcel of their lifelong association. In public debate and private conversation, Pauck's appreciation and apprehension to which Tillich responded with alacrity, had enlivened but never endangered their friendship. Indeed no one relished these stimulating exchanges more than Tillich himself.

How Pauck's inner conflict would have been resolved had he not run out of time is a matter for speculation. The chapter he has left us is mellow, sovereign, even distant. The tragic fact that Pauck did not finish this book may also be seen as a triumph of the spirit that refused to compromise scholarly standards either to the pressures of time or to the volatile climate surrounding contemporary Tillich research. Despite his grave illness, Pauck remained absorbed in work on this volume even in his last days. Such intensity was surely one of the factors which sustained his life beyond expectation.

---

*The original handwritten manuscript is in my possession.

When Wilhelm Pauck sensed that his life was drawing to a close, he and I discussed the possiblity of publishing a collection of his enduring essays. After his death, I continued these discussions with interested scholars and friends, who unanimously agreed that the most creative solution to the problem would be to publish the chapter on Tillich in a book of portraits of theologians and historians suggested by Pauck. In so doing, we feel that Wilhelm Pauck's labors have not been in vain, and that Tillich's work has been set in a broad historical context. Except for minor stylistic changes, the chapter published here is unaltered from the handwritten manuscript in my possession.

I wish now to express my gratitude to those who helped me bring this work to a conclusion: Robert Lynn, Vice-President of Religion, The Lilly Endowment, Inc., whose grant enabled me to do some research at the Paul Tillich Archive in Cambridge, Mass.; Mrs. Maria Grossmann, Librarian, Andover Theological Library, Harvard University, Cambridge, Mass.; Jack Forstman, Dean of the Vanderbilt University Divinity School, Nashville, Tn., who acted as trustee for the Lilly grant during my husband's lifetime; Claude Welch, Dean of the Graduate Theological Union, Berkeley, Ca., who acted as trustee for the Lilly grant after my husband's death; June Hunt, Business Manager of GTU; and Otto Büsch, chairman of *Die Historische Kommission zu Berlin,* whose stipend enabled my husband and me to spend the summer of 1976 in Berlin. The chapter on Paul Tillich is enriched by research done at that time.

Many faithful friends have participated in the making of this book: James Luther Adams, Robert McAfee Brown, the late William A. Clebsch, Brian Gerrish, Carl Hester, Paul L. Lehmann, David W. Lotz (who provided the sub-title for this book), Charles M. Nielsen, Jaroslav J. Pelikan (who gave his gracious permission to use a slightly edited version of his *Wilhelm Pauck: A Tribute* as the introduction to this book), and Lou H. Silberman. I am deeply grateful to them all.

I wish also to thank Mrs. Hannah Tillich and Robert Kimball, Tillich's literary executors, for granting their permission to quote from Paul Tillich's unpublished papers. Finally, I salute my friends at Harper & Row, especially Clayton Carlson and Dorian Gossy, for their patience, expertise, and support.

A month before my husband's 8oth birthday the American Society of Church History held a special session in his honor. In expressing his gratitude for the occasion, which he was unable to attend on account of illness, he wrote:

All that I have advocated in the course of my career has been designed to emphasize ideas and enterprises which can be understood only if they are expressions which reflect the nature of the church as a communion of believers. In advocating this I am aware of my desire to keep the heritage of the Reformation alive.*

May this book play a role in preserving and extending Wilhelm Pauck's legacy. May his students, past and future, "regretfully go against him or joyfully with him as one still alive, and still abundantly enlivening in our present midst."*

MARION PAUCK
Literary Execurix of the
Wilhelm Pauck Estate
Palo Alto, California
4 July 1984

---

*Letter from Wilhelm Pauck to Dale Johnson, chairman of the session. Dated 24 January 1981.
*Baron F. von Hügel, "Introduction", von Hügel, ed., E. Troeltsch, *Christian Thought: Its History and Application* (New York: Meridian Books, 1957), p. 32.

Introduction
Wilhelm Pauck: A Tribute

JAROSLAV PELIKAN

"Vos pauci estis superiores":[1] These words of Luther's lectures on 1 John (albeit in an eighteenth-century edition) express the eschatological consolation of the church as a little flock; and in the American edition we have therefore translated them: "You, who are few in number, are superior."[2]

Yet by a kind of tropological exegesis, which Luther rejected in principle but could never bring himself to give up in practice, these Latin words could be translated, or perhaps paraphrased: "You who are students of Pauck have a definite advantage." Philologically indefensible though such a translation may be in the light of Luther's own *Sendbrief vom Dolmetschen* of 1530, it does express the respect and gratitude which *"nos Pauci,"* speaking for many hundreds of their fellow students and colleagues, bear for Professor Wilhelm Pauck.

To his students over a period of five decades Whilhelm Pauck was the teacher we have all striven to emulate and, for that matter, have sometimes presumed to imitate; the devastating critic who never lacked the grace of a twinkle in his eye; the platform virtuoso who lived himself into the person and thought of the great figures in historical theology so convincingly that many of us must still make a conscious effort to avoid supposing that Luther's favorite gesture was a nervous fingering of the lower lip or that Schleiermacher always mumbled silently for a moment before tossing off an epigram. Many of Professor Pauck's phrases have become our own phrases, which we now hear our students repeat—and, as often as not, attribute to us. Thus, in one of those Pauckian phrases, he was our professor once, but he is our teacher still.

Nevertheless, it would be both a mistake for us and an embarrassment for him if we were to dwell on the personal aspects of his thought and teaching. Indeed, one of the most precious lessons he taught us, primarily by indirection and example, is to temper our admiration of any charismatic *Geist*, past or present, with a hard-nosed assessment of the objective situation. Chastened romatic that he was, Professor Pauck neither permitted his historical imagination to obscure his identification with "modern man" nor so absolutized modernity as to render the history of Christian dogma incomprehensible. This combination of perspectives—or, to employ a phrase that used to be his before theological faddism wore it out, this "creative tension"—shaped his role in American scholarship.

Perhaps the best way to summarize Wilhelm Pauck's vocation is to say that he kept theologians historically aware and historians theologically responsible. Having maintained for many years that "the major trend of contemporary theological thought is marked by a blindness to . . . [the] insistence that Christianity must be understood as a historical movement and that it must be interpreted by the historical method,"[3] he sought to make this insistence an unavoidable element in the theological work, not only of his own students, but of his colleagues as well. That historical "blindness," significantly, was a disease affecting theological schools that otherwise diverged widely in their methods and conclusions. What Dr. Pauck called "radical theological liberalism" was marked by the attempt to "subject the historical faiths to an examination on the basis of norms which are derived from the sciences or inspired by scientific philosophy," but it seemed to him that "in the light of the history of Christianity, [its] prospects appear questionable."[4] For although this philosophical theology could not have arisen except in the wake of the radical historical criticism of the Christian tradition, its own historical sophistication was insufficient to support its theological program. The antidote to theological liberalism proposed during the past generation has been no more richly endowed with historic sophistication; for it "says that church history is merely an auxiliary theological discipline." This ahistorical bias made it blind to the actual theological predicament, namely, that "what we need most is historical understanding and not theosophy."[5] One of Wilhelm Pauck's primary tasks was to demand that theologians, regardless of denomination or party or "school," take history seriously.

He was no less insistent, though considerably less explicit, in his demand that church historians remain theologically responsible. His programmatic declaration of allegiance to the work of Adolf von Harnack was "interested not primarily in Harnack's contribution to church historical knowledge but in his conception and interpretation of Christianity as an historical phenomenon."[6] For Professor Pauck, the "conflict between these three principles [theonomy, autonomy, and heteronomy] was the most interesting aspect of the history of religion."[7] Its implication is that Protestantism "must avoid a resuscitation of antiquated theological and ecclesiastical heteronomies as well as a reliance upon secular autonomies."[8] Thus it was not the historical investigation for its own sake (if, indeed, there is such a thing), but the historical as a resource for the theological that finally claimed his interest and loyalty. In a critique of Harnack delivered in 1939, Professor Pauck spoke out against a historicizing of the doctrine of the Trinity which would explain it "in such a way that it appears merely as the expression of the historical effort of ancient Christians to interpret their faith in terms of the philosophy of their civilization," for this would overlook "the permanent Christian concern around which [the controversies over the Trinity] arose."[9] Although the primary danger, as he saw it, has come from a theology that was not historically aware he refused to go to the opposite extreme of a church history that was theologically irresponsible.

In keeping with this dual commitment, Professor Pauck was one of the first to call the theology of Karl Barth to the attention of the English-speaking world; but he also consistently affirmed the abiding validity of the liberalism against which Barth protested. When *Karl Barth—Prophet of a New Christianity?* was published in 1931, very little of Barth was known in this country. *The Word of God and the Word of Man* had been translated by Douglas Horton and published in 1928, but it was not until 1933 that the English translation of Barth's *Römerbrief* appeared. Placing Barth's work into the context of the development of Protestant theology during the preceding century, Pauck's monograph probed the deeper meaning behind the Barthian protest against liberalism. He recognized the power of the new emphasis upon the distinctiveness of biblical language, and he acknowledged the validity of Barth's attack upon the easy optimism of a *Kultur-protestantismus*.[10] Nevertheless, Wilhelm Pauck could never be a party-line Barthian; for, as he asserted in the conclusion of his examination of Barth, "we cannot go back behind Troeltsch, Harnack, Ritschl, and Schleiermacher. We can only go beyond them."[11]

The commitment to the validity of liberalism as a critique of the orthodox tradition, if anything, became stronger in the course of Professor Pauck's development. In part, this may well be due to the theological ambience of the 1950s and 1960s, when the historical insights of liberalism were being bypassed in the name of a repristination of Reformation theology. By 1935 he had already stated his position:

We do not separate ourselves from the movement of liberalism. We clearly accept the liberation from arbitrary historical or traditional authority which it has achieved. We do our thinking on the basis of the liberal protest against heteronomous authority. We refuse to submit to the decrees of councils and popes, creed-makers, and self-appointed guardians of orthodoxy as we should refuse to consider the validity of the claim of one who should today rise and declare that by the grace of God he had obtained the right to rule over us.[12]

A decade or so later he had to remind those who cheered the rise of a neo-Reformation theology that "the 'Luther Renaissance' and the 'Calvin Renaissance' are the direct results of the preoccupation of historically minded liberal theologians with the Reformation."[13] And yet another decade later he delivered a critique of the *Church Dogmatics* that was all the more scathing because of his obvious admiration for Karl Barth as a theological mind.[14] Never one to repeat a cliché either in word or in deed, Pauck in some ways became less conservative rather than more conservative as he grew older. It would perhaps be more accurate to say that as, in the name of liberalism, he protested against some of the superficiality being propounded by liberals, so, still in the name of liberalism, he protested against an overly facile evasion of its implications and affirmed its abiding validity as a theological method.

This refusal to follow the clichés was also evident in Professor Pauck's mediating position between his native culture and his adopted culture. Many émigré scholars, not least some from Germany, have trafficked on their exotic status and elevated it into a way of life, carefully cultivating their accents and superciliously dismissing American scholarship as shallow and derivative. If anyone had reason to assume such a pose, it was a theological professor who had listened to the lectures of the giants of German theological *Bildung*—Holl and Harnack, Seeberg and Troeltsch. His debt to these men is undoubtedly a great one, and one which he has freely acknowledged. His store of anecdotes about various scholars, especially about Adolf von Harnack, was seemingly inexhaustible, and there always seemed to be a *mot juste* for any occasion. To us, for whom these golden names tend to be either reduced to items in a bibliography or elevated beyond all realism into keepers of the flame, he served as a sympathetic but not uncritical interpreter of the heritage of Teutonic scholarship. But withal he managed to acquire not merely the trappings, but the *Geist* and the *Gefühl* of American culture, language, and life with remarkable fidelity. A lecture by Wilhelm Pauck was a pleasure not only because of the erudition he conveyed through it and the analytical insight he applied to it, but also because of the aesthetic gratification of watching a true *Sprachkünstler,* who, like Joseph Conrad or Vladimir Nabokov, was in complete control of the nuances of a language that was not his mother tongue.

Yet another way to express the subtleties of the interrelations described in these several antinomies—and in some respects, the way that comes closest to Professor Pauck's own scholarly work— is to characterize his thought, *pace* Albrecht Ritschl, as an ellipse, with one focus in the Reformation and the other in the modern critical temper. Student tradition at The University of Chicago used to present him (once, so the story goes, in a skit) "with one foot in the Reformation and the other on a banana peel." Only from today's perspective is it possible to measure what his work as a Reformation scholar meant. Despite the work of Harvey and others,[15] the English episode in the career of Martin Bucer had not been properly evaluated, leaving a lacuna both in the study of the Continental Reformation and in the research into British Protestantism. Stating a motif which he did not, alas, pursue into later history, Pauck the young historian described the relation between political reality and theocratic idealism[16]—a relation which came to play an important part both in Reformed Christianity on the Continent and in Anglicanism, Presbyterianism, and Puritanism in the British Isles. The recent critical edition of Bucer's *De regno Christi* has rightly given attention once more to the discussion of "utopianism" called forth by Pauck's *Das Reich Gottes auf Erden.*[17]

But even while his mind was on Bucer, his heart was with Luther, and it may be that some future historian will regard it as Wilhelm Pauck's most important scholarly achievement to have continued in the New World and transmitted to a new generation the interpretation of Luther and of the Reformation that had emerged from the historical and theological work of the first half of the twentieth century.[18] There is, for example, no finer presentation anywhere of Luther's religiousness than Professor Pauck's essay on "Luther's Faith," published both in German and in English.[19] It would likewise be difficult to find a more authoritative summary of Luther's early theological development than the magisterial introduction to the English translation of the *Lectures on Romans* in the "Library of Christian Classics."[20] In countless other essays and lectures—many of them, regrettably, not yet in print—this student of Karl Holl has done for American Protestantism what Holl and his colleagues had done in the Old World. He was speaking autobiographically, and not merely analyzing the impact of Karl Barth upon the American theological scene, when he exclaimed:

But Protestants, particularly those of America, are hardly able to tolerate this confrontation with Luther's teaching! They have lost the sense of the vitality of Luther's Reformation to such an extent that they continually misunderstand some of its most vital tenets.[21]

The confrontation of American Protestantism with Luther's teaching is more real today than it has ever been before, thanks largely to the work of Wilhelm Pauck.

It seems appropriate, therefore, that the volume of essays in tribute to him entitled *Interpreters of Luther*—as well as this volume of essays by him—should combine his interest in the Reformation with his attention to modern theology. Whitehead's familiar *bon mot* that "the safest general characterization of the European philosophical tradition is that it consists of a series of footnotes to Plato"[22] could certainly be matched by the observation that much of Protestant theology has been a series of footnotes to Luther, or rather a series of monographs on Luther.[23] As a result, the *Lutherbild* of a particular theologian or school of theologians is frequently a most reliable index to their understanding of the Christian faith. As the controversial Polish literary critic Jan Kott has said of Shakespeare, so we may say of Luther that he "is like the world or like life itself. Every epoch finds in him what it itself is seeking and what it itself wants to imitate."[24] Therefore a study in depth of several Reformation figures and several "modern" thinkers may illuminate the subtlety of Luther's life and thought by raising the question how each of these men could, with at least some justification, find in him what he did. It may at the same time help to interpret the development of Protestant theology since the Enlightenment, as that theology has repeatedly sought to come to terms with the heritage of the Reformation.

To tell the truth, the perspectives of the students of Wilhelm Pauck are no less diverse than are those of the "interpreters of Luther" which are analyzed in the chapters that follow. And that is in its own way the most profound possible tribute to Wilhelm Pauck as a scholar and teacher. Some of us have become more radical because of him; others of us have come to appreciate the Christian tradition as we had never seen it before; yet others have been infected with a relativism which he, at least in principle, repudiated. But all of us have learned the truth of what (if I may be permitted a personal reminiscence) he told me when, as a nineteen-year-old boy, utterly devoid of any academic degrees, I came to discuss with him the prospects of doing a Ph.D. under him: "Just remember," he said, "that you will never be the same." And we are not the same—neither the same as we were nor the same as Wilhelm Pauck. For none of us will call himself his disciple, even as he, in his own affirmation of the Protestant principle, refused to be the disciple of any. Thus he has taught us all that

we must learn to be humble in the awareness that it is God, the Lord of all life, who has laid his hand upon us in this crisis. And we must learn to pray: We believe, O Lord, help thou our unbelief.[25]

NOTES

1. *WA* 20, 732.*
2. *LW* 30, 289.†
3. Wilhelm Pauck, "Adolf von Harnack's Interpretation of Church History," *Union Seminary Quarterly Review* (January 1954) 14 *[The Heritage of the Reformation,* 2d ed. (Glencoe: The Free Press 1961), p. 338].
4. Wilhelm Pauck, "The Prospect for Ecumenical Theology Today," *Journal of Religion,* XXV (April 1945) 81 *[Heritage,* p. 364].
5. Wilhelm Pauck, "A Brief Criticism of Barth's Dogmatics," *Union Seminary Quarterly Review* (May 1957) *[Heritage,* p. 358].
6. Pauck, "Adolf von Harnack's Interpretation," p. 13 *[Heritage,* p. 338].
7. Wilhelm Pauck, "The Nature of Protestantism," *Church History,* VI (March 1937) 15 *[Heritage,* p. 175].
8. Ibid., p. 23 *[Heritage,* p. 182].
9. Wilhelm Pauck, "The Idea of Revelation and the Nature of Protestantism," *Harvard Divinity School Bulletin,* XXXVII (April 16, 1940) 15 *[Heritage,* p. 190].
10. Wilhelm Pauck, *Karl Barth—Prophet of a New Christianity?* (New York: Harper & Bros., 1931), pp. 119–21, 102 ff., and *passim.*
11. Ibid., p. 220.
12. Wilhelm Pauck, "What Is Wrong with Liberalism?" *Journal of Religion,* XV (April 1935) 158 *[Heritage,* p. 322].
13. Wilhelm Pauck, "A Defense of Liberalism," *Journal of Religion,* XXXVII (January 1947) 53 *[Heritage,* p. 334].
14. Wilhelm Pauck, "A Brief Criticism," pp. 107–10 *[Heritage,* pp. 353–59].
15. A. E. Harvey, *Bucer in England* (Marburg: Privately published, 1906).
16. Wilhelm Pauck, *Das Reich Gottes auf Erden. Utopie und Wirklichkeit* (Berlin and Leipzig: Walter de Gruyter, 1928); cf., for example, the discussion of Hooker, pp. 159 ff.
17. Francois Wendel, "Introduction," *Martini Buceri Opera Latina,* XV, *De regno Christi libri duo* (Paris: Presses Universitaires, 1955), p. xxxix, n. 155.
18. For his own summary of this work, cf. "Luther and the Reformation," *Theology Today,* III (October 1946) 314–27 *[Heritage,* pp. 3–17].
19. Wilhelm Pauck, "Luther's Faith," *Religion in Life,* XVI (Winter 1946/47) 3–11; "Martin Luthers Glaube," *Deutsche Beiträge zur geistigen Überlieferung,* edited by A. Bergsträsser (Chicago, 1947) pp. 58–71 *[Heritage,* pp. 19–28].
20. Wilhelm Pauck, ed. a tr., *Luther: Lectures on Romans* (Philadelphia: The Westminster Press 1961), pp. xvii–ixvi.
21. Wilhelm Pauck, "Luther and the Reformation," p. 318 *[Heritage,* p. 7].
22. Alfred North Whitehead, *Process and Reality* (Torchbook ed.; New York: Harpest Bros., 1960), p. 63.
23. For excerpts from some of these monographs and comments on others, cf. Heinrich Bornkamm, *Luther im Spiegel der deutschen Geistesgeschichte* (Heidelberg: Quelle & Meyer, 1955).

---

*All quotations are translated from the Weimar Edition *(WA)* of Luther's works. The quotations taken from the Table Talk *(Tischreden)* are indicated TR; those taken from the letters *(Briefe)* are indicated B.
†The American Edition of Luther's Works is indicated *LW.*

24. Jan Kott, *Szekspir współczesny* (Warsaw: Państwowy Instytut Wydawniczcy, 1965), p. 13.
25. "The Crisis of Religion" in H. Richard Niebuhr, Wilhelm Pauck, and Francis P. Miller, *The Church Against the World* (Chicago and New York: Willett, Clark & Co., 1935), p. 69.

1. Luther's Faith

In his sermon on the occasion of Luther's burial on February 22, 1546, Bugenhagen characterized the reformer, his long-time friend and colleague, with the following words: "... he was without doubt the angel of which the Apocalypse speaks in Chapter XIV: 'And I saw an angel flying through the midst of heaven, who had an eternal gospel to preach,' ... the angel who says: 'Fear God, and give glory to him!' These are the two articles of the teaching of Martin Luther, the law and the gospel, by which the whole Scripture is opened and Christ made known as our righteousness and eternal life."[1]

Luther—an angel of God! Such a description suggests that his contemporaries understood his person and work in a religious sense.

I

Luther himself thought of himself and of his work in the same way. He did not wish to be called a prophet (only once[2] did he speak of himself as "the prophet of the Germans"), but he had the sense of a *divine mission*. In opposition to the defenders of the old faith who called him a heretic, he thought of himself as an *"ecclesiasticus* [churchman] by the grace of God."[3] God had called him, he felt, to use his office of "Doctor of the Holy Scripture" for the reformation of the church according to the gospel. So he wrote: "I have received my doctrine by the grace of God from heaven, and, what is more, I have kept it in the presence of one who can do more with his little finger than a thousand popes, kings, princes, and *doctores* could do."[4] In the same spirit he once described his mission in the following Pauline way: "If I should want to boast, I should glory in God that I am one of the apostles and evangelists in German lands, even though the devil and all his bishops and tyrants do not want me to be such; for I know that by the grace of God I have taught and still teach faith and truth."[5] Such high claims he justified with the certainty that he was speaking "Christ's word" and not his own. Therefore, he did not hesitate to conclude: "So my mouth must be his whose words it speaks."

Because he knew himself to be an instrument of God and because he felt "more acted upon than acting,"[6] he argued that the whole cause of the Reformation could not be measured by human norms. When in his old age he looked back upon the beginnings of the Reformation and contemplated "the very great, heavy care and trouble" which the work of the Reformation had cost him, he exclaimed: "Had I known all in advance, God would have been put to great trouble to bring me to it."[7] Remembering the days of the Diet of Worms, he pondered: "Truly God can drive one mad; I do not know whether now I could be so daring."[8] However, in the midst of the crisis of his trial, he had written: "The die was cast, and so I did not want to do anything else than what I did. I began to put all my trust upon the Spirit who does not carry on a lazy business."[9] Thus he explained that all that took place at the height of the Reformation occurred, not because he had planned it so, but by "divine counsel."[10]

This feeling of being divinely led he expressed best in the following charateristic words: "God has led me on as if I were a horse and he put blinkers on me that I could not see who came running up upon me. . . . A good deed rarely issued from planning wisdom and cleverness; it must all happen in the vagaries of ignorance."[11]

These descriptions of the feeling of being called to a work that he had not chosen for himself are all the more impressive because Luther did not derive any pretensions of personal authority from his sense of mission. He did not wish his own special gifts and abilities to be regarded as extraordinary or authoritative. He resented it that his opponents called his teaching "Lutheran," and he got no satisfaction from the fact that his followers called themselves by his name. "Who is this Luther?" he wrote. "My teaching is not my own, and I have not been crucified for the sake of anyone. . . . Why should it happen to me, miserable, stinking bag of worms that I am, that the children of Christ should be called by my insignificant name? . . . I am and will be nobody's master. With the one church I have in common the teaching of Christ who alone is our master."[12]

When, on one occasion, he wrote: "So say I, Dr. Martin Luther, the unworthy evangelist of our Lord Jesus,"[13] he desired to appeal to the authority of Christ, who alone, according to his opinion, should be heard as a prophet.[14] But, at the same time, he wished to be taken seriously in his judgment of himself as an unworthy servant of Christ. He dared to appeal with certainty to God's word, but he also confessed frankly that Christian obedience was a daily task for him and the cause of never-ending efforts. That is why he did not want to justify his right to speak in the name of God by his own Christian attainments. "Let everyone," he wrote, "be responsible for his own feelings. As for me, I regard myself as a Christian. Nevertheless, I know how dificult it has been for me, and still is, to apprehend and to keep this cornerstone [Christ]. But they certainly do me wrong [who call me a Lutheran], for—God strengthen me!—I am a small, poor Lutheran."[15]

No one understands Luther who does not pay attention to the two aspects of his sense of calling: on the one hand, the assertion of being held and supported by God, and, on the other, the rejection of any personal worth and authority.

II

His *faith* corresponded wholly to the spirit that guided him in his work.

His deepest convictions were determined by his conceptions of God. God, as he saw him, was the restlessly working, driving power in all that is, the ever-active, creative livingness which lets no creature stand still. God is at work everywhere and in all, also in the godless, even in the devil.[16] The whole universe is his "masquerade in which he hides himself while he rules the world so strangely by making a hubbub."[17] The almighty power of God is nowhere and yet everywhere. Because it moves everything, it is immanent in all; but because it creates everything, it transcends all.

It must be present at all places, even in the smallest leaf of a flower. The reason is this: "It is God who creates, works, and preserves all things by his almighty power and by his right hand, as we confess in the creed. He sends out no delegates or angels when he creates and preserves, but everything is the working of his own divine power. But if he is the creator and preserver, he himself must be present, creating and preserving his creature in its most inward and most outward being. That is why he himself is in the very inwardness and in the very outwardness of every creature, from end to end, below and above it, before and behind it. Nothing can be more present and be more really within all creatures than God himself."[18]

"God is smaller than anything small, bigger than anything big, shorter than anything short, longer than anything long, broader than anything broad, slimmer than anything slim, and so on; he is an inexpressible being, above and beyond all that one can name or think."[19]

This all-comprehending, all-penetrating creativity is the fountain and spring of life and of all good. It is closer to every one of us than any of us are to each other.[20] As it is God's nature to create all from nothing, so he is able "to help the forsaken ones, to justify sinner, to resurrect the dead, and to save the damned."[21]

He is the life of every being. He determines everything. He is present everywhere. But he is impenetrable and inscrutable. In such a way Luther spoke of God—most articulately in his book against Erasmus, *Of the Bondage of the Will,* and in his treatises on the Lord's Supper, called forth by his controversy with Zwingli. There he disclosed his profoundest thoughts on the creative power by which he felt himself driven and overcome. But he had still more to say.

It makes a difference whether you say that God is present or whether you say that he is present for you. But he is there for you, when he adds his word [to his presence] and binds himself, saying: Here you shall find me. When you have the word, you can grasp him and have him and say: Now I have thee, as thou sayest. So it is with the right hand of God; it is everywhere, as no one can deny; but it is also nowhere, therefore you cannot apprehend it anywhere unless it binds and confines itself for your benefit to one place. This happens when it moves and dwells in the humanity of Christ. There you will most certainly find it. Otherwise you must run through all creation from end to end, groping and fumbling about, here and there, without finding it. Although it is really there—it is not there for you.[22]

In Christ, the mysterious, inscrutable Lord of everything has made himself accessible. In him he is comprehensible, because he has revealed himself in him without abandoning his mystery. He is hidden in the humbleness of the child in the manger. In the cross he is not *directly* visible as the victor over hell, death, and the devil. He is abscondite in the message of Christ about the mercy that seeks the sinner. And yet—"Whosoever does not apprehend this man born of Mary, simply cannot apprehend God; even if they should say that they believe in God, creator of heaven and earth, they believe really only in the idol of their heart, for outside of Christ there is no true God."[23] In Christ, men have the "mirror of God's paternal heart." In him, God is a God for them, their God. In Christ, he is really the ever-renewing fountain of all good.

But men do not want to accept this teaching of God, for, so Luther argued, "Man by nature does not want God to be God; he would much rather that he himself were God and that God were not God."[24] Because of his self-sufficiency and selfishness, he is God's enemy. Though, when relying upon himself, he is driven from presumptuous security to despair in himself without being able to extricate himself from this dilemma, he refuses to acknowledge that he is a created being responsible to his creator. This unfaith is his sin. It is incomprehensible to him that he is a creature of God (this is proved by the fact that when he engages in worship he tends to fashion an idol for himself); but it is utterly unfathomable for him that God should be Father of sinners. His moral sense rebels against such a thought. If there is a God at all, so he thinks, God is the Lord of the righteous, in whose sight only the worthy ones are acceptable.

Such is man's natural religiousness, according to Luther's opinion. Faith is its opposite. It is the acknowledgment of God's sovereignty and the belief in his accessibility in Christ and his word. Faith meant to Luther simply to have God. "Having God," he wrote in the *Larger Catechism*, "is nothing else than heartily to believe and trust in him; ... this trusting and believing makes both, God and idol; for these two belong together, faith and God."[25]

This faith, Luther taught, must be seen as the personal act of the believer ("If you believe, you have,"[26] he repeated unceasingly), but he knew also that it is the work of the Holy Spirit and, as such, a gift of God. Faith can therefore be an event only if the Christian becomes a new person. It is Christ who forms this new person. "I do not live in my own person, but Christ lives within me.

To be sure, I live as a person, but not in myself or for my own person."[27] The person of the believer transcends itself, so to speak.[28] This was the experience of Luther's prophetic religion.

He tried to interpret this experience of faith in many ways, for all his thinking circled around it. "Faith," so he defined, "is the knowledge of things not seen; it is directed to things that are not apparent. In order that faith may occur, it is therefore necessary that all that is believed be hidden."[29]

Faith is a miracle that can't be understood according to ordinary criteria. Particularly when one has found God merciful, such faith appears as a blindly trusting audacity. "For this is the nature of faith, that it dares trust in God's grace. . . . Faith does not require information, knowledge, or security, but a free surrender and joyful daring upon an unfelt, untried, unknown goodness."[30] From here, Luther came to the remarkable conclusion that all certainty must be founded not upon human experience but upon divine revelation. "Our theology is certain," he said, "because it places us outside of ourselves; I do not need to rely upon my conscience, my senses, and my doing, but I rely upon the divine promise and truth which never deceive."[31]

And yet—faith must be a personal experience in order to be valid. A Christian must have faith by virtue of a personal deed and decision. "You yourself must decide; your neck is at stake. Therefore, unless God says to your own heart: This is God's word, you cannot comprehend it. . . . If you do not feel it, you do not have faith, but the word merely hangs in your ears and floats on your tongue as foam lies on the waters."[32]

III

In what a terrific tension Luther held his faith! On the one hand, he viewed it with radical seriousness as the work and gift of God who acts upon man from without. On the other hand, he experienced it as a concrete personal decision and commitment. In contemplating his tension, one understands why religion was a perpetual crisis and an unceasing battle for Luther.

This is the meaning of the *tentationes,* the agonies of faith, into which he was drawn again and again.[33] He felt that the merciful

God was withdrawing from him. He was overcome by doubts concerning his work, when he questioned whether he should have dared to upset age-old customs and traditions in the church. He felt that, in the light of the human need for security, the ambiguity of divine grace was unbearable. He then sensed the nearness of God, not as love and consolation, but as wrath and damnation. When such thoughts beset him, he felt that he was being attacked by the devil and thrown into a battle for his faith. He attributed such agonies to his psychological propensity to melancholy, but he knew also that he did not understand their true significance by such a psychological interpretation. Indeed, he held these agonies of faith to be unavoidable because he was aware that, from the viewpoint of ordinary human experience, faith was an impossibility.

He overcame these *Anfechtungen* (assaults), as he called them in his own tongue, by appealing to Christ and by relying upon the First Commandment: I am the Lord, thy God; thou shalt have no other gods before me. When he was free again and restored in the faith, he knew more definitely than ever before that the inborn and acquired human certainties and safeguards are nothing ultimately sure and that man deceives himself when he pretends to possess certainty in himself. Thus, these agonies appeared to him as a means by which the truth of faith, as a truth from beyond man's reach, was confirmed. A Christian, so he concluded, must be continually in the process of becoming. As he is a forgiven sinner who, despite being forgiven, again and again falls into the sin of unfaith, so he is thrown into agonies of faith until the end of his days, in order that he might test his faith by being compelled to fight for it. So Luther could say of himself: "I did not learn my theology all at once; I have had to brood and ponder over it more and more deeply; my *tentationes* have brought me to it, for one learns only by experience."[34]

He once said that the greatest of these *tentationes* was to know of none at all;[35] for such an attitude appeared to him the height of self-deception. He believed it to be an incontestable fact that every man has a bad conscience in spite of all the masks of self-confidence he wears, for at the bottom of his heart he knows himself to be in the wrong before God. Even though he rebels against the gospel of the forgiveness of God, because faith in this gospel involves the surrender of his self and the undoing of his self-determination, he will nevertheless experience faith as a liberation not only from himself but, particularly, from his bad conscience.

Luther best described the human situation that leads to the agony of faith in the following words. They describe the fright and terror by which one can be seized at the sound of a rustling leaf, and they symbolize all the insecurities of pride from which one can be liberated by faith alone.

So it can happen that conscience feels all misfortune that befalls us as the wrath of God, and that even a mere rustling leaf seems to be God's wrath. . . . There is nothing more worthless and more despised than a dry leaf that lies on the ground; worms crawl over it; it cannot ward off even the smallest speck of dust. . . . But there comes a time when its rustling will scare man and horse, spike and armor, kings and princes, the power of a whole army, and even such spiteful and angry tyrants as cannot be scared either by the fear of hell or by God's wrath and judgment, but only become still prouder and more hardened by such threats. Aren't we fine fellows? We do not fear God's anger but stand stiffly unmoved by it. But we can be scared and frightened by the anger of an impotent dry leaf, and the rustling of such a leaf can make the world too narrow for us and become a wrathful God to us.[36]

IV

From this analysis of Luther's faith we can conclude that his interpretation of the Christian religion corresponded exactly to his conception of the meaning of his mission in the world. In his faith he related himself only to God in Christ; he did not base it upon the content of his experiences. With respect to his work, he relied upon the almighty Lord of history and not upon his own qualities of leadership, of which he did not think much anyway. In his faith as well as in his work as a reformer, he really believed himself "more acted upon than acting." This way of thinking has nothing whatsoever to do with quietism, of which Luther has often been accused. Rather, it is "prophetic"—through and through. This can be proved by the fact that Luther felt himself called to a most personal, active participation in the work which, as he believed, God performed in the world through him. It was God himself, the ever-active creative power, who, by means of the Reformation, made room in the world for his word, and Luther was drawn into this divine work with his whole person. He felt that God had overpowered him; he did not think that he had thereby been drawn into a heteronomous servitude. He was moved, rather, to commit himself to him who had overpowered him and to cooperate with him. Such was Luther's own conception of his faith. His principles of action were: Do not rely on men, but trust in God. Do not fear men, but fear God. That is why Luther acted on the historical scene without special consideration of political and historical consequences. Whosoever wants "to help the cause of the gospel," he wrote in a letter to Wolfgang Capito,[37] must preach it without fear and regard of men, in order that "the free, pure and plain truth" may assert itself by itself alone.

In explaining the beginnings and the course of the Reformation to the people of Wittenberg after his return from his exile in Wartburg castle, he said: "All I have done is to further, preach, and teach God's word; otherwise I have done nothing. So it came about that while I slept or while I had a glass of beer with my friend Philip [Melanchthon] and with Amsdorf, the papacy was so weakened as it never was before by the action of any prince or emperor. I have done nothing; the word has done and accomplished everything. . . . I let the word do its work."[38]

These words sound quietistic and politically naive, but they were spoken by one who, in the name of God, changed the course of history. What Luther meant to express was that his decisions and actions were motivated only by his concern for the word of God, and not by political calculations and predictions. By, and on account of, his faith, he became a reformer. His work, the Reformation, will live as long as this faith finds a response in the hearts of men.

NOTES

1. Ernst Wolf, *Martin Luther* ("Theologische Existenz heute," Heft 6 [Munich, 1934]), p. 7.
2. *WA* 30, III: 290, 28.
3. *WA* 10, II: 105, 17.

4. *WA* 10, II: 228, 27.
5. *WA* 8: 683, 13.
6. *WA* B. 11: 39.
7. *WA*, TR 1: 42, 17.
8. *WA*, TR 5: No. 5342b.
9. *WA* 6: 157.
10. *WA*, TR 4; No. 3944.
11. *WA*, TR 1: 176, 15.
12. *WA* 8: 685, 6.
13. *WA* 30, III: 366, 8.
14. *WA*, TR 5: No. 6409.
15. *WA* 31, I: 174, 26.
16. *WA* 18: 709, 21.
17. *WA* 15: 574, 14.
18. *WA* 23: 133 f.
19. *WA* 26: 339 f.
20. *WA* 19: 492, 12.
21. *WA* 40, III: 56.
22. *WA* 23: 151.
23. *WA* 40, III: 56.
24. *WA* 1: 225, 1.
25 *WA* 30, I: 28.
26. *WA* 18: 118.
27. *WA* 40, 1: 546, 25. See Erich Vogelsang's illuminating discussion, "Die Unio mystica bei Luther," in *Archiv für Reformationsgeschichte* XXXV (1983), 73 ff.
28. See Fritz Frey, *Luthers Glaubensbegriff* (Leipzig: M. Heinsius, 1939), p. 110.
29. *WA* 40, I: 228, 15.
30. *WA* 10, III: 3, 329.
31. *WA* 40, I: 589, 8.
32. *WA* 10, I: 2, 335.
33. See Roland H. Bainton's interesting analysis of Luther's struggle for faith in *Here I Stand: A Life of Martin Luther* (New York: Abingdon-Cokesbury Press, 1950) pp. 359–72.
34. *WA*, TR 1: 146, 12.
35. *WA* 3: 424, 4.
36. *WA* 19: 226, 12.
37. *WA* B 2: 430 f.
38. *WA* B 3: 18 ff.

2. Luther and Butzer

The Strassburg reformer Martin Butzer (1491–1551) is remembered chiefly by scholars who specialize in the history of early Protestantism. He does not live in the memory of Protestants as one of their great leaders. But in his day he was a very influential person. Not only Strassburg, but all Germany, needed his energy, his practical advice, and his political skill. Many a diet and many an ecclesiastical conference heard him phrase formulas and doctrines that were intended to relieve tense situations and to make for reconciliation in religion. But the result of his work has been forgotten, it seems, with the memory of his energetic, spirited face. The new copies of his books that have been carried over to our generation adorn the rare book rooms of great libraries. The catalogues of common book collections remember him only by a chapter on divorce that he incorporated in his swan song, *De regno Christi*, written for the English king, Edward VI, which young John Milton happened to discover when his divorce kept his mind occupied with appeals to the parliament.[1] His secretary planned to publish his collected works after his death in ten big folio volumes, but he succeeded in getting only the *Scripta anglicana* (Basel, 1577) into print. The mass of the other material rests in Strassburg. Perhaps one day it will be revealed to interested historians, enabling them to judge thoroughly the man, his thoughts, and his influence. The writings of his that are now accessible have been studied mainly in reference to Calvin, and there seems to be proof enough that Butzer was Calvin's foremost teacher. They reveal, not an original mind, but one rich in many suggestive ideas which, in their full scope, remained unrealized and were not successfully applied by Butzer himself. Therefore, they were forgotten and left to emerge in the minds of later generations under new conditions. Anglicanism and Puritanism alike could rightly claim him as their godfather.[2] The ideas to which we here refer are concerned with practical religion, with the church and the state in their essential nature and their relationship to each other.[3] These ideas we shall here compare with those of Luther, in order to exhibit them in their full character and to estimate them at their own value. Perhaps the result will be a clarification of our own thought about the principles of practical religion in relation to the secular order. Such ideas are generally comprehended under the concept of the Kingdom of God. It may be well, therefore, to commence this comparative study with Luther's and Butzer's understanding of this notion.

Luther identifies the kingdom of God with the invisible church, the *communio sanctorum,* i.e., the communion of those who have accepted the word in faith,[4] the communion of those who have become real children of God through their God-given faith. Driven and inspired by the Holy Spirit, they love God and their neighbor because they cannot do otherwise. Through their faith they are able to fulfill the commandments of the Sermon on the Mount.[5] The Kingdom of God is "that which binds hearts and consciences together in a living communion." "It is a communion of love of purely spiritual character which comprehends all times and all lands."[6] The constitutive element of the Kingdom of God is faith. This conception is thoroughly religious. The citizens of the Kingdom are thought to be those to whom God grants, out of his mercifulness, justification by sanctifying them with the Holy Spirit and by assuring them, in the preaching of the word, of full certainty of salvation. "The Kingdom of God is a kingdom of grace in which, through the name of Jesus, all sins are forgiven."[7]

In his thought on the Kingdom of God, Butzer emphasized its *moral* character. He understood the gospel primarily as a moral phenomenon. It was to become a moral power. When, by the fulfillment of the Scripture, the communion of love is established among men, the Kingdom of God is realized; Christ rules.[8] He does not stress, like Luther, the religious content of the gospel as being of first importance. That accounts for the different conception of the relation between gospel and law. Luther sharply distinguished them from each other. But Butzer appreciates the gospel also as a law.[9] The Old and the New Testaments belong closely together.[10] The Scripture as an entity is obligatory.

Roughly speaking, then, the two reformers have a different concept of morality. For Luther, it is mainly a good inner attitude put into action, nourished by the grace of God. Butzer has the attitude originate out of the conscious and strict observation of the will of God given in the gospel, which is to be realized as such in all orders of life and is to comprehend the whole social and cultural life of man.[11]

It is to be noted that Butzer's concept of the Kingdom of God is not unified. Two circles of thought are interwoven with each other. The Kingdom of God has come when the commandments and the truth of the Bible have permeated *all* human conditions; but, on the other hand, it is present only in the church of the elect, the invisible communion of the predestinated saints.[12]

If we observe how, by using the narrower concept, the two circles are combined with each other, we touch the fundamental difference between Luther and Butzer.

Both of them consider the Kingdom of God as the communion of the true believers whom Christ governs and whom he leads to love. This means for Butzer that the Kingdom of God consists of the elect. But how can their communion become real? Election can never produce a vital contact between men, but concerns only individuals. This "communion," it seems, lacks that connecting link which Luther finds in the word, given and effective in history. How does Butzer find it? He considers the election realized by the incorporation of the Christian in the Corpus Christi, the church of Christ. The idea of predestination is combined with a peculiar idea of the church: Christ, who grants election by his spirit, has by his word constituted the church, an organization with offices and polity, so that his followers, the elect, can form a communion.[13] In this church, which is ordered by Christ himself and which is directed by him through his instruments, the *ministeri,* the flock of saints represents a communion of sanctification and of love. Membership in the Kingdom of God, which is possible only through conformity with the visible organized church, reveals itself in love, in ethical obedience to the commandments of God and Christ.[14] In such thinking, Butzer's strong emphasis on church discipline originates. The principle of election, however, is changed and enlarged. Anyone may consider himself elect who is a member of the Christ-ordered church and who contributes to the common welfare by leading a life that conforms to biblical prescription, thereby promoting God's glory and mankind's salvation. Furthermore, because Christ's order is superior to all human orders, his word and his discipline are of the highest significance for the shaping of human life. In all human conditions the word must be obeyed as a law. Even the state is bound to it; it is obliged to propagate the kingdom of Christ on earth.[15]

At the center of Luther's church concept stands not predestination, but the word of salvation. Members of the true church and of the Kingdom of God are those believers who have received the promise of justification from the word and who express their gratitude for such a gift in an evangelical morality. They, too, are elected, but that is not decisive for the formation of the church. The Church, in its invisible character as a *communio sanctorum*, originates in the word.[16]

The office of the pastor or preacher is therefore a necessity; the development of a visible church is required. But its only purpose is the preaching of the word and the administration of the sacraments. The form, order, and constitution of this earthly organization, the visible part *(Kultgemeinde)* of the invisible church *(Gemeinschaft der Gläubigen)*, is absolutely voluntary and incidental.[17] Christ has given no special orders for it; the Bible does not prescribe its external character. No discipline can be exercised in this church; only the word and its promise of salvation must be proclaimed. The Holy Spirit uses it as a means to gather the communion of Christians, and they give expression to their faith in spontaneous acts of love. A church discipline does not make this morality obligatory for a wider circle. The gospel, truly received and accepted only by a minority, cannot be made a moral law for a disinterested majority. The communion of love, called the *regnum Dei*, is limited to the small number of the *fideles* or *sancti*.

If one thinks that Luther unjustly enlarged this concept of the church in his idea of the general priesthood of believers, he should consider the statement of Holl: "Inasmuch as the Kingdom of God is an invisible entity and it is reserved for God to call into it whom he will, no man has the right to deprive any other person of membership therein or of the possibility of such membership, thus denying him participation in the communion of love."[18] The idea of the general priesthood of all believers indicates the incidental character of all church organization and the merely relative religious significance of ecclesiastical offices. Furthermore, by claiming that a secular profession could not hinder the perfection of a man's Christian character, Luther came to appreciate the religious importance of all secular callings.

Butzer took over these notions from Luther, but he emphasized almost more strongly the religious character of the professions and vocations. Christ's call to salvation and the calling to a profession go hand in hand.[19] He sees the realization of the communion of love which the "word" requires guaranteed in professional and vocational work for the benefit of the commonwealth.

Luther stresses, much more energetically than Butzer, the idea that a calling, a vocation, is Christian only in so far as the persons engaged in it are Christians. In so far as the motivations of Christian persons active in professions are guided by a loving concern for their neighbors, the orders of the world are Christianized. All orders of the world as such are non-Christian. Luther also regards state and magistrate as such an order. It is akin to the family and to artisanship, or craftmanship. It is merely the divinely controlled, natural world-order that is fulfilled in these "offices." A non-Christian is capable of administering them just as well as a Christian, if he accomplishes the task with "reason." "The procedure becomes Christianized only in the consciousness of the Christian person who knows that in filling his office he serves his neighbor."[20] As if directly refuting such an opinion, Butzer writes, in the discourse on the magistrates: "The task of a magistrate is another task than to make shoes, clothes, and such things which fulfill bodily needs."[21] Here, we touch upon a very important point of difference between Luther and Butzer, particularly with reference to their concept of the state.

Luther completely separated the sphere of the Kingdom of God from the sphere of secular orders.[22] State and Kingdom of God stand in strict contrast to each other: in the latter is freedom; in the former, coercion; the latter is dominated by love, the former by force; in the latter there is freedom for the inner man, untouched by external power, while the former disciplines the outer man.[23] What has the inner communion of love, which fulfills the Sermon on the Mount, in common with the external order that is founded upon compulsion, might, power, and the authority of the sword! But, nevertheless, the state is a God-ordained, natural order.[24] It even stands in the service of the kingdom of God.[25]

Without the state, i.e., the power of the civil magistrate, the flock of the true Christians could never exist, because they would be suppressed by evil men. The state furnishes to the Kingdom of God (not only to the church!) the possibility of growth, since it uses its coercive power to limit the expansion of evil and because it creates by its laws a morality which protects the extension of the gospel. In its fight against crime, the state is related to the Kingdom.[26] As a "police régime" it becomes a "left hand" for the Kingdom of God.

How different Butzer! He also knows of the limitation of political power in regard to conscience, which it cannot rule.[27] But under no circumstances does he put it in antagonism to the Kingdom of God. The political magistrate has a spiritual task. By having received with the power of the sword the power over the *lives* of its subjects or citizens, it is responsible for the best *living*. It has to see to it that life is lived *bene beateque*. According to its utmost ability, it must promote the highest type of morality, not only peace and concord on the principles of the "law of nature." Because the highest morality is founded on religion, it is the duty of the magistrate to establish true religion in his country, i.e., the moral powers of the Kingdom of God must have absolute influence in the lives of its subjects. Butzer does not hesitate to declare that the secular government must propagate the Kingdom of God by its own means. However, he makes the important presupposition that the true magistrate is Christian. All others he calls tyrants. The State is in the service of the Kingdom of God, directly and not indirectly. It does not only provide the setting and the conditions for the highest morality; it is obliged to spread the true moral life among its subjects. "It is the duty of the government to see to it that its subjects live right and well. This is not possible where they are not drawn, above all else, to the true service of God. On this depend all virtues, as well as felicity and well-being. For they who seek the Kingdom of God and his righteousness will themselves obtain all good things, said Christ the Lord. The pious rulers must therefore not use religion as a means for the maintenance of external peace as impious tyrants do, but the establishment of religion itself must be their aim. Therefore, they will leave nothing undone which glorifies the name of God among their subjects by their activity of governing and which propagates His Kingdom and builds it up in the best way."[28] So it follows that political rulers promote and serve the church; they must even be subject to her, as they hear and receive from the ministers of the church the word of Christ. The result is a Christian state which endeavors to develop all its life under the law of the biblical word. A distinction between the political and ecclesiastical power is recognized, but their separation is not stated.

For Luther, it was a fixed principle that church and state comprehend two separate spheres.[29] The idea of a Christian state was for him impracticable, if not inconceivable.[30] The gospel, which, in any case, is received only by a small number of men and, moreover, in its moral consequence is valid first of all for the individual, can never become, as for Butzer, a rule for political life. Throughout his lifetime, Luther complained about the fact that there were not enough Christians. Although he, too, related life in the world to the highest moral order (the *communio sanctorum*) by saying that love ought to regulate and permeate all secular activities, he hesitated to make it obligatory or binding. He only wanted to see the moralizing influence of the Kingdom of God at work in practical results. Butzer had probably the same aim in mind. But he wanted to make the observance of religion and its moral expression a requirement of law, thereby tending to secularize religion itself. Luther wanted to prevent just that.

Luther gives to religion its own sphere, clear and precise, and assigns to the secular orders a legal status of their own, *Eigengesetzlichkeit*. This shows his profound insight into the reality of things, for as long as economics are economics they are ruled by economic laws, and as long as politics are politics they are governed by political laws. Luther sees that the connection between the secular orders and religion can come about only through persons who, in their Christian consciousness, may raise affairs to a higher moral level, while the church, in preaching the word, enables them to review things *sub specie aeternitatis*, under the aspects of the invisible Kingdom of God.

Butzer's ideal state is a "commonwealth"[31] wherein the common welfare is guaranteed by the Christian nature of the government and its actions. Thus, he blends two spheres that are essentially foreign to each other. The true Christian communion seeks more than welfare. Butzer's own ideas regarding the realization on earth of the Kingdom of God promoted by the state display traits which concern happiness and utility. He claims that a Christian state will be the most *powerful* and the wealthiest one,[32] not feeling that the very existence of *such* a state would destroy the most distinctive features of the Christian religion.

One may read, as though a direct answer of Luther to Butzer, the rather pessimistic, gloomy words: "But see to it that you fill the world with true Christians before you rule it in a Christian and evangelical way. You will never be able to do so, for the world in the mass is un-Christian and will remain un-Christian, although all are baptized and are called Christian. But the Christians (as it is said) live far apart from each other. Therefore, it cannot be in this world that a Christian government becomes common everywhere, not even over a country or over a good number of men."[33]

That is why Luther does not demand that a prince *must* be Christian.[34] He recognizes—surely in contrast to Butzer—that an unbeliever can sometimes rule and govern in a better way than a Christian.[35] Though, naturally, he would greet a Christian prince with joy, he is of the opinon that the office of government *per se* is not influenced by the Christian character of its responsible leader. It is his function to maintain power in his country, to keep right and peace, to punish the criminals, and to protect the orderly citizens. Legislation is therefore governed by the common "positive law," and not—as Butzer advised—by Christ's precepts or by the decalogue. For the gospel does not contain a rule about the method of government; it prescribes only that one shall honor the civil magistrate. How superior is Luther, with his profound description of the Mosaic law as the Jews' "Saxon Mirror," i.e., common law, which may be used as a pattern for a law code and as a good example,[36] to Butzer, who was always inclined to consider the Mosaic law not as a code of natural or common law but as the law of God, deserving preference to all human laws! How much superior is Luther to Butzer when he writes: "Thus God has subjected secular government to reason, because it is not supposed to rule the soul's salvation or eternal things, but only goods of body and of time which God has subjected to men *(Genesis,* chapter 2). That is why the gospel does not teach how to govern and how to rule. It merely commands that one shall honor the magistrate and not rebel against him."[37]

However, this is not to say that Luther does not want the preacher to exhort the prince to morality and to the fear of God. Such attitudes are required on the basis of the natural world-order. Hence the rejection of atheism, the punishment of blasphemers, the fight of the state against heretics, as far as they are unbelievers and skeptical of the fundamental truths of Christianity.[38]

In this respect, owing to the point of view of their time, Butzer and Luther followed the same lines. A compulsory oppression of members of another Christian group, e.g., Catholics, a coercion of conscience, was unacceptable to them both, but they were of the conviction that a state with two confessional groups could not be governed.

This law against heretics suggests that the state has to pursue positive politics in regard to religion. It is a task required by the "law of nature." On the same basis, Luther considers it the state's duty to ensure the welfare of its citizens. Establishment of universities and schools, the issuance of marriage laws, propaganda for relief of the poor, suppression of begging and vagabondry, of usury, and exorbitant luxury,[38] belong to its program. These propositions for civic improvement, published in the "Manifest to the German nobility," are identical with those of Butzer, in his *De Regno Christi,* for the reorganization of social and cultural life in England. But the presuppositions out of which they grow differ radically from each other. The place of religion in their plans for a *Kultur und Wohlfahrtsstaat* is not the same.

Finally, we have to deal with the ideas concerning the relationship between church and state. It has been made evident that Butzer never felt the contrast between the two orders as sharply as did Luther.

When, in the course of time, in order to complete the work of reformation, Luther saw himself compelled to use the help of the prince in church matters, he did not thereby surrender his principles. The duty to *reform* is conferred upon the prince as the *praecipuum membrum ecclesiae,* on the basis of the general priesthood of all believers, and as *Notbischof.* It is true, all this led finally to the establishment of a church government appertaining to the sovereign, but Luther did not desire this result. According to Butzer, however, the sovereign is obliged, in fulfillment of the divinely ordered purpose of his office, to promote a reformation and supervise the church. He formulated the first Protestant theory for the church supremacy of the English kings.

As, in conclusion, we state that the difference between Luther's and Butzer's church concept is the result of a difference in world views, we are led to a general historical comparison. Though Butzer became a Protestant reformer through the direct influence of Luther, he remained, throughout his life, a loyal disciple of that school to which he was introduced as a student at Schlettstadt and Heidelberg. He never ceased to be a Humanist.[40] Hence the moralistic color of his Christian ideal. The difference between his and Luther's concept of the Kingdom of God is, therefore, largely due to the antagonism between Humanism and Lutheranism, between Erasmus and Luther, between an anthropocentric, rationalistic, and moralistic use of the Bible and a theocentric Biblicism.

NOTES

1. Martin Bucer, *The Judgment of Martin Bucer Concerning Divorce*, trans. John Milton (London, 1644).
2. Cf. Wilhelm Pauck, *Das Reich Gottes auf Erden: Eine Untersuchung zu Butzers "De regno Christi" und zur englischen Staatskirche des sechzehnten Jahrhunderts* (Berlin and Leipzig: Walter de Gruyter & Co., 1928), p. 111. The ideas of Butzer, to which this article refers, are fully discussed in this book. Cf. now the to date fullest treatment of Butzer's work in England, by Constantin Hopf, *Martin Bucer and the English Reformation* (Oxford: Blackwell, 1946).
3. Cf. *De regno Christi*, in *Scripta anglicana*, pp. 1–170 (now easily accessible in the critical edition by François Wendel, published as Vol. XV of *M. Buceri Opern Latina* (Paris: Presses Universitaires, 1955). *"De vera cura animarum*, ibid., pp. 260–356. *Dialogi oder Gesprech von der gemainsame [res publica;* commonwealth!] *und der kirchenübungen der Christen, Und was yeder Oberkait von ampts wegen aus Göttlichem befelch an denselbigen zu versehen und zu besseren gebüre* (Augsburg, 1535).
4. *W.A* 11: 271, 20.
5. Ibid., 11: 249, 36 ff.
6. Emanuel Hirsch, *Die Reich-Gottesbegriffe des modernen Denkens* (Göttingen: Vandenhoeck & Ruprecht, 1922), p. 7.
7. *WA* 52: 266, 16.
8. *Script. angl.*, p. 20.
9. Ibid., p. 55. Butzer defined faith as *persuasio* (e.g., *Enarrationes in quatuor Evangelica* [1536], pp. 219 ff.); Luther speaks exclusively of *fiducia*. Cf., on this point, the remarks by Hans Emil Weber, *Reformation, Orthodoxie und Rationalismus* (Gütersloh: Bertelsmann, 1937), p. 212.

10. *Dialogi*, p. O3v. Cf. Pauck, *Reich Gottes*, pp. 60 ff.

11. *Script. angl.*, p. 11. The same point is emphasized by Henri Strohl in his article, "Bucer Interprète de Luther," in *Rev. d'histoire et de phil. rel.*, XIX (1939), 223 ff. He asserts that Butzer was a better interpreter of Luther than Melanchthon was. But this book should not be read without reference to Robert Stupperich, "Die Kirche in Martin Bucer's theologischer Entwicklung," *Archiv für Reformationsgeschichte*, XXXV (1938), 81 ff.

12. Ibid., p. 157.

13. Ibid., p. 31. The fullest discussion on Butzer's ecclesiology now available is that by Jaques Courvoisier, *La notion d'église chez Bucer* (Paris: Alcan, 1933). He, too, compares Luther and Butzer, but he inclines to judge Luther from a prejudiced Reformed point of view.

14. Cf. Gustav Anrich, *Martin Bucer* (Strassburg: K. J. Trübner, 1914), p. 83.

15. Cf. Pauck, *Das Reich Gottes*, pp. 19 ff. Butzer says expressly in *De regno Christi* (*Script. angl.*, p. 149) that no law deserves the name of law unless it contains the fundamental law of love as it is given in the Bible.

16. Cf. Ferdinand Kattenbusch, *Die Doppelschichtigkeit in Luthers Kirchenbegriff* (Gotha: Klotz, 1928).

17. Cf. Henri Strohl, *L'épanouissement de la pensé religieuse de Luther* (Paris and Strassburg: Librarie Istra, 1924), p. 322 ff.

18. Karl Holl, *Gesammelte Aufsätze*, Vol. I: Luther (Tübingen: Mohr Verlag, 1923), p. 186. The interpretation of Luther's theology as it is given in this article depends largely upon Holl's work.

19. *Script. angl.*, pp. 32 ff., 136.

20. Karl Holl, *Gesammelte*, p. 347.

21. *Dialogi*, p. U4b.

22. Cf. Karl Müller, *Kirche, Gemeinde und Obrigkeit nach Luther* (Tübingen: Mohr Verlag, 1910); Hermann Jordan, *Luthers Staatsauffassung* (1917); Julius Binder, *Luthers Staatsauffassung* (Erfurt: K. Stenger 1924). J. W. Allen, *A History of Political Thought in the Sixteenth Century* (London: Methuen & Co. Ltd. 1928). The point of view of R. H. Murray in *Erasmus and Luther* (London: Society for Promoting Christian Knowledge, 1920), pp. 320 ff., and in *The Political Consequences of the Reformation* (New York: Russell & Russell, 1926), is not always convincing, though stimulating.

23. *WA* 6, 258, 31 ff.

24. Ibid., 11, 257, 39.

25. Ibid., pp. 258, 3.

26. Ibid., pp. 248, 29. Butzer's views of the Christian magistrate are instructively, if incompletely, discussed in the Freiburger dissertation by Rudolph Schultz, *Martin Butzer's Anschauung von der christlichen Oberkeit [Zella Mehlis* (Thüringen): Nordheim, 1932].

27. *Script. angl.*, p. 5.

28. *Dialogi*, p. N4v: *Die regierung sollen sehen, dass ihre unterthonen recht und wol leben. Das mag nun nit sein, wa sie nicht vor allem zum waren Gotsdienst gezogen werden. An dem hangen alle tugenten, auch alles glück und heyl. Denn die das reych und die gerechtigkeit Gottes suchen, wirdt alles gutes selb zufallen, sagt Christus der Herr. Darum müssen die gottsäligen obren die Religion nit als ein mittel zum eusserlichen friden brauchen, wie die gottlosen tyrannen thund, sondern die Religion selb lassen jr end sein, darumb sy alles thun und anrichten, das bei den jren durch jr ampt der regierung der nam Gottes als mehr gehailigt, und sein reych mehr ausgepreytet und bass erbowen werde.*

29. *WA* 11: 262, 7.

30. Ibid., 12: 330, 30.

31. Butzer preferred to speak of the state as *respublica*. This is due to the fact that his political thinking was formed primarily by his experience in the city-state of Strassburg. Cf. Hans Baron's important study on "Calvinist Republicanism" in *Church History*, VIII (1939), 30 ff.

32. *Script. angl.*, p. 158.

33. *WA* 11: 251, 34.

34. Ibid., 32: 307, 19; 440, 9, 23.

35. Ibid., 51: 242, 6.

36. *WA* 16: 377, 6.

37. Ibid., 51: 242, I.

38. Ibid., 51: 239, 21.

39. Ibid., 6: 457, 28 ff., 467, 17 ff., 450, 21 ff., 466, 13 ff., 465, 25 ff.

40. When Butzer met Luther for the first time, he was an enthusiastic Erasmian (cf. Anrich, *Martin Bucer*, pp. 4 ff.). He heard Luther in a disputation on the *theologia crucis* at an Augustinian convent in Heidelberg, 1518 (WA I, 353 ff.). Butzer wrote his impressions to his friend, the Humanist Beatus Rhenanus (cf. Daniel Gerdesius, *Introductio in Hist. Ev. Secluo xvi* [Groningen, 1774], pp. 175 ff.). His comparison of Luther with Erasmus is interesting: *Cum Erasmo illi conveniunt ommia, quin uno hoc praestare videtur quod quae ille duntaxat innovat, hic experte docet et libere* (1). Even at Butzer's funeral, his friendship with Erasmus is mentioned *Script. angl.*, p. 885). The following references on Butzer's Erasmian character are worth remembering: Erasmian influence upon Butzer's method of exegesis (A. Lang, *Evangelienkommentar Mart Butzers*, (Neukirchen & Darmstadt: Wissenschaftliche Buch Gesellschaft, 1941 & 1972) pp. 20 f., 30, 54 f., 58); humanistic influence upon Butzer's attitude in the controversy about the Lord's Supper (Cf. W. Koehler, *Zwingli und Luther*, Vol. I [Leipzig: Verein für Reformationsgeschichte von M. Heinsius Nachfolger, 1924]). The same influence governed Butzer in his political efforts to bring about a religious union (cf. P. Vetter, *Die Religionsverhandlungen auf dem Reichstage zu Regensburg* [Jena: Frommanschen Buchhandlung, 1889], pp. 79 ff.; M. Lenz, *Briefwechsel Philipps des Grossmütigen mit Butzer* [Leipzig: Heinsius, 1880], I, 271, ff., III, 31 ff.; Robert Stupperich, *Der Humanismus und die Wiedervereinigung der Konfessionen* [Leipzig: Heinsius, 1936]). The moralistic concept of religion and the plan to bring about a moral reformation of the world was common to all Humanists (cf. W. Sohm, *Die Schule Joh. Sturms und die Kirche Strassburgs* [München: Kaiser, 1912], p. 112; R. Seeberg, *Dogmengeschichte* [Leipzig: Heinsius 1920], IV, 2, 629; Otto Ritschl, *Die reformierte Theologie des 16. und des 17. Jahrh.* [Dogmengeschichte des *Protestantismus*, Vol. III, Göttingen: Vandenhoeck & Ruprecht, 1926], p. 123 ff.). Hans Emil Weber (*Reformation*, pp. 203–17) interprets Butzer's thought in terms of a *"christozentrische ethische Geistesmystik,"* For further literature, consult the *Bibliographia Bucerana* by Robt. Stupperich published together with H. Bornkamm's lecture, *M. Butzers Bedeutung für die europäische Reformationsgeschichte* (Gütersloh: Bertelsmann, 1952).

3. Calvin and Butzer

Calvin belonged to the second generation of Protestant reformers. It does not necessarily follow from this fact that he was an epigonus; that he was not, is proved by the existence of that strong type of Protestantism generally called Calvinism. But it cannot be doubted that he owed decisive stimuli to his evangelical predecessors and that, in the formulation of his theological and ecclesiastical system, he was not entirely original. It is the general opinion of historians that Calvin depended—at least in the first years of his career as an evangelical theologian—largely upon Luther; particularly the idea of justification, it is claimed, has no better interpreter among the later Reformers than Calvin. Neither will one go very far astray if he assumes that Melanchthon and Zwingli exerted some influence upon the reformer of Geneva. Recently, we have begun to pay attention also to another man with whom Calvin is known to have entertained a cordial and close friendship: Martin Butzer of Strassburg.

Seeberg and Lang were the first to demonstrate Calvin's dependence on Butzer. They were preceded by Usteri,[1] who dealt with the ideas and customs of baptism common to Strassburg and Geneva; by Erichson,[2] who proved that the Genevan order of worship which, later on, became of worldwide importance, is of Strassburgian origin; and by Scheibe,[3] who called attention to the identity of Butzer's and Calvin's doctrine of predestination. Seeberg[4] claims that "Butzerianism was the preparatory stage for Calvinism," and Lang declares that without Butzer the roots of Calvin's religious system cannot be clearly understood.[5] He also stresses the fact that the most significant ideas in Calvin's theology, namely, those on predestination and on church organization, show a direct influence of Butzer.[6] The findings of Lang were emphasized by Anrich, who wrote the first, short biography of Butzer. He asserts boldly that "the triumphant course of Calvinism throughout the world signifies a continuous influence of the ideas of Butzer," who must be called "the father of Calvinism before Calvin."[7] All these suggestions were found fruitful by O. Ritschl in his discussion of Butzer and Calvin in the *History of Protestant Dogma*. He not only gives a full presentation of Butzer's theology, but in his chapters on Calvin he refers also very frequently to the influence of Strassburg on Geneva and to the identity of Calvin's and Butzer's thoughts."[8] He even goes so far as to declare that the latter was superior to the former in "theological originality."[9]

The proof of such assumptions, however, is somewhat difficult. It must be more or less indirect; to a large extent, one must be satisfied with the demonstration of similarities. This becomes most evident in connection with the doctrine of predestination, which stands in the foreground of interest. Community of thought seems to have existed since 1536, when Calvin published the first edition of the *Institutes*. Mr. Van den Bosch,[10] who made a careful investigation of Butzer's concepts of predestination before the appearance of Calvin in the Protestant public, reaches the conclusion that "in the first edition of the *Institutes* Calvin attributes to the doctrine of predestination the same religious significance as Butzer." It is interesting to note that he feels unable to assert a direct dependence of Calvin upon Butzer,[11] Scheibe,[12] and especially Holl,[13] pointed out that in order to understand Calvin, it suffices to refer to Augustine and Luther, from whom also Butzer received the first stimulus to pay attention to God's *Alleinwirksamkeit*. But, in contrast to such an opinion, which, at first glance, seems to be quite conclusive, one must seriously consider the interpretation of Lang, who calls attention to an original trait in Butzer's and Calvin's idea of predestination. The idea of election was, to them, of the same value as the idea of conversion was to the Pietists and the Methodists.[14] It enabled them to explain why a great number of men accept the gospel and why others do not.

A pragmatic analysis of the religious status of a human group, namely the observation of the fact that there seem to be nonreligious individuals, led Butzer to advance his doctrine of predestination. Only later did he also develop its full theological consequences. It is noteworthy, however, that he never admitted that the predestination idea excluded the possibility of belief in free will.[15] Although a considerable change took place in his theological development, he never surrendered those features of his theory of predestination which he exhibited in his earliest writings. His concept of predestination was based on his idea of the spirit, an idea which gave to all his thoughts a characteristic, regulative note and which distinguished him particularly from Luther, while it related him closely to Zwingli. It is not at all impossible that Butzer was here indebted to the reformer of Zurich. The elect are those who have the spirit, and those who have the spirit are enabled to believe in the word and to live a virtuous life according to the Scripture. The foundation of the church is not the word, but the spirit which renders the word effective.[16] Both supplement each other, since both emanate from Christ, to whom God has given all power. The Kingdom of Christ is his rulership over those whom he has elected, i.e., those to whom he has given the spirit so that they can gather around the word, preach, and observe it in practice. In this respect the Kingdom of God is identical with the church. The same interest prevails in Calvin's thought; not only his doctrine of predestination, but also that of the word and the spirit, are first to be found in Butzer.

But in spite of this community of thought in connection with these leading phases of their theology, a dependence of Calvin upon Butzer could hardly be maintained if there were not indications of an actual relationship between them. The literary influence of Butzer on Calvin cannot be doubted. The latter expresses his gratitude to the Strassburger in most complimentary words in the Prefaces to his commentaries on the Epistle to Romans,[17] on the Psalms,[18] and on the Gospels.[19] Lang supposes also that Calvin already used Butzer's works in connection with his work on the first edition of the *Institutes*.

How Calvin became acquainted with the Strassburg reformer during his years of study in France cannot be made out with certainty. Traditional opinion refers frequently to the famous discourse of Nicolaus Cop (All Saints Day, 1533, Paris), which Calvin is supposed to have written for his friend, the rector-to-be. Lang[20] has shown that the author used a sermon from Luther's church postil in Butzer's Latin translation. But, of course, that does not prove anything about the kind, or even the possibility, of Calvin's acquaintance with Butzer's books. Pannier[21] thinks that young Calvin heard his cousin, Olivétan, who seems to have studied in Strassburg, speak of Butzer (in 1528)[22] and that, at Bourges, his professor, Volmar, fully introduced him to the work of the latter. The first certain indication of Calvin's acquaintance with Butzer is to be found in a letter of Calvin to Butzer, which Herminjard[23] dates on September 4, 1534, and which is written from Noyon to the "Bishop of Strassburg," imploring him for help in favor of a poor minister. In conclusion, Calvin writes: *"Hoc pro tempore, Vale erudissime vir,"*[24] as if he had had previous connections with Butzer. It is much more probable that he was on friendly terms with Butzer's fellow pastor, Capito, as the first letter from Butzer to Calvin (Strassburg, November 1, 1536)[25] seems to suggest. It is written in a tone of respect which very significantly contrasts with the familiar language Capito used in writing to Calvin.[26] Its purpose was to arrange for a meeting with Calvin (now at Geneva) at a place of his convenience, where all mutual and common problems were to be discussed until an agreement of opinion was established. The last sentences read as follows: "Farewell, most learned and holy man, and do not despise my request, giving me thereby new cause of sorrow. Words fail me to express my regret at the fact that I was not privileged to make your acquaintance and to speak to you when you were here. At other times, Capito shared everything with me. I do not know what dark spirit made him so forgetful that he did not think of introducing you to me. Now he himself is very sorry about it."

These words refer to Calvin's visit in Strassburg at the end of 1534,[27] or, which is more probable, to that of October, 1536.[28]

It is most likely that the two reformers did not become personally acquainted with each other until the synod of Bern, which took place in 1537. Calvin refers to this meeting in his letter to Butzer of January 12, 1538.[29] This was written under the impression of the dismissal of Megander from the church of Bern, while the lutheranizing pastors Peter Kuntz and Sebastian Meyer, whom Calvin despised, were retained. He felt that Butzer's efforts toward a union between the Swiss and the Wittenbergers on the basis of the Wittenberg Concord of 1536 were responsible for this upheaval at Bern. He addresses Butzer in a way that continued to be characteristic of his attitude toward the busy and famous man from Strassburg, even after their relationship had developed into a cordial friendship. He reviews the opinions of Luther and of the

Swiss from an impartial point of view, asserting that he, too, is vitally interested in a church union. However, he still favors the Swiss rather than the Lutherans. He appeals to Butzer that he attempt to bring the obstinate, narrow-minded Wittenbergers to their senses. With some superiority, he himself takes the position of an impartial, although interested, observer. As such, he, a man of twenty-nine years, boldly ventures to extend a severe admonition to the renowned theologian and churchman, seventeen years his senior. He criticizes Butzer for his diplomatic restraint in theological discussion, which, he says, originated in a desire to provoke no one. Calvin writes to him: "If you want a Christ who is acceptable to all, you must not fabricate a new gospel for that purpose. . . . Having said that the veneration of Saints is produced from human superstition rather than founded on God's word, you add at once that one must, nevertheless, have regard for the writings of the church fathers, and that in so far as they recommend this veneration, it ought not to be entirely condemned. Thus you reintroduce constantly that authority by reference to which every error can be represented as truth. But does it mean to keep God truly holy if one grants so much to man that His truth no longer rules over us?"[30]

The letter shows the royal freedom and superiority of Calvin. He was willing to cooperate wherever, without sacrificing fundamental truths, he could see the promise of success. This emphasis upon clarity in theological purpose and this impartiality are characteristic of him through his relationship with Butzer.

Butzer does not seem to have been offended by the severity of the criticism—perhaps he was accustomed to such a treatment! For when Calvin was forced to leave his position at Geneva during the year 1538, he and Capito stretched every nerve in order to persuade Calvin to come to Strassburg. Butzer's forceful appeal was finally successful.[31]

While in Strassburg, Calvin was exposed to the full influence of Butzer. In the letters to his friends,[32] one discovers an attitude much friendlier than before toward the man who bore, not only the burden of the ecclesiastical reform of Strassburg and of Hesse, but also that of the upbuilding of a Protestant united front throughout the European world. Although he still mentions differences of opinion between them, and though he states his unwillingness to follow Butzer in every respect, he defends him with cordiality and with a forcefulness that indicates clearly that their acquaintance had become close and intimate. This was the more important, as Calvin spent a highly formative period of his life in this close proximity to Butzer. It is, therefore, quite right that, in his admirable study on Calvin in Strassburg, Pannier stresses the possibility that, during the years from 1538 to 1541, Calvin became in many regards Butzerian.[33] He had many precious experiences; he deepened his theological views; and he made valuable observations of practical church organization. His views on predestination and on the Lord's Supper became more precise. In regard to these doctrines, he was, when he left Strassburg, a pupil or follower of Butzer. Furthermore, there can hardly be a doubt that it was in Strassburg that Calvin was introduced to the idea of a universal Protestantism, for the cause of which he was to work so enthusiastically and ceaselessly during the last years of his life. It was Butzer who called him to Frankfurt and asked him to accompany him to the memorable religious peace conference, synods, and disputations of Hagenau and Regensburg in 1541. Through the mediatorship of Butzer, Calvin thus came in contact with German Protestantism, and especially with Melanchthon. From that time on, he was almost another Butzer in his concern for a union of the Protestant churches.[34] In many respects, he brought to Butzer's plans a partial realization. However, he never was interested in being Butzerian. He became, rather, more himself. Pannier has well said: "When he left Strassburg, Calvin was more himself; he was more Calvinistic—and that due to the nearness of Butzer."[35] Whatever he took away with him, he had made fully his own. Indeed, one cannot say that he transplanted thoughts or institutions into his world without correcting or improving them. Whether it is baptism, the Lord's Supper, predestination, and the whole type of theology for which it stands; whether it is the idea that the school is most significant for an effective church discipline, and the curriculum and organization of the Strassburg Academy; whether it is the order of worship or of church organization itself, and the idea of a united, worldwide Protestant church—he made them all Calvinistic when he accepted them for himself and took them to Geneva. But, nevertheless, in all this lives Butzer. What he thought out and planned and recommended and inspired in all these respects was made real through the understanding mind and the efficient hands of Calvin.

The type of church which we call Calvinistic or Reformed, is really a gift of Martin Butzer to the world, through the work of his strong and brilliant executive Calvin.[36] The peculiar relationship between the two men becomes quite clear in connection with the formation of the Reformed church polity. In his study[37] on this very subject, Gustav Anrich has shown, very convincingly indeed, how strangely the two worked hand in hand. Being of a fundamentally similar religious disposition—both were under the influence of Humanism—thinking and acting, therefore, more or less in the same direction; tied to such cities as Strassburg and Geneva, which were so similar in character and need, they finally found each other. What the elder envisioned in plans that busied his life, the younger man eagerly made his own. He erected a structure he could rightly call his own, but he never could have built it without the enhancing, stimulative, productive thought of the other.[38]

As we describe the building and its growth, we present the arguments of Professor Anrich: When Calvin returned to Geneva in 1541, he proposed at once to the city magistrate a new church organization, and within a few weeks, he had won his case in the "Ordonnances ecclésiastiques." Their most characteristic feature was the installment of the four offices of pastors, teachers, elders, and deacons. The pastors were combined in the *Congrégation,* later on called the *Vénérable Compagnie.* The soul of the whole organization was not this pastoral group but the *Consistoire,* consisting of the ministers and the elders. Its task was the administration of church discipline. Only for these two outstanding offices was the method of appointment and election clearly stated: A pastor was selected by the *Vénérable Compagnie,* presented to the magistrate, and, if accepted, elected by the congregation, this election being ratified by the magistrate. The twelve presbyters were appointed upon the proposal of the pastors; all had to be members of the city council.

If one asks for the source of this order, one is inclined to follow Calvin, who points to the New Testament. In the 1543 edition of the *Institutes,* he offered proof by using the enumerations of the officers and gifts of the spirit in 1 Cor. 12 and Eph. 4. But after a careful study and examination of these references, it becomes evident that it was not the early Christian pattern that was applied to the conditions of Geneva, but rather that it was the needs of the Genevan situation that were projected into the New Testament. Since a scriptural source of the church order seems not to be indicated, it might be found, so one could assume, in Calvin's own proposal for church discipline of 1537. But, there, one does not encounter the term "elder," nor the doctrine of the four offices as *ius divinum*, nor collegial ecclesiastical magistrates. Neither do the *Institutes* of 1536 or 1539 present the case differently; nor is the hint at other cities where church discipline had been introduced before, e.g., Basel, of value, since the characteristics of the Genevan order are lacking. One has to turn to Strassburg.

Begun in 1531 under the leadership of Jacob Sturm as the representative of the magistrate, church discipline had been fully constituted in the church order of 1534, with the collaboration especially of Butzer. Three *Kirchenpfleger*, or wardens, assist the pastor of each parish in his work of discipline. All pastors and three of the helpers, who take turns in attending the meetings, form the church assembly, convening twice a month. Pastors are called in the following way: After having passed an examination, the candidate preaches before the congregation, and the elders of the parish with twelve members of the congregation undertake the election, which has to be ratified by the magistrate.[39]

This order was developed in order to protect the church against the Anabaptist sects. It resulted from a practical necessity. It is most interesting to note that Butzer devised the theological theory for these institutions. In the Strassburg Catechisms of 1534, 1537, and 1543, in his book, *De vera cura animarum*, of 1538, and especially in his church order for Hesse (accepted at Ziegenhain in 1538, published in 1539), he deduced from 1 Cor. 12 and Eph. 4 the theory of the divinely ordered offices of pastors, presbyters, deacons, and also that of the teachers, although they became never so prominent as in Geneva.

These orders, it is true, were not fully realized. Butzer could never obtain the full cooperation of the magistrate—only in Hesse was he quite successful. But there can be no doubt that he introduced Calvin to the Strassburg system of discipline. From Butzer, Calvin learned the theory of the *ius divinum* of ecclesiastical offices, especially that of the presbyters. So far Anrich.

It is, then, quite evident that the so-called Calvinist type of church organization originated very largely in Strassburg and in the mind of Butzer, whose ideas Calvin put into practice. The growth of this organization illustrates better than anything else to what an extent Calvin was Butzerian in order to be himself. Professor Von Schubert has rightly said: "What the contact with the spirit of Rome was to the founder of the order of the Jesuits, the contact with the spirit of Strassburg and of Butzer was to Calvin."[40] If we add to all the theological views they shared their identical estimation of social ethics, which Klingenburg has fully investigated,[41] and, particularly, Calvin's dependence on Butzer in his defense of elective government,[42] the affinity between the two reformers appears as truly astonishing. But whether this minimizes the originality of Calvin or of Butzer, we cannot say. We must be satisfied with the fact that there existed between them a very close community of thought and judgment. *"Bucer et Calvin,"* says Pannier, *"étaient bien faits pour se comprendre."*[43]

We know that after the Strassburg days, their friendship was cordial. But its expression in correspondence is largely unknown to us, because only a few of their letters are preserved. It is characteristic of both of them that, when Calvin was about to return to Geneva, Butzer wrote to Bern that Calvin was needed in Strassburg for the French congregation and the Academy as well as for the great tasks of Protestantism,[44] and that Calvin wanted Butzer to accompany him to his city.[45] A few examples of the intimacy that marked their relationship are still existing. On October 15, 1541, Calvin wrote to Butzer, in a letter of thanks for the hospitality he had received in Strassburg: "If I should not live up to your expectations, you know well that I am in your power. Admonish, chastize, do all that a father is permitted to do to his son."[46] And Butzer, who believed that Calvin's brilliance was equaled only by that of Melanchthon,[47] and who longed for Calvin just as much as for Capito, who had been taken by the plague of 1541,[48] was no less intimate in his letters to Calvin. He closes a cordial letter of consolation and encouragement with the following words: *"Sed tu meum cor, meus animus* [thou, my heart, my soul], *semper tuo, imo Christi bono, omnium omnia mala vinces, quoad licuerit . . . Tuus totus* [thine wholly] *Bucerus.*"[49]

The few letters of Butzer that were written during the following years and that have come down to us deal chiefly with political and ecclesiastical affairs.[50] But, beginning with the year 1547, the letters became more frequent and also more direct and open in tone and feeling. The dark days of the Emperor's warfare against the Protestants and of the Interim were approaching. Butzer saw his life work endangered: God's avenging hand was stretched out over his unfaithful people.[51] God himself was demanding the supreme sacrifice for the sake of faith. Butzer was willing to give it.[52] In these years, he proved that he was a man of firm, courageous decision. But his heart was faltering, and in sorrowful letters he deplored the situation of the German church, beseeching his friends for their prayers, so that the faint hope for a victory of the gospel might perhaps be fulfilled.[53] He prepared himself for exile. He learned that he would have to leave the city he loved with all his heart, in order to dwell in a foreign land. But, in the fall of 1548, he expressed the hope that in such a case the Lord might give him the opportunity of seeing the churches of Geneva.[54] When his fate became more certain and when he had already decided to go to England, he still wished to bid farewell to his friend personally.[55] Evidently, Calvin was again close to his heart, for he signed his letters again: *"Tuus totus Bucerus."*[56] His hope was not to be fulfilled; he fled to England, never to return, on April 6, 1549.

None of Calvin's letters of this period are preserved. But we can still read a few he wrote to England. They are examples of his fine, noble sensitiveness and tact, for it cannot have been easy to deal with Butzer, who was broken in health and in spirit and who saw his course ended. But Calvin's affection for him remained strong and fresh.

Butzer was homesick in London and in Cambridge. He longed for his friends, and he suffered because they did not write to him. He suspected that they had left him, turning to the Zurichers under the leadership of Bullinger, who saw in him a menace to the cause of the Gospel, blaming him for having obscured the doctrine of the Lord's Supper. The Swiss animosity against Butzer had turned into hatred. Already, in 1546, referring to the death of Luther (February 18, 1546), Bullinger had written to A. Blarer,[57] who was not only his but also Butzer's friend: "But I should begin to hope for the better, if Butzer also would be called by the Lord; for there lives no other man in our days, who gives more hopes to the Papists and who disputes about the Lord's supper in an obscurer way than this Butzer. . . . So much is certain: Now that Luther is dead, Butzer will delve more deeply into his union efforts, because until now he was miserably afraid of Luther, in his cause." About Butzer in England he wrote: "Butzer is in England and remains fully himself. What Germany has accepted from him, England will also accept. May the Lord protect her from evil and may He give him a better mind or a better end *(meliorem mentem vel meliorem metam)*. In such an ungrateful and evil time, however, there must be instruments of anger and corruption. The Lord Jesus may have mercy on his people."[58]

Calvin knew all about this. He not only consoled Butzer, but he also defended him. He requested Bullinger,[59] informing him of Butzer's complaints, that he should tell Hooper, who was taking Bullinger's side, to treat Butzer as he, one of the foremost servants of Christ, deserved. He assured Bullinger constantly of his friendship with Butzer: "I should do wrong to the church of God, if I should hate or despise him, not to mention anything about what he has meant to me personally."[60] Or: "Of course, I am sometimes of another opinion than you, but my heart is not at all estranged from you; just as I keep up my friendship with Butzer, although, in all freedom, I sometimes think differently than he."[61] To Butzer himself he wrote cordial letters, though they were not quite as intimate as one might expect. He wrote to Edward VI and to the Lord of Somerset,[62] assisting Butzer in his efforts for a reformation in England. He expressed his regret that it had not been possible for him to ask Butzer's advice in connection with a letter to Melanchthon.[63] He advised him—the best counsel to a homesick man—to write books in order to make his wonderful gifts useful to the church.[64] And—what was probably of more value to Butzer than anything else—he succeeded in having the Consensus Tigurinus accepted. Not without having asked for Butzer's opinion and not without praising his assent,[65] he here had pursued a work that was dearest to Butzer's heart. When he announced the friend's death (February 28, 1551) to Bullinger, he said that he felt lonesome, like an orphan.[66] No doubt he loved him much. If we remember that Butzer had been one of his chief teachers, we know why.

One wonders why Butzer never received proper credit for his contributions to Calvin and how it could happen that Calvin so entirely overshadowed him. We can find an answer to this question if we compare the goals the two men had set themselves in their work.

During the controversy of 1544 between the Lutherans and the Swiss, Bullinger once used the expression *bucerisare*[67] *(verbutzern* or *butzern),* having in mind Butzer's method of reconciling the divergent views on the Lord's Supper. By coining that word, he testified to the fact that Butzer represented an original type of Protestant theologian. It was because of this very fact that the Strassburger had so many enemies and that even his friends disagreed with him. He himself was well aware of the animosity his activity and viewpoint caused, but although he sometimes grew weary, he never ceased to pursue his ends. He was driven on by a decision which he had clearly defined to himself and which was the heart of all his work. It is prominent in all his writings, in commentaries, pamphlets, and letters. For our purpose it must suffice to concentrate our attention on the correspondence with the Blarers, of whom at least Ambrosius (of Konstanz) always understandingly tried to take his side.

Butzer was blamed for conceding too much to the Lutherans or to the Catholics. But he declared: "I condemn the Erasmian caution and the Saxon ambition; I seek the simplicity of Christ."[68] What he meant by this he explained at another occasion: "My aim is, although I pursue it not always with the necessary warmth and broadmindedness, that Christians should recognize and embrace each other in love; for all defects in customs and judgment result from the fact that, because of weak concord, the spirit of Christ misses its effect. . . . How well do I understand now, since my attitude toward Luther, Philipp (Melanchthon), and others is purer, their pious writings of which I had before so much to criticize."[69] He wanted to overcome the differences in theology, because a theological faith as such did not seem to him to comprehend the essence of Christianity. "In true theology," he wrote, "everyone knows correctly as much as he expressed in life."[70] The same principle is described in the gospel Commentary, in these beautiful words: "True theology is not theoretical or speculative. Its aim is rather action, i.e., a godlike life."[71] Through a faith that was effectively expressing itself in love, he wished to see the realization of the *communio sanctorum*,[72] "Communion"—that was his great ideal. Everything had to serve this end. "For nobody truly knows Christ who does not feel the necessity of a communion, of mutual care and discipline among his members.... Christ suffered and taught for no other purpose but that we should be one and embrace each other with the same love with which he embraced us, and that we should seek our mutual salvation with the same eagerness with which he sought ours."[73] Hence his emphasis upon church discipline. No communion of love could exist, he thought, without discipline.

Such an ideal was new and original in the compass of Protestant theology. It is interesting to note that Butzer attributed the ideal of communion now to the local congregation and then to the church at large. In this latter respect, he was still under the powerful impression of medieval ecclesiasticism and Catholic universalism. Christ, the head of the one church, the *corpus Christi*—to this medieval church concept he gave a Protestant flavor. He pointed out: "Christ, the head, is working in one body which is connected with him and consists of well connected and cooperating members. O pernicious blindness, that even the best Evangelicals do not recognize what it means to believe in the Catholic church and in the communion of saints, and to be members of Christ."[74] These are terms and words by which the medieval Catholics used to define their universalism.[75] When Butzer spoke or wrote them, he filled them with a new passion, described by "faith and love,"[76] which he had learned from Luther and Zwingli. But one still senses the atmosphere of the Dominican Order, in which Butzer received his education, and one hears, if even so softly, the great Thomas, when one reads: "The Kingdom of God is the church of Christ";[77] but the Protestant explains: "It consists of nothing that is external *per se*, but of faith and justice, and in such a use of external things as faith dictates." Butzer was a Catholic with a Protestant heart.

As such, he desired to be a Paul to his contemporaries; and, indeed, he had the wide-open heart of the great apostle.

If we cannot agree *[congredi]*, we are neither against nor of Christ. He promised that he would be in the midst of those who gather together in his name; if we cannot come together in his name, we cannot pray to him either.[78] All who read Paul must know how Paul and all true Christians promoted the protection and the development of the communion of saints and their agreement *[consensus]* in all things. By the ministry of the word, faith is born and nourished; that is why the apostle traversed land and sea and sent out his [pupils] with such eagerness; now another spirit is at the helm, which flees all union *[congressum]*.[79]

The same passion that sent Paul restlessly around the world was driving him on to make Christ the ruler "to whom the Father has given not only some regions of Germany but the whole globe."[80] One is almost tempted to say that, like the apostle, he desired to be a Jew to the Jews and a Greek to the Greeks in order that Christ might become the true king of all his believers.

But Luther and Calvin appealed to another Paul, the Paul who knew no compromise. If Butzer stressed the words "love" and "communion" most of all, Calvin emphasized, one may say, "faith" and "faithful." The famous saying of Hundeshagen: *"Die Dogmatik ist bei den Reformierten nur ein locus in der Kirche, bei den Lutheranern umgekehrt die Kirche nur locus in der Dogmatik,"* [81] is more appropriate with regard to Butzer than to Calvin.

Butzer thought of religion first of all as ministering to man's salvation, while Calvin related it primarily to the eternal God. Butzer was a humanistic, social Biblicist, Calvin a theocentric Biblicist. Calvin could always hold fast to one steady, firm pole, which he called *majestas Dei*, but Butzer was shifting and changing for the sake of the *communio sanctorum*. That is why the doctrine of predestination finds a logical place in Calvin's theological system, while Butzer at first used it as a means to analyze and to command a practical sociological situation, only later on compelling himself to think it out to its full theological consequences. That is why Calvin could afford either to differ from others in his opinions and yet keep friendship or to differ and break radically, while Butzer could neither stop to seek in friendship also some agreement of opinion nor radically break with anyone. Calvin could be cruel; Butzer could not, and he was no less energetic than Calvin!—for the *cura animarum* came first.

All this leads us to understand why Butzer was barely remembered by the side of Calvin. And yet—he was the father of Calvinism.

NOTES

1. J. M. Usteri, *Studien und Kritiken* (Zürich: Füssli, 1884), p. 417.
2. Alfred Erichson, *Die calvinische und die altstrassburgische Gottesdienstordnung* (Strassburg: Treuttel & Würtz, 1894).
3. Max Scheibe, *Calvins Prädestinationslehre* (Halle A. S.: Karras, 1897), pp. 17 ff., 69 ff.
4. Reinhold Seeberg, *Dogmengeschichte* (Leipzig: A. Deichert, 1898), II, 254; now IV, 2, 556.
5. A. Lang, *Der Evangelienkommentar Martin Butzers* (Neukirchen & Darmstadt: Wiss. Buch Gesell., 1941, 1972). p. 373.
6. A. Lang, *Calvin* (Tübingen: Mohr, 1909), *Reformation und Gegenwart* (Gütersloh: Bertelsmann, 1918), p. 176; cf. E. Doumergue, *Calvin*, (Lausanne: G. Bridel & Co., 1927), IV, 401 f.; V, 23 f.
7. Gustav Anrich, *Martin Bucer* (Strassburg: K. J. Trübner, 1914), p. 144.
8. O. Ritschl, *Dogmengeschichte des Protestantismus* (Göttingen: Vandenhoeck & Ruprecht, 1926), III, 122 ff. In respect of the theological relationship between Butzer and Calvin, cf. also Joh. Adam, *Evangelische Kirchengeschichte der Stadt* (Strassburg: Heitz, 1922), pp. 217 ff., and the remarks of H. Strohl in his interesting study on "Martin Butzer, précurseur du Christianisme social en Alsace du XVIe siècle," in *Le Christianisme social* Strassburg: L'trane Istra, 1922), pp. 992–1011. Professor Strohl has often emphasized the influence of Butzer upon Calvin; see particularly his detailed study, "La notion d'église chez les réformateurs," in *Rev. d'hist. et de phil. relg.*, XVI (1936), 265 ff.
9. O. Ritschl, *Dogmengeschichte*, p. 125.
10. Van den Bosch, *De ontwikkeling van Bucers praedestinatie-gedachten* (Hardewijk: Mooij, 1922).
11. Scheibe takes a similarly careful attitude; *Calvins Prädestinationslehre*, p. 73.
12. Ibid., p. 146.
13. Karl Holl, *Calvin* (Tübingen: Mohr, 1909), p. 47, n. 15. Cf. E. Doumergue, *Calvin*, IV, 424.
14. A. Lang, *Calvin*, pp. 78 ff.
15. Cf. Butzer's discussion in *Metaphras, et Enarrat, in Epistolam ad Romanos* (Strassburg, 1536), pp. 358 ff.
16. Cf. Richard H. Grützmacher, *Wort und Geist* (Leipzig: A. Diechert, 1902), pp. 116–22; O. Ritschl, *Dogmengeschichte*, pp. 129 ff.; W. Pauck, *Das Reich Gottes auf Erden* (Berlin: Walter de Gruyter, 1928), pp. 5 ff.; 13 ff.
17. *Calv. opp.*, 10, p. 404. Published in Strassburg, 1539. Cf. Scheibe, *Calvins Prädestinationslehre*, pp. 69 ff.
18. *Calv. opp.*, 31 (1557), p. 13.
19. Ibid., 45 (1555), p. 4. *Bucerum praesertim sanctae memoriae virum et eximium ecclesiae doctorem sum imitatus.* Cf. Paul Wernle, *Calvin* (Tübingen: Mohr, 1919), p. 34, 81. Lang mentions an influence of Butzer's book, *De vera cura animarum*, Cf. *Ref. und Gegenwart*, p. 183. Opposing view: Doumergue, *Calvin*, IV, 39.
20. A. Lang, *Calvin*, p. 21.
21. Jaques Pannier, *Calvin à Strasbourg* (Strassbourg: Imprimerie Alsacienne, 1925), p. 11, 13.

22. This assumption is based on a letter of Butzer to Farel, dated May (most probably 1528), which Kampschulte used for his theory that Calvin was a student of Butzer. Herminjard refuted this theory, suggesting that Butzer speaks of Olivétan. Cf. H. Eells, "Martin Butzer and the conversion of John Calvin," *Princeton Theol. Rev.* (1924), p. 402.

23. A. L. Herminjard, *Correspondence des réformateurs (Genéva: H. Georg, 1866).*

24. Ibid., p. 204, Cf. the discussion by Eells, "Martin Butzer & the conversion of J. Calvin," *Princeton Theol. Review* (Princeton: 1924), pp. 407 ff.

25. Herminjard, op. cit. IV, 117 ff.; cf. the correction of the date (not Dec. 1) by Eells, *op. cit.* pp. 412 ff.

26. Herminjard, p. 119;.

27. Ibid., p. 119, nn. 7, 9, 10.

28. Cf. Eells, "Martin Butzer," pp. 415 ff.

29. *Calv. opp.,* 10, pp. 137 ff.

30. Ibid., pp. 142 f.

31. See Calvin's own account in *Opp.,* 31, pp. 25 ff. Cf. Doumergue, *Calvin,* II, 225 ff.

32. *Calv. opp.,* 10, pp. 341; 344 ff.; 348.

33. Pannier, *Calvin à Strassbourg,* pp. 9, 54 f. Cf. also the fascinating accounts of Doumergue in *Calvin* (1902), II, 203 ff., and of Hastings Eells, *Martin Bucer* (New Haven: Yale University Press, 1931), pp. 229 ff. This detailed biography of Butzer unfortunately lacks attention to theology.

34. Cf. Joseph Bohatec, in *Calvin-Studien* (Tübingen: Mohr, 1909), p. 440; A. Lang, *Calvin,* pp. 78, 192. Compare also John T. McNeill, *Unitive Protestantism* (New York: Abingdon, 1930), pp. 68 ff. and 178 ff.

35. McNeill, *Unitive Protestantism, p. 55.*

36. This is also the judgment of Courvoisier *La Motion d'église chez Bucer* (Paris: Alcan, 1933), p. 147.

37. Gustav Anrich, *Strassburg und die calvinische Kirchenverfassung* (Tübingen: Mohr, 1928). See also Francois Wendel, *L'église de Strasbourg: Sa constitution et son organisation* (Paris, Renes Universitaires, 1942).

38. See the full discussion of this relationship in Joseph Bohatec, *Calvin's Lehre von Staat und Kirche* (Breslau: Marcus, 1937), pp. 460 ff.

39. The old Butzer seemingly wanted to exclude the congregation in this respect. According to *De regno Christi,* the ministers elect the elders, in contrast to the order of Strassburg, where he had the presbyters elected by the congregation. (Cf. W. Sohm, *Die Schule Joh. Sturms und die Kirche Strassburgs* [München: Kaiser, 1912], p. 163.)

40. Hans Von Schubert, *Calvin* (Tübingen: Mohr, 1909), pp. 13 f.

41. Georg Klingenburg, *Das Verhältnis Calvins zu Butzer auf Grund der wirtschaftsethischen Bedeutung bei den Reformatoren* (Bonn: Marcus, 1906). Cf. Doumergue, *Calvin,* V, 688 f.; compare also R. H. Tawney, *Religion and the Rise of Capitalism* (New York: Harcourt, Brace & Co., 1926), pp. 105 ff., and Bohatec, *Calvins Lehre,* pp. 719 ff.

42. Cf. Hans Baron, "Calvinist Republicanism", *Church History,* VIII (1939), pp. 38 ff., who proves Calvin's dependence on Butzer's *Lectures on the Book of Judges.*

43. J. Pannier, *Calvin à Strassbourg,* p. 12.

44. Herminjard, *Correspondence des réformateurs,* VI, 242 f.

45. Doumergue, *Calvin,* II, 701.

46. *Calv. opp.,* 11, p. 299: *Et si qua in re spei vestrae non respondeam, scis me sub tua potestate esse. Admoneas, castiges, omnia facias quae patri licent in filium.*

47. Herminjard, *Correspondence des réformateurs*, VI, 235 (letter to O. Myconius of Basel [Sept., 1541]; *Datis ergo operam ut juvete virum certe eximium, et cujus perfecto parem, excepto Philippo, nullum habemus, ardore, eloquentia et judicio).*

48. To A. Blarer; T. Schiess, *Briefwechsel der Gebrüder* Blarer (Freiburg: F. E. Fehsenfeld, 1910), II, 133.

49. Herminjard, *Correspondence des réformateurs*, VIII, 150 f.

50. E.g., *Calv. opp.*, 10, pp. 414 ff. (July 7, 1542); pp. 456 (Oct. 28, 1542); pp. 634 f. (Oct. 28, 1543); ibid., 12, pp. 152 ff. (Aug. 29, 1545); pp. 162 f. (Sept. 8, 1545).

51. Cf. *Calv. opp.*, 12, pp. 507; 520 f.; 555 f.

52. Ibid., 13, p. 5.

53. Ibid., pp. 147 ff.; 181 f.; 197 ff.

54. Ibid., p. 56: *Tum forsan dabit, ut quod expetii toties, videam vestras ecclesias.*

55. Ibid., p. 199.

56. Ibid., pp. 350, 358, 574.

57. Schiess, *Briefwechsel*, II, 442 f.

58. August 11, 1549, to A. Blarer; Schiess, *Briefwechsel*, III, 56. Note the following lines of a satirical poem on Butzer (communicated by A. Erichson in his little book, *Martin Butzer, der elsässische Reformator* [Strassburg: Heitz, 1891], p. 33): *Butzer der butzt auch am Rhein, Nimmt zuletzt ganz England ein.*

59. *Calv. opp.*, 13, p. 489. To Farel he wrote (August 18, 1550, ibid., pp. 624 f.) that he would not mention the Zurichers again in his letters to Butzer, in order not to hurt his feelings.

60. Ibid., 12, p. 729: *Sed obsecro te, mi Bullingere, quo iure nos a Bucero alienaremus quum huic nostrae confessioni quam posui subscribat? Ego virtutes et raras et permultas, quibus vir ille excellit, in praesentia non praedicabo. Tantum dicam me ecclesiae Dei gravem iniuriam facturum, si hunc vel oderim vel contemnam. Taceo ut de me privatim sit meritus.*

61. Ibid., 13, p. 165.

62. To Seymour: ibid., 13, pp. 16 f., 18 f., 64 ff., 528 ff. To Edward VI: ibid., 13, pp. 669 ff.; 14, pp. 30 ff., 38 ff., 341 ff.

63. *Calv. opp.*, 20, p. 401 f. This letter was written a few days before Butzer's death. Butzer never read it.

64. Ibid., pp. 393 f.

65. Ibid., 13, pp. 424, 457, 534 f.

66. Ibid., 14, p. 106: *Nuncius de Anglia nondum rediit. Sed interea de Buceri morte certior factus magnum accepi dolorem. Quod nollem, brevi sentiemus quantum ecclesia Dei iacturam fecerit. Satis dum vivebat reputabam quam praeclaris dotibus excellerit: quam utilis adhuc nobis foret, melius nunc demum ex orbitate ipsa agnosco.* To Viret he writes a few weeks later (ibid., pp. 121 f.): *Moeror quem ex Buceri morte concepi sollicitudinem ac metum auget. . . . Quam multiplicem in Bucero iacturam fecerit, quoties in mentem venit, cor meum prope larcerari sentio.* And still a few weeks later to Farel (ibid., p. 133): *De Buceri obitu nihil attigeram, ne vulnus meum scinderem.*

67. Schiess, *Briefwechsel*, II, 308.

68. Ibid., I, 721.

69. Ibid., I, 742.

70. Ibid., I, 648: *In vera theologia tantum quisque rite novit quantum vita exprimit.*

71. *Enarr, in quat. Ev.* (Basel, 1536): *Vera theologia non theoretica et speculativa, sed activa et practica est. Finis siquidem ejus agere est, hoc est vitam vivere deiformem.*

72. Schiess, *Briefwechsel*, I, 774; *Religio nititur fide efficiente communionem sanctorum.*

73. Ibid., II, 131 f.

74. Schiess, *Briefwechsel*, II, 119
75. It is most interesting to observe how often the judgments of Gierke, Maitland, Figgis, apply also to Butzer, Cf. O. Gierke, *Genossenschaftsrecht*, Vol. III (Berlin: Weidmann, 1887; English translation by F. W. Maitland, *Political Theories of the Middle Ages* [Cambridge: The University Press, 1900]); F. N. Figgis, "Respublica Christiana," in *Transactions of the Royal Hist. Soc.*, 3d series (London: Longmans, Green & Co., 1911), V, 63 ff.
76. *"Fides et caritas"* is another slogan in Butzer's theology. Note how F. W. L. Baum (*Capito and Butzer* [Elberfeld: Friderichs, 1860]) emphasizes it in his representation of Butzer.
77. Herminjard, *Correspondence des réformateurs* VI, 20. This is the theme of his last work, *De regno Christi*.
78. Schiess, *Briefwechsel*, I, 773.
79. Ibid., I, 772 f.
80. Ibid., I, 641.
81. O. Ritschl, *Dogmengeschlichte*, p. 129, n. 26.

4. Luther and Melanchthon

Until recently, historical studies of the Reformation were concentrated upon Luther research. Thus the impression was created that the heritage of the Lutheran Reformation, i.e., the spiritual attitudes displayed in Lutheran piety and doctrine, morality and ecclesiastical practice, must be understood and evaluated chiefly with respect to Luther.

But such a judgment does not correspond with the historical facts. The spiritual substance of Lutheranism has been at all times both more and less than what was embodied in Luther's person and teaching—*less*, because his prophetic spirit proved itself to be inexhaustible; and *more*, because, from the beginning (in contrast, for instance, to Calvin), his work was being preserved by the labors of others who gave it form and body. In all this Melanchthon played a decisive role. Hence it is of greatest significance that Luther scholars should concern themselves also with Melanchthon.

In my opinion, Ernst Troeltsch has stated most aptly what this means specifically. He writes:[1]

It was not Luther but Melanchthon who determined fully what the exact consistency of Lutheranism was to be. He was the chief teacher and instructor, the scholarly publicist, and the theological diplomat of early Lutheranism; as such he passed Luther's ideas through the sieve of his formulations. Through these formulations the wonderfully rich and highly varied ideas of Luther became theological doctrines stated in definite forms. It was Melanchthon who was mainly responsible for the education of the new theological generation and for the formulation of all official utterances. Through all this Luther's thinking was presented in a form which was derived from Melanchthon's 'theology of definitions'.

Indeed, it was through the scientific system of the *loci communes* that Melanchthon became the theological teacher of Lutheranism for more than a century. This system had originated in Humanism. It was therefore Melanchthon, the humanist, who rendered these significant services to the Reformation. What this has meant, has been impressed upon us only recently in a fresh way by the suggestive dissertations of Wilhelm Neuser and Adolf Sperl.[2] Melanchthon was the only humanist with whom Luther came to terms and whom he tolerated. We may even go so far as to say that he entered into an alliance with him.[3]

This is all the more remarkable in view of Luther's hostility toward Erasmus and his negative attitude toward the humanistic program of reform. We Protestant church historians must remind ourselves again and again of this circumstance, especially because of the fact that in this strange alliance the humanist Melanchthon proved himself to be the stronger of the two, insofar as he achieved a more direct concrete effectiveness than Luther, in the theological teachings and in the ecclesiastical orders of Lutheranism.

Luther never stressed the differences between himself and Melanchthon insofar as they were rooted in Humanism, yet he knew exactly what they consisted of and what they meant. We shall come back to this, later on. Here it must suffice for us to refer to a letter, written in 1536 by Chancellor Brück to the Elector of Saxony, in which he reports about a conversation with Luther. Luther had told him, he writes,[4] that students frequently complained to him saying that they had noticed a conflict between his teaching and that of Melanchthon and that they feared that a split might develop between them, especially if it should turn out that Melanchthon would move to Tübingen. And then Brück continues as follows: "Martin said that he (Melanchthon) was a learned man whom he esteemed highly, but that his reason occasionally caused him trouble; he would have to be on his guard lest he end up at the same point where Erasmus came out. If it should ever happen that they would have to write against one another and dispute with one another, a great *scandalon* would certainly arise."

It is noteworthy that things did not come to this; Luther never broke with Melanchthon, and Melanchthon remained loyal to Luther. They both were resolved to do all in their power to make their alliance a lasting one, i.e., to keep combined the ways of an unphilosophical evangelist and those of a philosophical humanist.

I shall try to show the nature of this mutual resolve by dealing (1) with the character and the aims of Melanchthon's humanism, and (2) with the nature of the friendship between the two, paying special attention to the fact that Luther had a deep understanding of Melanchthon's humanistic way of thinking, even though he was conscious of his own reliance upon totally different sources.

I

Most of the Reformers (I am thinking of Spalatin and Melanchthon; Zwingli and Oecolampadius; Capito and Butzer; Farel, Calvin, and Beza; Latimer and Cranmer; Jewel and Richard Hooker; i.e., the founders of the Lutheran, Reformed, and Anglican church orders) came to Luther or the Reformation out of a Christian Humanism which was largely determined by Erasmus or as the chief representative of which one regarded Erasmus. But as they became reformers, i.e., as they were brought under the sway of Luther's powerful teaching with the result that their thinking was changed insofar as they were forced to break with the authority of the Pope and to submit instead to the sole authority of the word of God, they all remained, each in his way, humanists. In this they all were different from *the* Reformer. Even at the time when he called himself *Eleutherius,* his thinking was fundamentally not humanistic but evangelical.

Young Melanchthon, then twenty-one years old, came to Wittenberg a persuaded humanist. He joined the Reformation and became a Lutheran through and through—and yet he remained a humanist. Even when he became the main spokesman, next to Luther, of the Saxon-German Reformation, he understood himself to be a humanist and thought as such, and this in a more definitive way than Calvin did, later. Also the world view of *this* reformer was sustained by Humanism, but, in his lifework in Geneva, he let his thinking be determined so decisively by the Scripture and the theological thought of the Reformation, that his humanistic way of thinking was almost entirely absorbed by his Biblicism. We can even go so far as to say that his understanding of the gospel compelled Calvin to undertake in his main work a sharp and pointed attack against the representative views of certain humanists, even though he was thoroughly trained in Humanism and well aquainted with the Erasmian *philosophia Christi,* with the biblical-platonic philosophy of Faber Stapulensis, and with the critical thinking of Guillaume Budé.

Melanchthon, however, as far as I know, never subjected Humanism as a world view and as a program of intellectual, moral reform to basic criticism, even though he frequently took the part of Luther and the Reformation, in a clear and resolute way, over against the humanistic defenders of the Roman Church, including Erasmus. Despite the definitive break between Erasmus and Luther in connection with their discussion on free will, indeed, despite Luther's radical and occasionally even contemptuous rejection of Erasmus, Melanchthon turned again and again to this prince of the humanists and stayed in connection with him.[5]

He always regarded himself as a humanist. It was probably for this reason that he refused to yield to Luther's pressure that he exchange his Greek professorship in the faculty of liberal arts with a theological one,[6] despite the fact that as a theologian he had a much larger following among students than as a philologist and philosopher. In the end, he was given double professorial status in the University of Wittenberg: he was appointed a member of the artistic as well as the theological faculties. Thus he was a teacher both of biblical-theological and humanistic scholarship.

He refused to obtain the degree of Doctor of Theology. In order to qualify as a theological teacher, it sufficed him to take the examinations required for the B.D. degree. Thus, though he was a professional theologian throughout his life, he was and desired to be, at the same time, a humanist.

We too should, therefore, consider him a humanistic theologian and not, as Wilhelm Maurer suggests, a Lay-Christian.[7] It is true, to be sure, that, as Professor Maurer shows in his eloquent lecture, at no time in his life Melanchthon ever occupied a pulpit in order to preach. But the fact that he could or would not preach and that he never was a minister does not suffice to call him a "non-theologian." We cannot deny the title of "theologian" to the author of the *"Loci communes"* or *"theologici"* who also composed the "Augsburg Confession" and its "Apology." Indeed, we must regard him as a theologian whose main concern was the teaching of true doctrine.

The main features of his humanistic thinking, as it expressed itself specifically in his theological work and generaly in connection with his efforts for the realization of Luther's Reformation, were the following:

In the way that was characteristic of all Reformers, he too emphasized the absolute authority of the Scripture. Especially in his Lutheran beginnings, he was so insistent upon the idea that this must be the norm of evangelical Christianity, that we can readily understand that it was he who caused Luther to draw the consequences from the Leipzig Debate in declaring, over against the authority of the Pope, that the Scripture was the exclusive principle of Christian truth. In this connection, we should also remember that Luther undertook the translation of the New Testament at his suggestion.

In view of all this, we cannot be surprised to find that his interpretation of the Scriptural principle was conditioned by Luther's teaching, but there was also a strongly humanistic nuance in his biblical thinking. This reflected the Erasmian slogan *"Ad fontes!"* He thought that God's voice could be heard most clearly in the beginnings of his revelation rather than in later testimonies about it, no matter how important they were believed to be. He wrote: "It was not Luther's intention to keep us bound to what he had written but he wanted to lead everyone's mind to the sources; he wanted us to hear the very voice of God."[8]

We find this explanation of the authority of the Bible also in the teaching of men like Zwingli and Butzer. Like Melanchthon, they too never forgot the insights, mediated to them by Erasmus, which, at the beignning of their careers, had had such a liberating effect upon them. Hence it was true of them too that their understanding of the Bible as God's word was determined by the notion that it was the source, the *historical* source, of divine truth.

From here we can understand that the Bible became for them the only binding rule for the ordering of human life. This was their teaching as, later, it became also that of Calvin. And Melanchthon too thought so, at least during the first phase of his career in Wittenberg, until the shock of the iconoclastic riots in this town caused him to adopt Luther's teaching that one cannot derive from the gospel any rules for the ordering of man's life in the world. Nevertheless, he never gave up the humanistic notion that religion is the fountain and origin of virtue and that the practice of religion ensures the moralization of the life of man.

We must not interpret an occasional remark as if it were a declaration of principle. But we are permitted, I think, to regard the following work of Melanchthon as an utterance which was very characteristic of his whole thinking. It is to be found in a letter to his friend Joachim Camerarius: "I never wanted to become engaged in theological work for any other reason than that I might contribute to the improvement of life."[9]

Luther understood the nature of theology differently, namely, not as a method by the application of which life can be bettered but as the effort to clarify the teaching which is centered in God's *evangelica promissio* offering forgiveness of sin and eternal life.

Because he was a Lutheran theologian, Melanchthon also was basically of this persuasion. And other evangelical theologians who have been influenced by Humanism, e.g., Butzer, thought so too. But it was a mark of the many-sidedness of their thinking that, in their writings, they returned again and again to the humanistic ideal of the *emendatio vitae* without feeling in any way that thereby they deviated from their main theological theme. How often Butzer asserts, for example, that the welfare of every man and of a people consist in the knowledge of what it means *bene beateque vivere*. The humanists were especially fond of this phrase of Cicero's (which, as far as I know, Augustine introduced into Christian literature). A man like Butzer used it often in order to indicate that the goal of the Reformation was the moral ordering of human life. In this, Melanchthon, just like other humanistically inclined Reformers, especially Calvin, felt himself to be his spiritual kin.

Yet it was very telling of this Lutheranism that, despite the fact that he liked to emphasize good works as the fruit of faith and that he insisted on teaching the "third use of the law," it was impossible for him to understand the Bible in the moralistic-legalistic way of Zwingli, Butzer, or Calvin. Evangelical humanists, which they were, they attached special value to the connection between faith and morality. But Melanchthon was inspired by

Humanism to cultivate especially the connection between *faith* and *intellectual culture.*

Indeed, he felt it to be his calling to realize this connection. And the manner by which he fulfilled this vocation established his fame, because, by relating faith to intellectual culture, he gave German Lutheran Protestantism a special form.

Already in his inaugural lecture in Wittenberg, on August 29, 1518, he made a plea, over against scholastic method and "pseudo-science," for an alliance between theology and true scholarship, based on the discipline of humanistic learning. He asserted[10] that an unlearned theology was the worst of all evils, because he felt that such a teaching must necessarily produce innumerable mistakes and faults. Then he proceeded to advocate the return to genuine Aristotelianism and demanded of the theologians that they should rely on it. He must have made so convincing a plea that even Luther, who was in the audience, did not resent this praise of Aristotelian philosophy but was moved to join in the general, enthusiastic applause.

Shortly after this, Melanchthon became a convinced follower of Luther. For a time, he gave up his scientific, humanistic reform program.

But when, in the early 1520s, the establishment of a new ecclesiastical order became pressing, i.e., the actualization of the Reformation in the context of the common life, he resumed his old undertaking, but now under the auspices of the Reformation. He became one of the chief organizers of the Reformation in Saxony and he quickly acquired wide fame as the most prominent scholar in the University of Wittenberg and as the author of unusually influential textbooks and other pedagogical writings. He now pursued the task of building a bridge between school and church, scholarship and theology, education and faith, culture and religion. "Those who, in their preaching, now and then dissuade the young from the study of classical literature," he wrote, "should have their tongues cut off. If one permits barbarism to raise its head, the consequences will be that theology deteriorates, as it has happened before, and I fear that this will again be our lot, unless we defend God's most precious gift, namely learning, with all our strength."[11]

At this time (the beginning of 1523, one year before he published his appeal for the establishment of schools "To the Coun-

cilmen of Germany," which Melanchthon provided with a Foreword), Luther lent him his full support. He too wrote: "I am
firmly persuaded that there can be no true theology without literary learning... Indeed, I recognize that the word of God never was made fully known except where God first prepared the
way by causing languages and letters to rise and prosper as if
they were precursory John-the-Baptists ... I certainly wish that
many poets and rhetors may arise, for as far as I can see there is
no better means by which men can apprehend religion *(sacra)*
and practice it rightly."[12]

Luther allied himself with Melanchthon in this, partly because
he admired his intellectual power, partly because he hated Roman Catholic scholastic philosophy, and partly because he was
persuaded that nobody was able to understand the Bible without
some training in languages and without a general knowledge.
But he was unable to associate himself with Melanchthon in relation to the latter's interest in a universal system of knowledge[13] to
which also theology would belong. However, he did not interfere
with his friend's efforts to establish a humanistic educational program on the soil of the Lutheran Reformation (1) by reforming
the curriculum of the faculty of liberal arts in Wittenberg; (2) by
formulating a plan for the establishment of "higher schools,"
which was widely adopted under the leadership of the city of
Nurnberg;[14] and (3) by proposing new statutes for the theological
faculty in Wittenberg and by putting them into effect.

By taking these steps, Melanchthon tried to put all branches of
science and letters (in several of which, including medicine and
mathematics, he was himself an expert) into the service of theology, in order thus to realize the educational ideals of humanistic
rhetorics, eloquence, and erudition.

In the same seat of learning, in which Luther had declared war
on Aristotelian philosophy, particularly the "Metaphysics" and
"Ethics," and where he continued passionately to oppose it, his
friend Melanchthon now sponsored it as the model and pattern
of true philosophy. He declared that the writings of Aristotle
were indispensable[15] and that their teaching content was "quasi
the very voice of nature."[16] In view of the fact that Luther's violent
objection against philosophical-theological speculation was generally adopted by the Reformers, it is interesting to note that Me-

lanchthon's Aristotelianism was not a comprehensive one, for he disregarded the "Metaphysics" and kept silent about it. But he had a high esteem for the "Ethics," a work which persistently stirred Luther's anger. In 1527, he had it printed together with his own scholia. In the preface, he stated that it would be the advantage of the theologians if they knew how to distinguish between the philosophical and the Christian virtues.[17]

We can therefore understand why it was that Melanchthon chose to advocate a certain traditionalism by means of which he tried to combine the moral-intellectual legacy of Greece and Rome with the truth of Holy Scripture. His high esteem of historical tradition as a preparatory stage and basis of the Christian religion led him, on the one hand, to reject all innovations, and, on the other hand, to regard himself as an ally of all *boni et docti viri*, i.e., all who were trained in *humanitas* and in *pietas et eloquentia*, i.e., in the humanities. His slogan was: *Non nova dogmata!* In his writings, he frequently expressed himself in this vein. In the same letter to Erasmus which we have previously quoted, he wrote the following: "I have many times stated emphatically that I am neither an originator nor an advocate of new teachings."[18] Because of this conviction, he was so intolerant in this attitude toward the Anabaptists. He suspected them of *"amor novitatis."*[19]

However, this very manner of thinking permitted him to make common cause, to a considerable degree, with the theologians and spokesmen of the Roman Church, precisely for the sake of the common intellectual tradition which he believed himself to share with them. This too was an Erasmian-humanistic attitude, because of which he deeply differed from Luther and aroused his displeasure. Yet in this regard he resembled other Protestant Erasmians. Butzer, for example, also placed the tradition of antiquity next to the Bible and, in this connection, emphasized, even to a greater degree than Melanchthon did, the formative character of the doctrines of the Fathers.

In speaking of Butzer as a humanistic comrade-in-arms of Melanchthon, it is perhaps pertinent to mention that they both wanted to see the Christian religion established as a cultural force in the social-political commonwealth under the leadership of Christian magistrates. In this they followed the conviction communicated to them by Erasmus that rulers and princes are responsible not ony for the temporal but also for the eternal welfare of their subjects and must therefore enforce obedience to both tables of the law.

But enough of this—it is impossible for me to discuss all the traits by which Melanchthon gives evidence of his lifelong dependence on humanistic "philosophy." But I must mention at least briefly that he used the method of the *"loci"* in his theological exposition of Luther's teaching. This was that method developed in connection with humanistic rhetorics which made possible a new scholarly treatment of theology. For it compelled the theologians to formulate basic concepts *(loci communes)* by reference to which they then would define essentials. Thus a clear investigation and discussion of theological subjects *(res theologicae)* could be undertaken. As Paul Joachimsen has shown, Melanchthon's *Loci* are characterized by the fact that the polarity of Luther's thinking broke in upon an Erasmian mode of thought. In other words, in his opinion, this work represents the attempt to express the polarity of Luther's thought in systematic form by means of dialectics.[20]

In this connection, we must also not fail to note that Melanchthon tended to regard the church as a kind of school and that he was wont to put special stress on the teaching aspects of the ministerial office and the sermon, thus minimizing Luther's concept of the church as the *communio sanctorum,* especialy insofar as it was connected with the idea of the universal priesthood of believers. The older he became, the more he tended to think that the substance of the gospel was represented by "doctrines."

Hence his theological discussion of the evangelical faith was marked, on the one hand, by clear definitions and on the other hand, by carefully interpreted combinations of theological themes which, in the initial analysis, had been distinguished from one another. Reason and revelation, law and gosepl, sin and forgiveness, civil and spiritual justice—these were the basic concepts which he first distinguished from and then combined with one another.

What Luther understood to be a divine action which men must apprehend or "feel" by experience, a giving on the part of God to which, in the Holy Spirit, a receiving on the part of man corresponds, a divine speaking and promising which becomes actualized in human hearing and trusting, Melanchthon expressed by means of his "defining theology" and its "basic concepts." There was nothing in it which must be considered false or wrong from the viewpoint of Luther's major concerns. On the contrary, he understood very clearly what the Reformation was all about. But his manner of theologizing did not mirror that immediate, dynamic actuality of the gospel of Christ which Luther was able to express so directly and forcefully. This was noticeable particularly in his treatment of justification.

Because he discussed it in terms of distinctions between penance, forgiveness, the imputation of Christ's righteousness, renewal, good works, etc., he was accused by his own fellow Lutherans, indeed, by his colleagues and pupils, even during Luthers's lifetime, of having perverted the evangelical truth which Luther had rediscovered. Luther never adopted these criticisms of Melanchthon. Moreover, he never expressly rejected the Melanchthonian treatment of the doctrine of justification. And he was right in this. He knew that, in his fundamental teaching, Melanchthon had comprehended clearly what he (Luther) meant to say.

All this is plainly apparent in a letter of Melanchthon to John Brenz which deals with the subject of justification and to which Luther added a postscript. It lets us see that Melanchthon had understood thoroughly the Lutheran doctrine of justification and that Luther agreed with him. Nevertheless, precisely this writing makes clear wherein they differed from one another. Melanchthon writes.[21]

You are still confined to Augustine's way of thinking ... for he thinks that we are regarded as righteous because of the fulfillment of the law which the Holy Spirit accomplishes in us. And you too think that the doctrine that we are justified by faith means that by receiving in faith the Holy Spirit we can be righteous through the fulfillment of the law which the Holy Spirit accomplishes. This idea identifies righteousness with our fulfillment of the law, with our purity and perfection, but properly speaking, this renewal must be understood as a result of faith.

Now you must dismiss from your mind this idea of renewal and the law, instead, you must direct your attention to Christ's promise in order that you may see that it is for Christ's sake and not because of this renewal that we are righteous, i.e., acceptable in God's sight and capable of being consoled in our conscience. For the fact of our having become new is not sufficient for this *(Nam haec ipsa novitas non sufficit)*. We are therefore righteous by faith alone, not because, as you express yourself, it is the root of our renewal, but because it is directed to Christ. It is because of him that we are acceptable to God, regardless of our renewal, whatever that may be. This renewal is the necessary consequence of faith, to be sure, but it cannot give consolation to our conscience. So then, it is not love fulfilling the law which justifies us, but faith alone— and it justifies us not because it makes us somehow perfect but only because it apprehends Christ. We are therefore righteous—neither because we love nor because we fulfill the law nor because we have been made new (even though all this constitutes the gifts of the Holy Spirit), but because in faith we lay hold of Christ. Faith therefore justifies us not because it is the work of the Holy Spirit in us but because it apprehends Christ. It is for his sake and not because of the gifts of the Holy Spirit which may be ours that we are acceptable in God's sight.

This is Melanchthon speaking. We cannot deny that he here defines with clarity the essential nature of justification.

But now listen to Luther's postscript (which, as far as one can tell from the style, appears to have been written down in haste):

Let me add to this on my part, dear Brenz, that in order to understand this matter properly, I make it a rule to remind myself that there is in my heart no quality of any kind that could be called faith or love. But I put in their stead Jesus Christ and say: There is my righteousness! He is in fact what this quality and this so-called formal righteousness in me are supposed to be *(ipse est qualitas et formalis, ut vocant, iustitia mea)*. Hence I no longer need to concentrate my attention upon the law and good works nor upon a Christ who confronts me from without and whom I must take to be a teacher or a donor of something. Instead I understand him to be the one who is in and by himself what he teaches me and gives me as his gift *(sed volo ipsum mihi esse donum vel doctrinam per se)*. I therefore have everything. Remember that he himself says: "I am the way, the truth, and the life." He does not say: I give to you the way and the truth and the life, as if he effected all this on me from without. It is within me that he must be, stay, live, speak . . . so that we are righteous in God's sight in him and not in love and in the gifts that flow from faith.

What Melanchthon sought to make clear by doctrinal definitions, Luther explained by pointing to the actuality of the believers' communion with Christ. Here lay the deepest difference between them. This lack of any Christ-mysticism in Melanch-thon's theology has been interpreted as a humanistic legacy,[22] with the suggestion that also for Erasmus "knowledge of Christ" was never the same as "mystical communion with Christ." I am unable to judge whether this opinion is valid, but in view of the many-sidedness of Melanchthon's thought, it certainly does not seem to be impossible.

We thus come to the conclusion that, in his theology, Melanch-thon gave to Luther's understanding of the gospel a humanistic-scientific form which, in respect of its basic presuppositions, was foreign to Luther's spiritual outlook.

II

Despite and yet also because of the deep differences that pre-vailed between them, Luther and Melanchthon were dependent upon one another. The great impact which each of them made upon later generations would not have been possible without the other's influence. It is an extraordinarily interesting and even moving undertaking to analyze the nature of their friendship.

It was a strong comradeship nourished by common work re-sponsibly carried on. It commenced in their almost fervent dis-covery of one another and it matured in a trustful mutual sym-pathy in which each rendered available to the other what he possessed of insight, knowledge, and wisdom.

Luther transmitted to Melanchthon his understanding of the gospel as the free, unmerited forgiveness of sins which bestows salvation on man through personal faith, and Melanchthon gave Luther access to the Greek language and to philosophy as a whole and compelled him to attach value to the art of clear thought and precise formulation.

After some time, there occurred a cooling off in this relation-ship but never an estrangement. The friendship became calm and steady. They had much labor in common, and they visited each other frequently and without any formality.[23]

But it is noteworthy that they were never exactly intimate in their personal relations, although they had a deep acquaintance with one another, as Luther's many remarks on Melanchthon in his Table Talk show and as the latter's brief biography of his friend clearly proves. It was, of course, not without significance that Luther was more than thirteen years older than Melanchthon. For this reason, it is understandable that the latter found a close friend in Joachim Camerarius, who was almost of the same age as he and, moreover, was a persuaded humanist.

As far as Luther is concerned, he was personally related in a much closer and more relaxed way with Spalatin and Justus Jonas, and also with Johann Bugenhagen, than with Master Philip.

It was symptomatic of the special nature of this relationship that Melanchthon was not invited to Luther's wedding (only to the wedding feast, which took place later) and that Luther's sudden decision to marry caused him considerable embarrassment. Jonas, on the other hand, was a partner in almost all events in Luther's life which were of a personal significance to him. By accident, he even was present when Luther died. But Melanchthon gave the funeral oration.[24]

Melanchthon revered Luther as his fatherly friend. In almost all his letters, he addressed him as *pater carissimus*. This indicates that he kept at a distance from Luther. In his will, which he put on paper in 1539, when he was forty-two years old, he specified this by stating[25] that he had come to know Luther as a man gifted with heroic mental powers and distinguished by piety and many virtues and that he regarded the great many benefits he had received from him as an expression of special good will toward himself; for this reason, he wrote, he had always esteemed him most highly and it was therefore his wish that his family too should revere him as a father.

Moreover, he always had a clear sense of Luther's historical stature. When he got the news of his friend's death, he said to his students that that man had passed away who had been *the* guide of the church. In his memorial address, he placed him as a hero of the faith next to Augustine and the apostle Paul.

Luther on his part maintained toward Melanchthon the attitude of great admiration. Sometimes, so it seems, it was a little exaggerated, especialy when he could not find words enough to praise the intellectual powers of the shy, somewhat gauche Magister Philippus. A few days after the latter's arrival in Wittenberg, he wrote to Spalatin:[26] *"Philippum graecissimum, eruditissimum, humanissimum habe commendatissimum."* He saw embodied in this youth the sharpness of mind of an experienced, wise old man.[27] It is almost not believable that, in a letter he wrote to him from Augsburg, at a time when he himself was involved in the precarious negotiations with Cardinal Cajetanus, he took occasion to say[28] that he would gladly perish, if necessary, but that then he would have to miss forever the relationship with him which had been so precious to him.

This way of speaking is partly to be explained by the tendency to exaggerate, so characteristic of the humanists of that age, which also Luther occasionally adopted. He must really have been strongly impressed by Melanchthon's knowledge of languages and by his thorough humanistic acquaintance with ancient literature. On his return from Augsburg, he invited his friend to dinner, addressing the invitation as follows:[29] *"Philippo Melanchthoni Swartzerd, Graeco, Latino, Hebraeco, Germano, nunquam barbaro."*

Luther had a keen mind and was very sharp-sighted. He possessed a broad general knowledge, thorough theological learning, and particularly an amazingly accurate knowledge of the Bible. He sensed himself called to his work and, from this consciousness of his calling, he was aware of his great gifts and their significance. But despite this, he tended to entertain a low opinion of his books and the products of his pen. With few exceptions, they seemed to him to be nothing but occasional writings which deserved to be forgotten. He wore his heart on his sleeve (or, as the Germans say, *er trug sein Herz auf der Zunge*) and he was an artist of speech of great creative power; yet he regarded himself as a "babbler"[30] when he thought by comparison of Melanchthon's skill of making definitions. His ease of expression and his talkativeness (which he once characterized with a view toward the laconic way of Charles V by saying: "I think he does not talk as much in the course of a whole year as I do in the course of a single day")[31] appeared to him as wordiness: "I cannot manage brevity and perspicacity as well as Philip can," he said.[32] He intimated that what he knew of the skill of applying dialectic distinctions to theological subjects, he had learned from Melanchthon.[33] Indeed, he considered him superior to all Graecists and Latinists as a teacher of dialectics.[34]

He called himself the pioneer of the Reformation and Melanchthon the builder and planter thereof. "I prefer the books of Master Philip to my own," he said,[35] "and I rather see them used, whether they be written in Latin or in German, than my own. I am here in order to do battle with the sectarians and the devil; this is why my books are very aggressive and argumentative. I must uproot stumps and tree trunks; cut down thorns and thickets, and fill in waterpools. I am the rough woodsman who must build a road and keep it open. But Master Philip moves about quietly and in an orderly fashion; he builds and plants, sows and waters according to the great gifts which God has given him so amply."

Melanchthon's art of teaching and his proficiency in communication were based, he believed, on his humanistic scholarship and education. By his exceedingly great praise of him he gave expression to his satisfaction and delight at the fact that Melanchthon placed these incomparable gifts[36] of his in the service of the Reformation.

Thus he regarded Melanchthon's Commentary on the epistle to the Romans (1532) as an exegetical work of the first rank. Augustine would have been delighted with it, he opined, while Jerome would have been angry at it.[37]

As far as the *Loci* were concerned, he thought that there was no theological work that could equal it. He assigned an almost canonical significance[38] to this piece of writing, which is of a clear and orderly character true to its nature as a textbook and, to be sure, Lutheran through and through, but it lacks all immediate power of persuasion. At the end of his life, in 1542 or 1543, he once said:[39]

Whoever wants to become a theologian has a great advantage today. For he has the Bible which now is available in so clear a translation that one can read it without any trouble. Then too, he must read the *Loci communes* of Philip. With the help of these two, he can be a theologian whom neither the devil nor any heretic can harm. The entire field of theology lies open before him, so that he can read all he wants to for his edification. If he wants to, he may also read Melanchthon's Commentary on Romans, and my Galatians—these books will give him *eloquentiam* and *copiam verborum*. You cannot find anywhere a book which treats the whole of theology so adequately as the *loci communes* do. If you were to read all the Fathers and *sententiarii* you would find that they are not worth anything. Next to Holy Scripture, there is no better book.

There can be no doubt that this judgment was well considered. For Luther seems often to have pondered the roles which individual persons have to play in the events of the times. He had an acute sense of the capabilities of his contemporaries and of the motives of their actions. His judgment of persons was almost always to the point, despite his tendency to bestow exaggerated praise upon his friends and to belabor his enemies with an uncouth, unrestrained disrespect. We are told that once he did not rise after dinner but remained seated and fell into thought and then wrote on the table:[40] *"Res et verba Melanchthon; verba sine re Erasmus; res sine verbis Lutherus; nec res nec verba Carlostadius."* (Philip knows the truth and can express it; Erasmus can express himself but does not know what the truth is; Luther knows the truth but cannot express it; Karlstadt knows neither the truth nor can he express himself well.)

However, we must also be mindful of the fact that this friendship was burdened with special difficulties which they both had to bear.

Melanchthon was pained by Luther's violent temper and argumentativeness,[41] by his monkish uncouthness, by his prophetic certainty of faith which was always dynamic and occasionally rumbling, and especially by his stubborn way of persisting in judgments once formed and of reaching to his opponents' criticism of himself with an irreconcilability that lacked all considerateness. He even went so far as to complain[42] that on account of Luther's behavior, he had been forced to live in shameful servitude. This complaint was in part an expression of timidity which, in times of crisis, could turn into hopelessness.[43]

To a man like Calvin, both Luther's bent toward anger and Melanchthon's fearfulness appeared to evidence weakness. For example, with respect to Melanchthon's hesitancy to take sides in the controversy about the Lord's Supper between Geneva and the arch-Lutherans of Hamburg, he once wrote to his friend Farel:[44] "You see . . . how weak this man is. Even greatest necessity does not cause him to speak up openly. He agrees with us but lacks the courage to alter his opinion freely! . . . If only he lived nearby. By talking to him for three hours, I could accomplish more with him than through a hundred letters!"

Here Calvin was overconfident! For Melanchthon's apprehensiveness was not merely an expression of an inborn timidity and irresoluteness. It was founded in deep-seated anxiety. Calvin did not count with this and probably could not do so. Even he would not have been able to change much in the course of a long talk.

But Luther was intimately acquainted with this trait in Melanchthon's character, for this anxiety was the burden which he (Luther) had to bear in this friendship.

Melanchthon was a complicated person. Though he was soft and reserved and in no way rambunctious (he called himself a "quiet bird"[45]), he was in no sense a weakling. From his youth, he had a tendency to lose his temper,[46] and he could be very severe. He often treated his students with great strictness, especially in the disputations;[47] and the intolerance he displayed toward the rebelling peasants[48] and toward the Anabaptists[49] clearly shows that he was not meek. He had a sense of humor, as is evidenced by the fact that, in his lectures, he loved to tell stories and anecdotes out of his own experience, but it was full of sarcasm and a certain sharpness. Luther said of him:[50] "Philip too can sting you, but he does so with needles and pins; these pricks hurt and are hard to heal. But I stab you with boar's spears."

Furthermore, he was canny. This was due to his sharp intelligence, which enabled him quickly to see through most situations. Indeed, all his ways were determined by his unusually broad knowledge and by his mastery of the methods of thought. He had the passionate desire of wanting to know everything and, in a certain way, he wanted to exercise a sort of control over life through knowledge. Luther tells in his Table Talk[51] that, at the diet of Augsburg in 1530, someone asked Melanchthon: "Philip, what are you up to?" and that he replied: "Stay on top" ((vincere).

Like many of his contemporaries, he was devoted to astrology: he wished to know what the future held, and he wanted to see human decisions determined by his prescience. Luther was astonishingly tolerant of this superstition. He once said[52] that astrology had the same significance for Melanchthon as a drink of strong beer had for him when his thoughts depressed him. But his general judgment about this matter is stated in the following:[53] "I could never believe that he was really serious about this. As for me, I do not fear the heavens, for our nature is higher than that of the stars; it cannot be subjected to them." Or: "I do not care for dreams and visions. I have something more certain, namely the word of God."[54]

This passion of the scientist in Melanchthon of wanting to test everything, including the things of faith and religion, was the root of the anxiety that lay upon him. It was a burden not only for himself but also for his friends, and especially for Luther.

But he (Luther) was able, in his own way, to see through it. Thus he was able to maintain full freedom of action in his relations with his friend. He compared himself with Isaiah and Melanchthon with Jeremiah, because this prophet too, he said,[55] was full of anxious concern.[56] Melanchthon's anxiety was continuously on his mind. This is indicated, for example, by the following remark to Justus Jonas, as he informed him of the death of Melanchthon's son George:[57] "You can imagine how very difficult it is for us to console this unusually tender-hearted and sensitive man." As he was dictating to his assistant Veit Dietrich a new exposition of the Psalms, he remarked in connection with the saying (Ps. 25:17): "The troubles of my heart are enlarged" (the Vulgata reads "multiplied"),[58] "Little Philip will know what is meant by this, I think."

In one of the many comparisons he made between himself and Melanchthon, he said:[59] "Little and insignificant things give me concern, but big ones do not. For this is how I think about larger problems; this is too high for you, you cannot comprehend it; therefore let it go. But Philip thinks differently. He is not even touched by the kind of things that cause me concern, he is worried instead about the large affairs of religion and politics. But to me only private things are important."

Now it is very instructive to see that Luther thought he knew wherein this difference in attitude between himself and Melanchthon consisted. He believed that his friend's anxiety was derived from his scientific-humanistic way of thinking. This is proved especially well by the letter he wrote in 1530 for the castle Coburg to his friends in Augsburg.

Before and after the public presentation of the Augsburg

Confession, on June 25, 1530, Melanchthon (who was its author and as such the theological spokesman and negotiator of the Lutherans) was troubled by terrible worries. On June 18, Justus Jonas wrote to Luther:[60] "Philip worries excruciatingly about this whole affair." And a few days later, Melanchthon himself informed Luther that he was terribly worried and that he was almost always close to tears.[61] He feared that if the Emperor and the other princely opponents of the Reformation should proceed to settle the religious issue by war, all of Germany would be torn apart.[62] Later he wrote:[63] "If war breaks out, a horrible change of the Empire and of everything else will ensue." In other words: he feared the dissolution of the whole Latin-Christian order.[64] He wanted to see the Christian cultural heritage preserved and therefore hoped that a final break with the Emperor or the Roman Church could be avoided, despite the fact that both had condemned Luther and all his works in a definitive way. He therefore felt that he was carrying a very heavy responsibility. In order to comprehend the historical consequences of the actions he would have to take, he employed all his intelligence and all his skill of analyzing and defining issues, hoping that he thus might help to avert a catastrophe.

He found himself surrounded by Luther and the Lutherans, who were interested only in a true confession of the evangelical faith; by the political opponents of the Emperor as, for example, Philip of Hesse in league with Zwingli and the Upper-Germans, who wished to use the religious conflicts in order to oppose the Habsburger *"Weltmonarchie,"* by the representatives of the Roman Church who refused absolutely to sanction the Reformation and who hoped to draw him over into their camp; and finally by practical politicians like the Prince-bishop of Salzburg[65] who wanted to settle the whole conflict through concessions.

In wonderfully graphic letters, which have become famous, Luther counseled Melanchthon to confess his faith boldly, to put the whole affair in the hands of God and to give up all attempts of constructing a philosophy of history. I cannot here go into detail; I only want to show what Luther thought about Melanchthon's motives and ways of thinking. For he maintained that his friend's anxiety and fear must be attributed to his philosophy and to his humanistic scholarship.

This is what he wrote:[66] "You are so terribly concerned about the end and issue of this affair, because you cannot comprehend it. But if it were possible for you to comprehend it, I for one should not want to have any part in it and still less I should want to be the one who started it. God has placed it under a certain basic concept which is not available to you either in your Rhetorics or your philosophy, and it is called faith.[67] This basic concept includes all things which are visible and not apparent (Heb. 11:3). Whosoever wants to make them visible, apparent, and comprehensible as you do, gets cares and sorrows as his reward as you do, etc." On the same day, he remarked to Justus Jonas:[68] "Philip is tortured by his philosophy and nothing else," just as somewhat earlier he had told him directly:[69] "It is your philosophy which tortures you so and not your theology."

What he meant by this, he explained in several letters of June 30, 1530. To Melanchthon himself he wrote[70] that he was trying, on the basis of his philosophy, to govern the matter before him as if it were within his power. And he admonished John Brenz to give a warning to Melanchthon:[71] "Philip is honestly concerned, but 'without knowledge' (Rom. 10:2), about peace and posterity. As if it were due to the worry and solicitude of our parents and not to the providence of God alone that we are what we are. When we are gone, he will still be God the creator just as he was before our time and still is today. He will not die nor cease to be God . . . I am writing this to you and the others hoping that one of you will be able to persuade Philip that he should stop trying to steer the world, i.e., to crucify himself." At the same time, he told Spalatin:[72] "I know with certainty in whom I put my faith, for he is able to do exceeding abundantly beyond what we can ask or think. Philip, however, believes and wishes that God should do what he does according to his (Philip's) counsel in order that he might be able to boast saying: See, this is how it had to be done; I too should have done it in just this way. But no, this is not right. This 'I' is much too small. It says (in the Bible): Thus I 'shall be who I shall be' For his name is 'Who I shall be' (Exod. 3:14). Nobody can see him as he is, but he will be he, as we shall see. But enough of this! As for you, be strong in faith (Eph. 6:10) and continue to admonish Philip in my name that he should not try to become God but that he should fight against the desire that is inborn in us and planted in our hearts by the devil, namely that we want to be like God. This drove Adam out of Paradise and it and nothing else will throw us out too and deprive us of all peace. We must be men and not God. This is the sum of it all. We are not able to change anything; if we were, only unceasing restlessness and sorrow would be our reward."

As descriptions of Melanchthon's behavior, these words sound perhaps exaggerated; but probably they are basically true. They delineate very sharply the spirit of Melanchthon. At the same time, they show clearly the difference between the two reformers. Luther was a man of faith who saw all human thinking and acting subject to the action of God, and Melanchthon was a man of science, a scholar, who tried to regulate as many things as possible by the power of his knowledge.

What is really remarkable in this is the following: Luther, the prophet, and Melanchthon, the humanist, were at one in their understanding of the gospel, and they served the Reformation for the same end. This is what both of them, but particularly Luther, desired.

When the diet of Augsburg had been adjourned, he expressed his approval of Melanchthon in these words:[73] "I shall canonize you as faithful members of Christ." Soon thereafter he praised the Confession of which Melanchthon had been the author and which had cost so much anxiety and worry. He declared it to be a theological masterpiece. In his opinion, it excelled the works of the most distinguished church fathers, even of Augustine.[74]

Thus Luther gave Melanchthon his blessing, in spite of all his differences from him.

We cannot but approve this positive judgment, for we know that Luther's work did not become historical without Melanchthon's contribution and that Melanchthon's work cannot be separated from that of Luther.

NOTES

1. E. Troeltsch, *Vernunft und Offenbarung bei Johann Gerhard und Melanchthon* (Göttingen: Vandenhoeck und Ruprecht, 1891), p. 58.
2. Wilhelm A. Neuser, *Der Ansatz in der Theologie Melanchthons* (Neukirchen: Buchhandlung des Erziehungsvereine, 1957). Adolf Sperl, *Melanchthon zwischen Humanismus und Reformation* (München: Kaiser, 1959).

3. Franz Hildebrandt, *Melanchthon, Alien or Ally* (Cambridge: The University Press, 1946), p. xii.
4. *WA* B VII; 412.
5. This is proved by Melanchthon's letter to the aged Erasmus (12 March 1536; Allen, op. ep. *Erasmi*, XI; 323. Cf. also his letter of 23 March 1528; ibid., VII; 731). Erasmus, to be sure, said, even at such a late date as March 1534, that Melanchthon impressed him as being more Lutheran than Luther himself (Ibid., X; 363).
6. Cf. *WA* B III; 528, 8 ff. (Luther to the Elector Frederick; 23 March 1524.)
7. Wilhelm Maurer, *Melanchthon: Humanist und Reformator. A lecture.* Karlsruhe, 1960.
8. *CR** VI; 170: *Volebat enim Lutherus non detinere (nos) in suis scriptis, sed ad fontes deducere omnium mentes; ipsam vocem Dei audire nos voluit.*
9. *CR* I; 722: *Ego mihi conscius sum, non aliam ob caussam tetheologekénai, nisi ut vitam emendarem.* In the last letter he addressed to Erasmus on 11 March 1536, a few weeks before the latter's death (11 July 1536), he wrote in the same vein. He stated that, in the new edition of his *loci* (1535), he had made an effort to formulate *"firma doctrina et utilis moribus ac pietati."* (Allen, op. ep. *Erasmi*, XI; 323.)
10. *CR* XI; 280. Cf. Franz Hildebrandt, *Melanchthon*, p. 2.
11. *CR* I; 666.
12. *WA* B III; 50, 21, to Eoban Hesse, March 29, 1523. Cf. E. Mülhaupt, *Die Reformatoren als Erzieher* (Neukirchen: Buchhandlung des Erziehungsvereine, 1956), p. 75.
13. Heinrich Bornkamm, *Melanchthon. A lecture,* 3rd ed. (Göttingen: Vandenhoeck & Ruprecht, 1960), p. 15 f.
14. In the long run, it did not prove successful.
15. *CR* XI; 654: *Carere igitur Aristotelis monumentis non possumus.*
16. *CR* XIII; 281: *Hanc enim doctrinam (Aristotelis), quasi vox est naturae, sequamur.*
17. Cf. Neuser, *Der Ansatz*, p. 40.
18. Allen, op. ep. *Erasmi*, XI; 323: *toties profiteor, me nec authorem nec suffragatorem novarum dogmatum esse.*
19. For a similar reason, he rejected the teaching of Copernicus. Cf. Hildebrandt, *Melanchthon*, p. 11.
20. Paul Joachimsen, *Loci Communes.* Luther-Jahrbuch VIII (1926), p. 27 ff. Cf. also E. Troeltsch, *Vernunft*, p. 60 ff. and W. Neuser, *Der Ansatz*, p. 51 ff.
21. *WA* B VI; 99, 3 (May 1531).
22. Cf. Neuser, Der Ansatz, p. 42.
23. Their wives, however, did not get along too well with one another. Melanchthon's wife, Katharine Krapp, daughter of a Wittenberg burgher, was no better a householder than her husband. But Luther's wife, Katharine von Bora, was a capable economist. One can even call her successful. The two women did not like one another. It seems that differences of social origin (Katharine Luther was of noble birth) were of some influence in this.
24. Bugenhagen preached the funeral sermon.
25. *CR* III; 827.
26. *WA* B I; 198, 40 (2 Sept. 1518).
27. *WA* II (Gal. 1518); 595, 19.
28. *WA* B I; 213, 12 (11 Oct. 1518): *Malo perire, et quod unum gravissimum est, etiam vestra conversatione dulcissima carere in aeternum.*

---

*CR = Corpus Reformatorum

29. *WA* B I; 252, 1 (22 Nov. 1518).
30. *WA* TR V; No. 5511 (1542/43); *ich bin ein wescher, magis rhetoricus.*
31. Kawerau, Gustav, ed. J. J. Köstlin, *Martin Luther: sein Leben und seine Schriften* (Berlin: A. Duncker, 1903) II; 283.
32. *WA* TR II; No. 1649 (1532).
33. *WA* TR II; No. 1545 (1532); TR V; No. 5646.
34. *WA* Tr II; No. 2300 (1531): *Philippus superat omnes Graecos et Latinos in tradendo dialectica.*
35. Preface to the German translation of Melanchthon's interpretation of the Epistle to the Colossians (1529): *WA* XXX, pt. II; 68, 8.
36. *WA* TR V; No. 5646: *Es ist auf Erden keiner, den die sonne bescheinet, der solche dona hette.* Cf. also *WA* X, pt. 10II; 309 f.
37. *WA* TR I; No. 316 (1532); cf. TR II; No. 1842.
38. In his treatise against Erasmus, he praised it as a book of immortal significance which deserved to be included in the canon of the church. (Cf. *WA* XVIII; 601, 3.)
39. *WA* TR V; No. 5511.
40. *WA* TR III; No. 3619 (1 Aug. 1537).
41. Allen, op. ep. *Erasmi* VII; 371: *Nunquam ita amavi Lutherum, ut probarem eius in disputando acerbitatem* (the text as given in CR I; 946, needs emendation).
42. In the famous letter to Carlowitz (28 April 1548), CR VI; 880; cf. also W. Ellinger, *Ph. Melanchthon* (Göttingen: Vandenhoeck & Ruprecht 1961.).
43. A short time after the bigamy of Philipp of Hesse had come to public knowledge (whereby also the Reformers were exposed to criticism), Melanchthon was en route to the important Colloquy of Religion in Hagenau. In Weimar, he fell seriously ill. He was so depressed, worried, and uncertain that he lost all will to live. Luther was called. When he arrived (28 June 1540), Melanchthon was apparently near death. Luther exclaimed: "Good God, what ill has the devil inflicted on this *organon!*" Then he stepped near the window to pray, as it was his custom to do, and he fervently implored God to save his friend: *"Allda musste mir unser Herr Gott herhalten, denn ich warf ihm den sack vor die Türe und rieb ihm die Ohren mit all seinen Verheissungen, dass er das gebet erhören wolle, die ich in der Heiligen Schrift aufzuzäblen wusste, dass er mich musste erbören, woanders ich seinen Verheissungen trauen sollte."* (G. Kawerau; ed; J. J. Köstlin, *Martin Luther: Sein Leben und seine Schriften*, p. 526 f.) Then he assured Melanchthon that he would stay alive and persuaded, nay compelled him, to take a little food. Melanchthon soon got well, and Luther was convinced that he had "prayed his friend back to life." (*WA* TR V; No. 5407, April–June 1542).
44. *CR* XLIII; 322 (27 Nov. 1554).
45. *CR* VI; 474 (to Butzer, 28 August 1544): *Ego sum tranquilla avis.* Cf. also CR VI; 880 (to Carlowitz, 28 April 1548); *Non sum philoneikos* (quarrelsome); ibid., 882; *Fortassis sum natura ingenio servili.*
46. R. Stupperich, "Die Kirche in Martin's Butzer's theologischer Entwicklung," *Archiv für Reformationsgeschichte*, XXXV (1938), p. 16.
47. Cf. Luther's remarks in *WA* TR IV; No. 4056.
48. Ellinger, *Ph. Melanchthon*, p. 212.
49. Cf. Stupperich, "Die Kirche in Martin Butzer's theologischer Entwicklung" p. 46 ff. Also his essay "Melanchthon und die Täufer" in: *Kerygma und Dogma* III (1957), 150 ff.
50. *WA* TR I; No. 348 (1532).
51. *Wa* TR II; No. 1992.

52. *WA* TR I; No. 17 (1531).
53. *WA* TR III; No. 3520.
54. *WA* TR IV; No. 4444 L. Hildebrandt remarks on this (*Melanchthon,* p. XVIII): Should this be the root of the problem that the "*solum verbum*" was not certain enough for Melanchthon? At another place he writes (p. XXVI): Melanchthon tests, where Luther trusts.
55. *WA* TR II; No. 2296a.
56. Namely, that he was scolding too much.
57. *WA* B V; 132, 10.
58. G. Kawerau, ed., J. J. Köstlin, Martin Luther: *Sein Leben und Seine Schriften,* II; 220: "*Ich meine, Philippche wisse wohl, was das heisse.*"
59. *WA* TR I; No. 80. Cf. also Luther's letter to Melanchthon (30 June 1530) (*WA* B V; 412, 19): "*In privatis luctis infirmior ego, tu autem fortior, contra in publicis tu talis, qualis ego in privatis, ut ego in publicis talis, qualis tu in privatis (si privatum dici debet, quod geritur inter me et Satanem),* etc."
60. *WA* B V; 367, 69.
61. *WA* B V; 396, 1.
62. *WA* B V; 602, 5 (1 Sept. 1530).
63. *WA* B V; 604 (4 Sept. 1530).
64. Cf. Georg Merz, *Glaube und Politik im Handeln Luthers,* 2d ed. (München: Kaiser, 1933), p. 33 ff.
65. On June 25, Justus Jonas informed Luther that when Melanchthon, desiring an audience with the Cardinal, referred to conscience, his eminence remarked contemptuously: "Ha! Conscience! What is conscience, conscience!" (*WA* B V; 390, 82). Five days later, Jonas wrote further details about these negotiations: the cardinal had declared himself ready to make concessions in relation to the Lord's Supper; reform of the mass; priestly marriage; fastings; and other traditions, but he had said that the fact that a bailiwick (i.e., Wittenberg) should want to reform the whole Empire was an intolerable disturbance of the peace. In his "Warning of his dear Germans" (1531) Luther referred to this (*WA* XXX, pt. III; 283, 26).
66. *WA* B V; 406, 54 (29 June 1530).
67. *Deus posuit eam in locum quendam communem, quam in rhetorica tua non habes nec in philosophia tua: is vocatur fides.*
68. *WA* B V; 409, 18 (29 June 1530).
69. *WA* B V; 399, 6 (27 June 1530).
70. *WA* B V; 412, 7.
71. *WA* B V; 417, 3.
72. *WA* B V; 414, 34.
73. *WA* B V; 622, 5.
74. *WA* TR I; No. 252: "*Hieronymus potest legi propter historias, nam de fide et doctrina verae religionis ne verbum quidem habet. Origenem hab ich schon in bann getan. Chrisostomos gillt bei mir auch nichts, ist nur ein wescher. Basilius taugt gar nichts, der ist gar ein munch; ich wolt nicht ein heller um ihn geben. Apologia Philippi (i.e. the Confessio Augustana) praestat omnibus doctoribus ecclesiae, etiam ipso Augustino. Hilarius et Theophilactus sind gut, Ambrosius auch, der geht zuweilen fein ad remissionem peccatorem, qui est summus articulus, quod illa maiestas divina ignoscat gratis.*"

5. Schleiermacher's Conception of History and Church History

The judgments of Schleiermacher's critics and interpreters about his conception of history and his historical work are surprisingly contradictory. Some attribute to him a profound historical sense, while others criticize him for the lack of it. Some admire him for the fact that he thought in historical terms, while others find fault with him because his historical knowledge, they say, was limited. Such negative opinions were even expressed by thinkers who felt themselves deeply attached to him and who believed that in their own work they were preserving ways of thinking they had learned from him. Thus, for example, Ernst Troeltsch,[1] being in this respect of the same mind as Albrecht Ritschl[2] and his son Otto Ritschl,[3] once stated that Schleiermacher did not know much about history. One of the bluntest statements I have found is that by Albert Schweitzer. He writes about Schleiermacher: "Precisely in his treatment of the history of Jesus, the great dialectician shows plainly that he was really an unhistorical thinker *[ein unhistorischer Kopf]*."[4] This statement is slightly less sharp than Dilthey's remark to the effect that Schleiermacher was "a thoroughly unhistorical thinker" *[ein ganz unhistorischer Kopf]*.[5] When Dilthey wrote this, he was thinking of the absolutistic features of Schleiermacher's Christology of which he was consistently highly critical, as the recently published second part of his *Life of Schleiermacher* shows;[6] he considered it irreconcilable with a true historical interpretation of the figure of Jesus.

But this was not Dilthey's complete judgment. He certainly would not have identified himself with H. R. Mackintosh[7] or F. Flückiger[8] who, though separated from one another by a whole generation but similarly influenced by Karl Barth, agree in the opnion that Schleiermacher "was not prepared to take history quite in earnest." Dilthey was too deeply aware, if I may apply to him R. R. Niebuhr's phrase, of Schleiermacher's "intense preoccupation with history and the historical."[9]

This remarkable divergence in the assessment of Schleiermacher's relation to history can be explained, I believe, not by reference to his interpreter's prejudices or lack of thoroughness, but rather by the consideration of the possibility that Schleiermacher's thought was burdened with a certain *ambiguity*. This appears to be the opinion of Friedrich Meinecke. He had a high opinion of Schleiermacher's importance as a historical thinker and he believed that by his rich use of the idea of individuality in his interpretation of religion and of human life generally, Schleiermacher developed an historical sense and communicated it to others. But he also felt that it was Schleiermacher's "fate" *[Verhängnis]* that the two sides of his highly gifted nature which went into the making of his distinctive view of the world—on the one hand, intuition and feeling, and, on the other hand, the sharpest conceptual thinking—did not reach a full mutual penetration in his later life. The contemplation of the concrete world receded, he said, but his ordinary dialectical talent spread out excessively and caused him to come under the sway of influence which restrained his individualizing way of thinking."[10]

I am inclined to agree with this characterization of Schleiermacher's mentality and I feel that it is supported by a study not only of such writings as the *Brief Outline on the Study of Theology* and the *Glaubenslehre*, but also of the lectures on "Ethics" and even on such specifically historical subjects as the "History of the Church" and the "Life of Jesus."

II

Before we analyze Schleiermacher's conception of history, it may be well to consider what he thought about historical method. He distinguished between three kinds of historiography, which he called atomistic, pragmatic, and organic. The *atomistic* approach to historical data produces at best a chronological record, but it fails to demonstrate a connection between historical events or actions. "It is of interest only to a vain curiosity that wants to know what once was. This kind of history contains everything and nothing, it must contain everything because even the smallest detail fills time, and it contains nothing because it cannot definitely determine anything."[11] Schleiermacher rejected this historicism. He said: "Nothing is more fruitless than a piling up of historical learning which neither serves any practical purpose nor offers anything for the use of others in its presentation."[12]

The second way of dealing with history is the *pragmatic* or psychological one. It attempts to explain present events by linking them to causes in the past. Schleiermacher made the following critical observations about it:

One cannot separate the present from the past as if they were opposites and one cannot detach certain parts from the present. What one thus arbitrarily sets aside [from the whole] is then viewed as having been caused not by a similar single corresponding factor but by a part of all single factors of the recent past. What is characteristic of ths view is therefore the tendency to attach small causes to great events and hence to consider historical results as accidental, because one has a wrong conception of what is necessary or inevitable.[13]

The true understanding of history is to view it in analogy to an *organism*. For, so Schleiermacher believed, in history all is one. One can separate any part of it from the whole only in the same way as when, in considering an organism, one views one system of vital functions in separation from all others.[14] "History is everything that is known as bound to time [*Die Geschichte ist alles was die Wissenschaft enthält als in der Zeit angeschaut*], namely, the organization of nature as a process [*ein werdendes*]: natural history; the organization of the mind process: moral history [*Sittengeschichte*]; and the identity of both of these as a process: world history."[15]

This means that for Schleiermacher history is, on the one hand, all that goes on in the world as a process of becoming and, on the other hand, the historian's account and representation of this process, indeed, his own involvement in this process. Hanna Jursch (whose dissertation, *Schleiermacher als Kirchenhistoriker*, published in 1933, is the only specific study of Schleiermacher's Church-historical work), rightly distinguishes between "objective" and "subjective" history.[16] *Objective history* is the interpenetration of principle and the concretely given; *subjective history* is the apprehension of this process by empirical observation and that divinatory generalization which Schleiermacher called "speculation." The "principle" manifests itself in universal life as a living, formative agent and it culminates in the polarity of reason and nature as displayed in human civilization. It is an *intensive* power which penetrates interiorly and an *extensive* power which expands internally—in analogy to the relationship between soul and body. It is always in process of becoming, either by way of a gradual development or through a sudden emerging in a new, original beginning.

Schleiermacher called the interpretative speculative science of the life of reason, or the "science of the principles of history",[17] "*ethics.*" In his view it corresponded to "*physics,*" the general science of nature, just as he set the empirical study of history *(Geschichtskunde)* in parallel to the empirical knowledge of nature *(Naturkunde).*[18]

This remarkable correlation of "objective" and "subjective" history is very well described by Schleiermacher himself in the *Brief Outline* at the beginning of his discussion of Church history. He says: "Every historical mass may be viewed (a) on the one hand, as one indivisible being and doing in process of becoming, and (b) on the other hand, as a compound of innumerable individual moments. Genuinely historical observation consists in the combination of both" (§150). "Accordingly, every fact has historical individuality only insofar as the two are posited as identical: the outer reality as the changing of what nevertheless maintains its identity, and the inner reality as the function of a force in motion. In this matter of speaking, the 'inner' is posited as soul, the 'outer' as body—the whole, consequently, as a life" (§151). The perception and retention in memory of spacial changes is almost a sheer mechanical operation, whereas the construction of a fact, the combination of outer and inner into *one* historical perspective, is to be regarded as a free action of the mind"(§152).

Now what is implied in this view is that history is not an accidental or arbitrary play of forces, but that it has a goal, namely, the triumph of reason or mind over nature. In the *Speeches on Religion,* Schleiermacher speaks of the finite as being on the way *(im Unterwegssein)* towards the infinite, and of the ultimate suspension of the contrast between the finite and the infinite.[19] He sees the goal of history as "the triumph of life over death," accomplished through the "redeeming work of eternal love."[20] In *Philosophical Ethics* he sees life as an "ethical process" in the course of which, through the interpenetration of reason and nature accomplished in the life of family, nation, Church, and free cultural association, the "highest good" or moral ideal will be realized in the universal community of mankind.[21] In the *Glaubenslehre,* he describes and interprets Christianity as a teleological religion directed towards the kingdom of God as its moral end. The redemption of all men which is being and will be accomplished through the communication to them of Christ's perfect God-consciousness in the common life and common spirit of the Church is viewed as a gradual progress. "In the historical development of the Christian Church," Schleiermacher writes, "redemption is being ever more completely realized in time, and the Holy Spirit is thus pervading the whole ever more perfectly . . ."[22]

In another context of the same work, the *Glaubenslehre,* he goes even further. In view of the idea that "all other religious fellowships are destined to lose themselves in Christianity, and hence that all nations are destined to pass over into the Christian fellowship," he envisages the possibility that "the common spirit of the Christian Church would then be the common spirit of the human race."[23]

At the end of his life, Schleiermacher was convinced that Christianity was the absolutely highest religion in which all other religions would be progressively absorbed and transcended and in which humanity would be fulfilled. In the Introduction to his lecture on the *Life of Jesus,* he said specifically: "I must here make the assumption (and I believe that it is unavoidable to do so because the whole idea of a Kingdom of God in its development on earth would otherwise be vain and empty) that we must think of life as a continuous progression *[Fortschreitung]* and by no means as an aimless cycle *[einen leeren Kreislauf]*."[24]

The term "progression" *(Fortschreitung)* is used by Schleiermacher also in his lectures on Christian morals *(Die christliche Sitte).* He says there: "Every progression is but a better understanding and appropriation of what is posited in Christ."[25] This sentence expresses an important qualification of the conception of history as a development. For the "progression" of which Schleiermacher speaks is not progress towards a goal by way of ascending stages, but the ever wider and deeper quickening of the life of mankind under the power and influence of Christ. The progression must be understood not so much as an advancement towards a goal, but as a growing conformity with Christ, whose person and work are normative for all men. As the founder of Christianity, he alone is the redeemer for all,[26] and "he alone is destined gradually to quicken the whole human race into a higher life[27] by "the highest enhancement of the human reason"[28] through the divine spirit. He is *not the goal of history,* nor can it be said that under the "influence" or "impulse" of his perfection all men, united in the common life of the Church, will one day reach the goal of history, but as Dilthey states, Christ is the *center of history* because his archetypal life and the discipleship of Christians actualized in communion with him are "the mystical context" [Konnex] in which Christianity actualizes what, from the philosophical point of view, is contained in the ideality of the world *[im idealen Weltzusammenhang],* for the realization of the highest good."[29]

It is therefore probably correct to say that for Schleiermacher there was only a hopeful or promising development of history but not an end of history.[30] This hope and this promise are grounded in Christ. By this basic assertion advanced in the *Glaubenslehre,* he went beyond the position he had taken in the *Reden.* But the ambiguity which he there expressed beset his thought to the end of his career. He wrote: "There will come a time, so says Christianity, when there will be no concern about a mediator but when the Father will be all in all. But when will this time come? I fear it will be beyond all time.[31]

One may perhaps say that he viewed the process of world history, which, beginning with the appearance of Christ, was identical for him with the life and development of the Christian Church, as determined by something immutable, *the divine,* which in ever new and different ways is connected with mutable factors as they arise in the conditions of life in the world. There is thus a continuous progression due to the determination of the mutable factors in the history of mankind or the Church by the divine immutable, but an *end* of this progression, i.e., a time when it will reach a goal, is inconceivable.

This seems to me implied in what Schleiermacher writes in §126 of the *Glaubenslehre:* "If the fellowship of believers as an historical body within the human race, is to exist and persist in continuous activity, it must unite in itself two things—a self-identical element whereby it remains the same amid change, and a mutable element in which the identity finds expression." The self-identical element must be seen in that "the mode in which the divine exists in the human ever remains the same"; also in that "the goal also remains the same to which the Church throughout all its movements is seeking to approximate"; and finally, in that "the relation of the Holy Spirit to the Church as its common spirit remains the same"; in other words, "the Church is ever self-identical as the *locus* of the Spirit in the human race."[32] But the mutable element is determined by human nature and its environment in the world, as the Holy Spirit works through it. The divine "permeates" the human in the world and thus Christianity develops as a "force in history."

In connection with this we must give attention also to Schleiermacher's idea of individuality and individualization. This idea was characteristic of his thought throughout his career. He gave forceful expression to it in his first publications, especially in the *Speeches* and *Soliloquies.* His conception of the religions as individual historical bodies in the *Speeches* and his idea of the manifestation of the infinite in many finite individualizations, as well as his interpretation of human persons and groups as unique historical individualities, constitute fresh insights and discoveries. They not only enriched his own thought by filling it with a historical sense insofar as his attention was from then on directed to the "new" and "original," but they also fructified the historical understanding of others. Certainly his interpretation of the religions of mankind as historical bodies which originate at a certain time and undergo changes in the course of their development, existing side by side in many forms, constitutes the basis of an entirely new, truly historical interpretation of religion and theology.

I do not want here to describe in detail how Schleiermacher proceeded to interpret the history of religions, i.e., how in the *Speeches* he endeavored to "discover religion in the religions";[33]

how religion itself, i.e., absolute religion, was then for him "the ever unrealizable essence of the innumerable individual historical religions";[34] and how, in the *Glaubenslehre,* he interpreted Christianity as the absolute religion in relation to which all other religions, the primitive ones as well as the world religions, represent only transitory and preparatory stages. The point I am here interested in making is that his emphasis on the individual character of historical phenomena unavoidably crossed his concern to see Christian faith and life in a teleological perspective. Thus, for example, he found himself unable to make a value judgment between Roman Catholicism and Protestantism. Indeed, he was forced to give recognition to plural embodiments of the Christian spirit. Modifying his statement that "every man has in him all that another man has, but it is all differently determined,"[35] we may attribute to him the view that every Christian group or Church has in itself all that another Church has but that all is differently determined.

Now, in order to see identity and difference in the historical development of persons and movements, one must focus one's attention upon the *center* to which they are oriented and by which they are determined. Schleiermacher the author of the *Speeches* knew this, and his thinking continued to be shaped by this knowledge. The individual as a single or as a social totality, he pointed out,[36] is determined by its *center.* It achieves a certain character and a wholeness when all its single parts are turned toward *one* center.

So much for and about my thesis that Schleiermacher's historical thought was determined by his double concentration upon goals as well as centers, upon *the goal* as well as *the center* of history and that this double concentration caused his historical interpretation to assume a subtle but pronounced ambiguity.[37]

III

In conclusion, I wish to make a few observations about Schleiermacher's conception of the historian's procedure.

He believed that the historical apprehension of life was "a talent . . . developed in each person . . . through the resources of his own historical life,"[38] a talent which he thought becomes better as one grows older. "The consideration of history," he said, "requires a certain distance."[39] Otherwise one tends to criticize things too quickly and too polemically because one assumes an inappropriate partisanship toward them.[40] It is interesting to note that in this connection Schleiermacher expressed the opinion that the present cannot be historically analyzed or interpreted. In his own work he did not consistently live up to what was implied in this, but in his lectures on Church history he refrained from dealing with recent developments in accordance with his conviction that only distance of time will allow the historian to obtain a proper perspective.

What technical historical scholarship amounts to he described succinctly in the *Brief Outline on the Study of Theology*.[41] Historical knowledge is "obtained in two ways: (a) directly through the use of primary sources," i.e., historical documents and monuments; "and (b) more easily, though only indirectly, through the use of historical presentations" (§156). The historian or anyone who desires to acquire historical knowledge and understanding must aim to achieve an historical account of his own. He will suceed best in this if he acquires the knowledge of historical facts and actions by his own direct examination of the sources and then goes on to use historical interpretations of others, being careful to eliminate "what has been interpolated by the author in each case" (§158). This is made easier if one studies as far as possible the works of recent authors with whose outlook and presuppositions one is more or less directly acquainted and "if one can compare several portrayals of the same series of facts, all the more so if these are taken from different points of view" (§158). Thus the result of historical research will be an objective presentation of the materials, but it will unavoidably be marked by subjective factors. All accounts and interpretations of the same historical events will be different. "The problem of presenting a [historical] subject in a correct way can be solved only in different, not the same ways. Each description contains a transformation of the continuum, which is a concrete subject, into a discrete one. It consists of single, separate statements which in every case contain a judgment of the one who describes. Moreover, it is inevitable that some things are passed by and are not described while others are contracted and drawn together, for otherwise the description would be infinitely extended."[42] The really important task of the historian is that he avoid a preoccupation with single, separable, and separate details and that he concentrate his attention upon the internal unity by which details are held together.[43] Only in this way can each new moment of history be comprehended in relation to the entire past.[44] At the same time, the present will then be illuminated in such a way that also the future can be prophetically determined.[45]

The inner unity of an historical action, event, or process must be comprehended as alive—this was Schleiermacher's conviction. This is why he could write in the *Brief Outline* about the task of obtaining a survey of the history of the Church as follows: ". . . this account will develop into a vital historical perspective, one which contains a forceful impulse of its own, only when the total career of Christianity is apprehended at the same time . . . as the depiction of the Christian spirit on the move . . ." Having said this, he added the following significant note: "Only when it has taken this form can knowledge of the total career of Christianity affect Church leadership as it should."[46]

In the light of this conception of the historian's work it is understandable that Schleiermacher advocated the combination of two methods, the empirical method and another, which he called "speculative," i.e., generally interpretative and critically evaluative. He advocated its use also in the *Glaubenslehre* and in the *Dialektik*.

"All so-called *a priori* constructions," he felt, "come to grief over the task of showing that what has been . . . deduced . . . is actually identical with the historically given. . . . the purely empirical method, on the other hand, has neither standard nor formula for distinguishing the essential and permanent from the changeable and contingent."[47] The peculiarity of any historical phenomenon, the Christian Church for example, cannot be comprehended or deduced by purely scientific (i.e., generalizing and abstract) methods nor grasped by mere empirical methods.

What Schleiermacher here recommends is undoubtedly the procedure any historian must follow if he wants to be more than a collector of data or a mere chronicler of events. But the big question is what historical empiricism is, what kind of "speculation" the historian is allowed to use, and just exactly how the empirical and speculative methods can be combined. If one seeks for an answer in Schleiermacher's own work, a conclusive one will not be found. He does not seem to have made any thorough empirical studies in any field—say in the manner of the pragmatic historians of his own day or the later positivists, nor does he appear to have been engaged like Hegel and the Hegelians in a speculative construction of historical developments. One can perhaps say that he observed intuitively and that he judged critically the ways of men in all cultural activities, and particularly in the field of religion, always helped by his own very great dialectical skill in making distinctions and by his love for constructing edifices of thought *(Gedankengebäude)*.

What he says in the *Speeches* and in the *Glaubenslehre* about the development of the religions is not exactly in accordance with an empirical study of the history of religions, nor is it deduced from any general theory about religion. Indeed, his correlations and distinctions are quite suggestive and have proved fruitful; but empiricists say of his thought that it is too philosophical and speculative, and some philosophers have criticized it for being too empirically descriptive. Hermann Süskind, who certainly was a careful and sympathetic interpreter of Schleiermacher, found himself driven to the conclusion that Schleiermacher dealt with the historically given as if the fact of its being given also proved its validity and, in order to illustrate this criticism, he referred to Schleiermacher's treatment of the relation between Protestantism and Roman Catholicism, marked as this is by Schleiermacher's refusal to make a judgment of truth or of value.[48] Süskind's observation probably does not do full justice ot Schleiermacher, because he did not regard it as the task of the historian to make judgments of truth or validity but to achieve understanding. He wrote: "Insofar as one tries to make do with a merely empirical method of interpreting Christianity, he cannot achieve a genuine knowledge of it. One's task is rather to endeavor both to understand the essence of Christianity in contradistinction to other churches and other kinds of faith, and to understand the nature of piety and of religious communities in relation to all the other activities of the human spirit."[49]

In all I have said in this lecture, I have kept in mind what Schleiermacher said about historical theology and especially about Church history in his *Brief Outline on the Study of Theology*, and how he treated the history of the Church in his own lectures.

(He offered a course on Church history three times in his career, in 1806 in Halle and in the winter semesters of 1821–22 and 1825–26 in Berlin.)

My characterization of his conception of history could be extended by a consideration of his total view of the theological task and of the central place which historical studies must occupy in it. But this would lead to an examination of the nature of theology from which I must here refrain.

I could also test his basic interpretation of Church history by his own performance as a Church historian. But this would not be of general interest, for he offered only a brief survey, mostly of the history of doctrine, which he had not had time to prepare thoroughly, either by a close study of the primary sources or by a careful outline of the general structure of the Church's development.

So I return now to the question I raised at the beginning and invite your discussion of it in the light of my analysis of his basic views. Was he or was he not an "unhistorical thinker"? *I* believe he had a deep and acute historical sense. He said rightly that "one who wants to master philosophy must understand it historically."[50] In all his work, particularly in relation to religion and Christianity, he was constantly in search of historical understanding.

NOTES

1. Review of Hermann Süskind, *Christentum und Geschichte bei Schleiermacher* (Tübingen: Mohr, 1911), *ThLZ*, 38 (1913), cols. 21–24.
2. Albert Ritschl, *Schleiermachers Reden über die Religion und ihre Nachwirkungen auf die evangelische Kirche Deutschlands* (Bonn: A. Marcus, 1874), pp. 90 f.
3. Otto Ritschl, *Schleiermachers Stellung zum Christentum in seinen Reden über die Religion: Ein Beitrag zur Ehrenrettung Schleiermachers* (Gotha: Friedrich Andreas Perthes, 1888), p. 31.
4. Albert Schweitzer, *Geschichte der Leben Jesu Forschung* (Tübingen: Mohr, 1913), p. 63.
5. Wilhelm Dilthey, *Schleiermachers*, 1, *vermehrt um Stücke der Fortsetzung aus dem Nachlasse des Verfassers*, Hermann Mulert, ed. (Berlin and Leipzig: W. de Gruyter, 1922), p. 776.
6. Wilhelm Dilthey, *Schleiermachers System als Philosophie und Theologie* (Berlin: W. de Gruyter, 1966), 2 vols.; issued simultaneously as vol. 14 of Wilhelm Dilthey, *Gesammelte Schriften* (Göttingen: V. & Ruprecht, 1966), 2 parts. See pp. 489, 589 f.
7. H. R. Mackintosh, *Types of Modern Theology* (London and New York: Nisbet & Co., 1937), p. 45.

8. F. Flückiger, *Philosophie and Theologie bei Schleiermacher* (Zollikon-Zürich: Evangelischer Verlag, 1947), p. 48.

9. R. R. Niebuhr, *Schleiermacher on Christ and Religion: A New Introduction* (New York: Scribners, 1964), p. 5

10. Friedrich Meinecke, *Zur Theorie und Philosophie der Geschichte*, Eberhard Kassel ed. (Stuttgart: W. Kohlhammer, 1959; his *Werke*, vol. 4), p. 344.

11. *SW,** I. 11, (Berlin: Reiner, 1835–1884) p. 263.

12. Friedrich Schleiermacher, *Brief Outline on the Study of Theology*, Terrence N. Tice, trans. (Richmond: John Knox Press, 1966), §191, p. 70.

13. *SW* I, 11, p. 624

14. Ibid., p. 625.

15. Ibid., p. 624.

16. Hanna Jursch, *Schleiermacher als Kirchenhistoriker* (Jena: Verlag der Frommanschen Buchhandlug, 1933), p. 61.

17. F. Schleiermacher, *Brief Outline*, §29, p. 27.

18. Cf. Süskind, *Christentum*, p. 55. See also Friedrich Hertel, *Das theologische Denken Schleiermachers* (Zürich: Zwingli Verlag, 1965; *Studien zur Dogmengeschichte und systematischen Theologie*, vol. 18), pp. 226 ff.

19. F. Schleiermacher, *Uber die Religion. Reden an die Gebildeten unter ihren Verächtern*, 3rd ed. (Berlin: W. de Gruyter, 1821), p. 165.

20. Ibid., p. 103.

21. F. Schleiermacher, *Grundriss der philosophischen Ethik*, F. M. Schiele, ed. 2nd ed. (Leipzig: Deichert 1911).

22. F. Schleiermacher, *The Christian Faith*, H. R. Mackintosh and J. S. Stewart, eds. (Edinburgh: T. & T. Clark, 1928), §129, p. 595.

23. Ibid., §121, p. 564. In this paragraph one can find the remarkable statement that "the Christian Church is one through this one Spirit in the same way that a nation is one through the national character common to and identical in all" (p. 563). This parallelism between Church and nation is noteworthy for itself, but even more so because, almost in the same breath, Schleiermacher goes on to point out that the common spirit of the Church is derived from one and the same source, Christ. Then the whole thought is given still another turn by the observation that "faith only comes by preaching, and preaching always goes back to Christ's commission and is therefore derived from Him" (p. 564).

So preaching is the medium and vehicle of the common spirit of the Church in which the redemption through Christ is effected. All this has caused me to give special attention to Schleiermacher's incidental remark in his "Church History" about the monks of Chartreux, the Carthusians. He says: they "attributed special merit to taciturnity, but to base a Christian enterprise primarily upon this is something monstrous, inasmuch as the word is the very principle of Christianity" *(SW*, I, 11, p. 508).

24. *SW* I, 6, p. 10.

25. *SW* I, 12, p. 72.

26. F. Schleiermacher, *The Christian Faith*, §11, 4, p. 58.

27. Ibid., §13, 1, p. 63.

28. Ibid., §13, 2, p. 65.

29. Dilthey, *Leben Schleiermachers II* (ed. Redeker), p. 511. Cf. also Süskind, *Christentum*, p. 25.

30. Paul Seifert, *Die Theologie des jungen Schleiermacher* (Gütersloh: G. Mohn,

---

*S.W. = Schleiermachers Werke

1960); "Beiträge zur Förderung christlicher Theologie, 49), p. 188. "Es gibt für Schleiermacher nur eine hoffnungsvolle Entwicklung aber kein Ende der Geschichte."

31. F. Schleiermacher, Reden 3rd. ed. (1821), p. 171.

32. F. Schleiermacher, The Christian Faith, §126, pp. 582 ff.

33. F. Schleiermacher, Reden 3rd ed. (1821), p. 238.

34. Süskind, Christentum, p. 150.

35. F. Schleiermacher, The Christian Faith, §10, 3, p. 47.

36. F. Schleiermacher, Reden 3rd ed. (1821), p. 260. Cf. Siefert, Die Theologie, p. 133.

37. Schleiermacher's insight into the nature of individuality and individualization led him to many kinds of suggestive historical observations and interpretations, for example, in what he had to say about the relations between a "mass" and the "great individual" and about the function of "great men."

"Where we observe a multitude of single lives that act upon one another and that fluctuate between one another, a multitude which is not formed in a truly organic way and in which the single individuals do not achieve personal independence, we deal with a mass" (SW III, 3, p. 77). Opposed to this mass in its plurality, Schleiermacher places the great individual who has achieved personal wholeness and unity and also the community which manifests in its life a common spirit.

Against this background, he speaks of the "great man." Through and because of him the mass ceases to be mass; through him it is formed into an "organic common life," or, after periods of degeneration, it becomes reformed and is started upon a new development (ibid., p. 80). Great men are thus founders of states, founders and reformers of religion, indeed redeemers! "A great man is what he is, not because of single achievements on behalf of single classes, nor is it his proper task to found a school in the arts or in science. He is not the founder of a school but of an age." (ibid., p. 83).

One can understand why Schleiermacher regarded the biography of a great individual as the foremost subject of historiography.

38. F. Schleiermacher, Brief Outline, §155, p. 61.

39. SW I, 11, p. 37.

40. SW I, 11, pp. 51 f. Cf. Jursch, Schleiermacher, p. 56.

41. §§156–159, p. 62.

42. SW, I, 7, p. 271. Cf. Jursch, Schleiermacher pp. 71 f.

43. Ibid., 6, p. 2.

44. F. Schleiermacher, Brief Outline, §186, p. 69.

45. F. Schleiermacher, Grundlinien einer Kritik der bisherigen Sittenlehre (Berlin: W. de Gruyter, 1803), p. 452; quoted by Süskind, Christentum p. 145.

46. §188, pp. 69–70.

47. F. Schleiermacher, The Christian Faith, §2, p. 4.

48. H. Süskind, Christentum u. Geschichte, p. 87.

49. F. Schleiermacher, Brief Outline, §21, p. 24. In this connection, Schleiermacher's conception of heresies should be discussed; but here such a discussion would lead too far afield.

50. "Wer die Philosophie besitzen will, muss sie historisch verstehen." Quoted by Dilthey, Leben Schleiermachers II (ed. Redeker), (Berlin: W. de Gruyter, 1966), p. 15.

6. Adolf von Harnack

I

Adolf von Harnack was born on 7 May 1851 in the Baltic city of Dorpat in Livonia, which was then and is now again a Russian province. His forebears had come there from Germany. His paternal grandfather, a tailor, hailed from East Prussia; his maternal grandfather, a professor in the University of Dorpat and, for many years, its rector, was a native Westphalian. His father, Theodosius Harnack, a strict Lutheran with peitistic leanings, was a professor of practical and systematic theology, first in Dorpat, then for thirteen years (1853–66) in Erlangen, Germany, and then, again, for the rest of his life in Dorpat (he died in 1889).

Harnack and his three brothers (they were all unusually gifted) were educated in Erlangen and Dorpat. In October 1872 Adolf left home in order to complete his studies in the University of Leipzig.[1]

In 1873 he wrote and published his doctoral dissertation on an early Gnostic text. Shortly thereafter (1874), he began his academic career as a church historian, first as a *Privatdozent* (1874), and then as a professor-extraordinary (1876) in Leipzig. In 1879 he was appointed to a professorship in Giessen. From there he moved to Marburg (1886). Two years later he was called to the University of Berlin. By then he had already acquired fame as a teacher, researcher, author, critic, and as an organizer of scientific projects.[2] This call was opposed by the Supreme Council of the Evangelical Church. As the highest office of the Prussian state church, it was entitled to exercise a veto right of sorts on appointments to the theological chairs in the universities. However, both the faculty and the Minister of Education strongly desired Harnack's appointment. On their recommendation and on that of Chancellor Bismarck and his cabinet, Emperor William II, then at the very beginning of his reign, overruled the church office and affixed his signature to the document of Harnack's appointment on 17 September 1888.

The objections of the churchmen were based chiefly on Harnack's *History of Dogma* (3 vols., 1886–89; 4th ed., 1909). They consisted mainly of the following charges: (1) that he doubted the traditional views concerning the authorship of the Fourth Gospel, of the Letter to the Ephesians, and of the First Epistle of Peter; (2) that he was critical of miracles and specifically, that he did not accept the conventional interpretation of Christ's Virgin Birth, Resurrection, and Ascension; and (3) that he denied the institution of the sacrament of baptism by Jesus. No attempt was made to refute these views on the basis of historical scholarship from which they were derived, only the irreconcilability of Harnack's views with the doctrinal authority of the church was stated.

All this cast a shadow on Harnack's academic position. Indeed, it darkened his entire career. Even at this time, to be sure, Harnack was of the conviction that the gospel of Jesus Christ had nothing in common with the doctrinal authority exercised by an ecclesiastical hierarchy or by a bureau of church officials. But the church to which he belonged felt it necessary to maintain this very authority. He could, therefore, hardly avoid some kind of conflict with it. Nevertheless, it was a source of deep sorrow for him that, throughout his life, he was denied all official recognition by the church. He was not even given the right to examine his own pupils as they entered into the service of the church. Yet, for many years, he was the most influential theological teacher.[3]

Hundreds, nay thousands of students who later became ministers gave him an enthusiastic hearing, and scores of them were inspired by him to prepare themselves for theological professorships, which then became centers from which his views were spread to ever-widening circles. As a member of the theological faculty of Germany's most distinguished university, which was maintained and supported by the state and protected by it as to its academic freedom, Harnack made an incisive contribution to the training of the leaders of the Protestant Church. This church was united with the same state, yet it never invited him to take a seat at its councils, synods, or boards, and it never gave him any assurance that as a theological teacher he was one of its spokesmen. Thus Harnack could not but be deeply disappointed in his strong desire to serve the church.[4]

In a wider sense, he served it, of course, through his prolific authorship. Most of his more than sixteen hundred large and small writings were devoted to the study of the history of the church.[5] The New Testament, the Church Fathers, but also the Reformation and Protestantism furnished him the main themes.

Certain of his works have already become classics. His *History of Dogma,* for example, will have a permanent place among the masterpieces of theological literature. Though it will be superseded in specific parts, it will always be recognized as a most suggestive work of historical interpretation, grandly conceived and executed with superior skill both as to style and content.[6] The work on *The Mission and Expansion of Christianity during the First Three Centuries* (2 vols., 1902; 4th ed., 1924) is almost of the same quality. His *History of Ancient Christian Literature* (3 vols., 1893–1904) laid the foundation for all further critical studies in patristics.

Few works of modern theological literature have created as much excitement and stirred up as much furor as Harnack's *Wesen des Christentums (What is Christianity?,* 1900; 15th ed., 1950). It is the transcript of a student's stenograph of a course of lectures delivered to students of all faculties in the winter semester 1899–1900. Troeltsch[7] thought that it was representative of all theological work based on historical thinking. It certainly has become generally regarded as the one book which more directly than any other represents so-called liberal Protestant theology.

Harnack continued to publish scholarly and popular writings throughout his life. His authorship extended over fifty-seven years, from 1873, when he published his dissertation on Gnosticism, to 1930, when his publications ended with an article on the name of Novatian. His first important scholarly work had been a prize essay on Marcion (unpublished) for which the University of Dorpat had given him a gold medal; his last significant book was devoted to an interpretation of the same heretical figure,[8] and it stirred up considerable excitement.

In his capacity as a historian, Harnack was elected, in 1890, to the Prussian Academy of Sciences in Berlin. Theodore Mommsen, one of its most distinguished members, gave him an enthusiastic welcome. Here he soon became the organizer and chairman of the editorial council of the *Cricital Edition of the Greek Christian Authors of the First Three Centuries.* Furthermore, he learned to relate theological scholarship to that of other disciplines. It was a signal honor that he, the theologian, was invited by the Academy to prepare its history, which was to be published in connection with the celebration of its two hundredth anniversary in 1900. Harnack punctually fulfilled the assignment. In three volumes, he offered not only an interpretation of the activities of the Academy but, in connection with it, also a history of modern scholarship.

At the dawn of the new century, he was at the height of his career. When the anniversary of the Berlin Academy was celebrated in a glittering ceremony, he was the official orator. It so happened that, just then, he also occupied the post of rector of the University of Berlin. Moreover, at this time his fame was spreading throughout the world in connection with the publication of the book *What Is Christianity?* He wielded great influence on educational affairs through the office of the Minister of Education who frequently sought his counsel.[9] Ever increasingly he became a representative personage. The public saw in him scholarship personified. William II, the German emperor, gave him special recognition, first by inviting him into his company and then by bestowing special honors upon him.[10]

All this had an effect upon his academic career. To be sure, church historical teaching and research continued to be his primary love and labor. But, in the course of time, he came to assume two further professional responsibilities. Indeed, he said of himself that he was active in three different careers. In 1906 he accepted the appointment to the post of Director General of the Royal Library[11] in Berlin, the largest and most important library in Germany. Some of his friends were disturbed; they feared that he might gradually abandon his theological career. But Harnack wrote to his friend, Professor Martin Rade in Marburg:

You come to know the world only insofar as you influence it. My new position will not make me a librarian so much as an organizer. I hope that my friends will find that theology is not made the loser thereby but that all branches of learning, including theology, will make a gain. I have *done* little in my life, and I should like, in a modest way, to supplement my work of lecturing and writing by a "doing" from which the whole community can profit. The church has not offered me an opportunity of this kind, and if such work were offered to me now, it would come too late for me.[12]

He proved to be an excellent organizer and a brilliant administrator. Hence nobody was much surprised when in 1911 he accepted also the post of president of the *Kaiser Wilhelm Gesellschaft*.[13] This was a foundation organized (in connection with the celebration of the centennial of the University of Berlin and sponsored by the German Emperor) for the purpose of launching scientific research institutes in which scholars would pursue basic and applied research of a kind in which the universities could not afford to become engaged, on account of their primary responsibility for teaching and professional training. Under Harnack's leadership and with the support of government and industry, the foundation rapidly established several research institutes chiefly in the natural and medical sciences. Almost immediately they won worldwide recognition and influence.

Harnack continued to be president of the *Kaiser Wilhelm Gesellschaft* until the end of his life. He led its affairs when it assumed broader and poignantly practical responsibilities during World War I, and he saw it through the turmoil caused by Germany's military defeat and through the ensuing period of monetary inflation and economic depression. In the spring of 1930, these duties led him to Heidelberg, where a new institute of medical research was to be opened. There he died, after a brief illness, on 10 June 1930.

In 1921 he had become a professor emeritus. He then gave up all administrative duties connected with his professorship and retired from the library, but he continued to teach (on a reduced schedule, of course) for several years.[14] In the spring of 1929, he delivered his last lecture in the University of Berlin, and at the same time he closed his seminar on ancient church history over which he had presided continuously for one hundred and eight academic semesters. It always had been the center of his work and the headquarters of his professional labors. For in connection with the broad influence he exercised and throughout the deep impact that went forth from him to all fields of cultural endeavor, he always remained first of all a church historian and a theologian. Indeed, he embodied in his person a kind of cultural Protestantism, which was deeply anchored in his personal faith and reached out broadly upon the wide field of human civilization. "Creator of unforgettable scholarly works, a master of organization, he impressed everyone, wherever he appeared, as a dominating personality through clarity, sureness, and strength of will."[15]

II

Whatever may have been the secret of Harnack's power and whatever was the source of his accomplishment as a scholar, administrator, public figure, and representative man, one can say that he was what he was and that he produced his great works in the way he did, because he was an unusually gifted teacher.

One of his students in Leipzig, at the very beginning of Harnack's career (in 1877–78), wrote almost fifty years later in the following enthusiastic way of the impression Harnack (who was then still in his twenties) made upon him and his fellow students:

We had the feeling that a new world was dawning upon us. We had been trained by capable teachers and we were taking courses from eminent professors and well-known scholars. But here we were touched by the aura of genius. Harnack combined in himself in a unique way the qualities required of a scholar with the gifts of a born teacher: concentrated inquisitiveness; tireless industry; the ability of ordering and forming his materials; a comprehensive memory;[16] a clear and considered judgment, and together with all this, a wonderful gift of intuition and combination and, at the same time, a marvelously simple, lucid, and appealing manner of presentation. And, to top it all, he also had not infrequently the good fortune of finding and discovering something new. To every subject and field of study he gave light and warmth, life and significance. In both theory and practice he was a master of the teaching method.

He came to his classes only after thorough preparation. He was never without notes, but he spoke extemporaneously . . . without affection or pathos and never seeking cheap effects. He talked eloquently and from an even inner participation in what he was dealing with, without trying to excite or overwhelm his hearers. Yet he was fascinating and convincing. He was illuminating through the gentle compulsion of complete objectivity. He was conscientious and accurate but not pedantic, nor did he get lost in details. Without minimizing or concealing difficulties, he explained the problems at hand with vividness as to their logical form and material content. He made the past live through the present and let the present explain the past.[17]

Many other testimonies prove that these striking words express the experience and judgment of the large circle of Harnack's students and pupils. Among these none is perhaps as telling as that of Dietrich Bonhoeffer,[18] who was a member of Harnack's last seminar and who spoke in the name of his fellow students at the memorial service on 15 June 1930 in Berlin. He said, among other things:

He got hold of us in the way a real teacher gets hold of his pupils. He shared our questions, even though he confronted us with his superior judgment. We assembled in his home for a serious piece of work on the history of the ancient church, and there we came to know him and his unerring striving for truth and clarity. All mere talk was foreign to the spirit of his seminar. He demanded absolute clarity. This did not exclude the possibility that very personal and inmost questions were raised. He was always willing to listen to questions and to answer them. All that mattered to him was the honesty of the answer. Thus we learned from him that truth is born only from freedom.[19]

We should note that as a teacher Harnack was an historian and that as an historian he was a teacher. The role of the teacher is almost identical with that of the historian. In a certain sense, every true teacher is a historian, and nobody can be a true historian unless he is willing to be also a teacher. For, in every present, men find that they must come to terms with the cultural legacy they have inherited from their fathers. They must take possession of it and incorporate it in their own lives. They must fit it to the requirements of their own situation and thus transform it and then transmit it to their children and their children's children.*

Civilization is a product of education and a learning process at the same time. Men are engaged in it in order to relate the values produced by past generations to the needs of the present; at the

---

*Here Pauck echoes also the Goethe dictum that he often quoted in the classroom: *"Was du ererbt von deinem Vätern hast, Erwirb es, um es zu besitzen!"*—Ed.

same time, they endeavor to hand them on to future generations. Whoever, therefore, furthers human culture is in a real sense a teacher as well as a historian, for as he hands down the cultural traditions of the past to those around him, he acts as a historically responsible educator.

In this sense, Harnack was a supreme teacher-historian.[20] His writings as well as his activities clearly prove that he believed it to be the highest task of the historian to prepare his fellow men for right action in the present.[21] "Only that history which is not yet past but which is and remains a living part of our present deserves to be known by all," he wrote.[22] Hence he regarded all history as mute as long as it is nothing but a display of an antiquarian interest or dealt with only in terms of archaeology, that is, as long as it is understood to be merely a record of past human life.[23]

The following statement sums up Harnack's fundamental conception:

We study history in order to intervene in the course of history, and it is our right and duty that we do this, for if we lack historical insight we either permit ourselves to be mere objects put in the historical process or we shall have the tendency to lead people down the wrong way. To intervene in history—this means that we must reject the past when it reaches into the present only in order to block us. It means also that we must do the right thing in the present, that is, anticipate the future and be prepared for it in a circumspect manner. There is no doubt that, with respect to the past, the historian assumes the royal function of a judge, for in order to decide what of the past shall continue to be in effect and what must be done away with or transformed, the historian must judge like a king. Everything must be designed to furnish a preparation for the future, for only that discipline of learning has a right to exist which lays the foundation for what is to be.[24]

We should misunderstand the import of these words if we should take them to imply that Harnack was not concerned about the objectivity of historical research. He was wont to say that he was doing his work as a historian on three levels, namely, source criticism, representation, and reflection, and that he felt most at home on the third level.[25] And it is a fact that he devoted much rigorous and time-consuming effort to the establishment of the accuracy and reliability of his sources, and, moreover, that he took great care to represent and interpret these sources as diligently and objectively as possible. But he was also painfully aware of the limits that are set to the historian as he attempts to reconstruct, to relate, and to interpret past actions and events. He shared to some extent the skeptical judgment of Goethe who is reported to have said in a conversation with the historian Heinrich Luden: "Not all that is presented to us as history has really happened; and what really happened did not actually happen the way it is presented to us; moreover, what really happened is only a small part of all that happened. Everything in history remains uncertain, the largest event as well as the smallest occurrence."[26]

As a historian, Harnack therefore did not try to tell *wie es eigentlich gewesen* (what really happened), and, indeed, he avoided all biographical history because he suspected that it represented, especially in regard to motivations, a necessarily unsuccessful engagement with insoluble puzzles and inscrutable enigmas. Instead, he chose to study the development of institutions, that is, states, societies, groups, and corporations and their established practices, customs, laws, codes, and authoritative rules. He interpreted institutional history as a history of ideas, for he judged that one cannot understand the development and the power of institutions unless one knows the direction along which they are moved by the ideas that govern and maintain them. For example, he believed it to be the historian's task to show to what extent an institution has succeeded in incorporating the idea or purpose for the concrete expression of which it was founded or in what way an institution may be striving to maintain itself even after it has lost the right to exist because the purpose that called it into being has become invalid or lost its directive power. He even dared define the norm by reference to which the historian can judge what institution or institutional function deserves to be maintained: that in them which preserves life. And he was persuaded that "only that line of action and that power preserve life which liberate men from 'the service to that which passes away,' from enslavement to mere nature, and from servitude to one's own empirical self."[27]

III

Among Harnack's books, the *History of Dogma* is the clearest expression of this basic conception of the historian's task. It shows concretely how and to what extent he tried to carry out his historical principles in his own field of study. He himself describes the importance of his interpretation of the history of dogma in the following way:

By delineating the process of the origin and development of the dogma, the "history of dogma" furnishes the most suitable means for the liberation of the church from dogmatic Christianity and for the speeding up of the irresistible process of the emancipation which began with Augustine. But it also witnesses to the unity of the Christian faith in the course of history by furnishing proof that the actual significance of the person of Jesus Christ and the principles of the gospel were never lost sight of.[28]

In writing the history of dogma, that is, the history of those authoritative ecclesiastical doctrines concerning the person and work of Christ, God incarnate, which every Christian had to accept on peril of being excluded from the communion of salvation, Harnack desired to show, in the first place, how it happened that the gospel of Jesus Christ, which in its nature has nothing in common with ecclesiasticism and with authoritarian statutes and doctrines, became embodied in the cultic-hierarchical practices and, especially, the doctrinal institutions of the church. But, in the second place, he wanted to offer proof, by historical analysis, for the thesis that if the gospel is to retain its living power today, it must be freed from identification with the dogma. Indeed, it was his major point that the dogma originated in the effort of the ancient Christians to render the gospel comprehensible in the concepts of the Hellenistic world view and that they therefore expressed it in the thought-forms of Greek philosophy and science. Then he drew the conclusion that, after having been maintained for centuries through the doctrinal authoritarianism of the church, the dogma has been coming to an end in the way the various Christian churches and groups have come to deal with it: in Eastern Orthodoxy it has become an uncomprehended relic kept alive only in the cultus and the liturgy; in Roman Catholicism it has become submerged in the hierarchical-sacramental order of the church culminating in the absolute authority of the Pope; the Reformation invalidated it in principle by the rediscovery of the gospel and by the assertion of its primary place in all Christian thought and life. However, the reformers failed to recognize the full revolutionary significance of this rediscovery: instead of making room in all Christian thought for the gospel alone, as they said it was their purpose, they coupled the reformation of the church on the basis of the gospel with the conservation of the dogma, in the interest, so they believed, of a scriptural catholicity. Thus it came about that the churches of the Reformation, namely, Lutheranism, Calvinism, and Anglicanism, exhibit in their orders and practices a personal faith in Christ in the context of authoritarian churchmanship. They have always required of the faithful obedient submission to the authority of ministers and ecclesiastical officials, and these are duty-bound to maintain conformity with the dogma.

It was Harnack's conviction that the Reformation must go on. Inasmuch as "every really important reformation in the history of religion was primarily a critical reduction,"[29] Luther's rediscovery of the gospel must be completed by the emancipation of Christianity from doctrinal authoritarianism. He believed that the Hellenization of the gospel, which began with the formulation of the Logos-Christology and culminated in the promulgation of the Nicene dogma of the Trinity and of the Chalcedonian dogma of Christ, very God and very man, was an historical decision through which the Christian church succeeded in maintaining its identity in its confrontation with Hellenistic civilization and the Roman Empire; but he was also convinced that this Hellenization need not be continued forever, especially if this perpetuation can be accomplished only through an authoritarianism and an intellectual servitude which are irreconcilable with the gospel and its spirit. Having in mind Luther and the Reformation, he summed up his basic view in the following words:

Christianity is something else than the sum of doctrines handed down from generation to generation. Christianity is not identical with biblical theology nor with the doctrine of the church-councils but it is that disposition which the Father of Jesus Christ awakens in men's hearts through the gospel. All authorities on which the dogma is based are torn down— how then can the dogma possibly be maintained as an infallible teaching! Christian doctrine is relevant only to faith; what part can philosophy then have in it? But what are dogma and dogmatic Christianity without philosophy?[30]

He concluded by asking: "How can there possibly be a history of dogma in Protestantism in view of Luther's 'Prefaces to the New Testament' and in view of his writings on the principles of the Reformation?"[31]

And with respect to the various historical forms Christianity assumes in the course of time, beginning with the so-called Jewish Christianity of the Apostolic Age, he wrote: "Either Christianity is . . . identical with its first form (in this case, one is forced to conclude that it came and went at a certain time) or it contains something which remains valid in historically changing forms. Starting with the beginnings, church history shows that it was necessary for 'early Christianity' to perish in order that 'Christianity' might remain. So too, there followed, later on, one metamorphosis upon another."[32]

We must acknowledge that this interpretation is thoroughly historical. By combining historical exposition with historical criticism, Harnack drew the full consequences from the application of the historical method to the Christian religion. In fact, he replaced the dogmatic method, which had been employed for so long a time in Christian thought, by the historical method. In doing so, he brought to a culmination the approach which had first been introduced into Christian theology by the historical theologians of the Enlightenment, especially Johann Salomo Semler (d. 1791), and which then resulted in the interpretation of Christianity as a "development" at the hands of Ferdinand Christian Baur (d. 1860) and Albrecht Ritschl (d. 1889), whom Harnack regarded as his immediate predecessors.[33] He relied on the work of these historical theologians and brought it to a climax insofar as, in following out the implications of the historical method, he substituted for the traditional dogmatic norm of Christian theological truth the historical concept of the nature of Christianity (Wesen des Christentums). Thus he hoped to replace theological dogmatism by historical understanding.

In the introduction to a new edition of his lectures on the nature of Christianity, he wrote: "Historical understanding is achieved only as one makes the effort of separating the distinctive essence of an important phenomenon from the temporary historical forms in which it is clothed."[34] In these lectures, which constitute a summary and a popularization of the results of his sholarly investigations, he tried to achieve this understanding by identifying the nature of Christianity with the gospel and its influences. He therefore dealt first with the gospel of Jesus Christ, then with the impact that Jesus himself and his gospel made upon the first generation of his disciples, and finally with the main types of the Christian religion as they developed from the changes it underwent in its encounter with different human conditions. He proposed to discover what these movements had in common by testing them by the gospel. Furthermore, he believed that he would be able to define the principles *(Grundzüge)*, that is, the main characteristics of the gospel, by verifying them through a study of the various ways by which the gospel was understood in the course of church history.

It is often said that Harnack identified the nature of Christianity with the teachings of Jesus. But this is an undiscriminating simplification of his view. He did not think it possible, it is true, to define the Christian religion apart from the gospel of Jesus Christ; but he did not isolate this gospel from its historical impact, nor did he absolutize it on the basis of the New Testament where it is recorded in its earliest form. No historical form of Christianity, he believed, should be absolutized or regarded as normative.[35] "One may say," he wrote, "that Paul or Augustine or Luther were right [in their conception of the Christian Gospel], yet one must never go so far as to regard their Christianity as Christianity itself."[36] He was persuaded that wherever the gospel of Jesus Christ is actually believed, that is, where it is really apprehended by way of a commitment to God derived from faith in this gospel (so that this commitment is a certain trustful disposition of the heart), there Christianity is realized: the impulse which motivates such an actualization, and the fountain which feeds it is the gospel—the gospel which Jesus proclaimed and of which he was the concretion in his historical humanity.

Harnack never stated in so many words what he conceived the nature of Christianity to be (and we should realize that no historian would attempt to offer a final definition), but he undertook again and again the task of defining the gospel. We must take care not to isolate certain ones of these definitions from the rest lest we illegitimately distort his thought.

He loved to quote Luther's saying, supposedly under the assumption that it summarized the gospel: "In forgiveness of sins there is life and bliss." Or he said: "The religion of the gospel rests upon . . . faith in Jesus Christ, i.e., because of him, this particular historical person, the believer is certain that God rules heaven and earth and that God the Judge is also the Father and Redeemer."[37] In the *History of Dogma*, he asserted that the gospel as the New Testament presents it is something twofold:[38] (1) the preaching of Jesus, and (2) the proclamation of Jesus as the Christ who died and rose again for the sake of sin and who gives the assurance of forgiveness and eternal life.

Many, therefore, misunderstand Harnack when they hold that he thought that the gospel consists ultimately only of the teaching of Jesus. There is, of course, no denying that he put great stress upon the teaching of Jesus. Indeed, he has become famous for the definition he offers in *What Is Christianity?* In the teaching of Jesus, he says there,[39] there are three circles of thought, each of which contains the whole proclamation: (1) the Kingdom of God and its coming; (2) God the Father and the infinite value of the human soul; (3) the better righteousness and the commandment of love. He was concerned to emphasize that this teaching must be received with full seriousness. For he was persuaded that it was not something merely provisional, which must be differently understood in the light of Jesus' death and resurrection,[40] as if only a certain conception of the person of Christ (for example, that he was the "Son of God," etc.) could ensure the proper comprehension of the gospel.

"Not the Son but alone the Father belongs in the gospel as Jesus proclaimed it."[41] By saying this, Harnack in no way intended to minimize the significance of Jesus. He wanted only to make sure that the gospel was understood as a religious-moral proclamation addressed to man's conscience, which requires from him a decision for or against it and will then bring about a transformation of his inner disposition. He desired thus to avoid the impression that the gospel must be taken to be a revelation of an extraordinary sort which can be maintained only on the basis of certain metaphysical views about God, Christ,[42] man, and the world. He felt it necessary to insist on saying that "Jesus does not belong to the gospel as one of its elements,"[43] for, in fact, he thought of him as highly as possible.

He was the personal concretion and power of the gospel, and we still perceive him as such. For one has ever known the Father in the way he knew him, and he gives this knowledge to others, thereby rendering "the many" an incomparable service. He leads them to God, not only by his word but still more by what he is and does and, finally, by his suffering. It is in this sense that he said not only this: "Come unto me all ye that labor and are heavy laden and I will give you rest," but also this: "This Son of Man is not come to be ministered unto but to minister and give his life as a ransom for many."[44]

Throughout his life, Harnack was certain that because of this gospel, Christianity was *the* true religion. "It is *the* religion," he wrote,[45] "because Jesus Christ is not one among other masters but *the* master and because his gospel corresponds to the innate capacity of man as history discloses it."

In order to do full justice to Harnack's basic conception, we must note also that he frequently pointed out what the gospel and the Christian religion are not. "The Christian religion is something lofty and simple and is concerned only about one point: Eternal life in the midst of time through God's power and in his presence. It is not an ethical or social arcanum for the purpose of preserving all sorts of things or of improving them. Even the mere question of what it has contributed to the cultural progress of mankind does harm to its spirit."[46] It is an error, therefore, to apply the gospel directly to secular affairs and to deduce from it detailed prescriptions and statutes for their regulation.[47] It is something religious; indeed, it is religion itself and as such a disposition of mind marked by worship in spirit and in truth. Hence it cannot and must not be expressed in laws and regulations or in a worship through signs, liturgical rituals, and idols.[48] Its true nature is threatened if it is linked with or confined to authoritative forms of faith and order, dogma and liturgy, law and hierarchy. Ecclesiasticism, so Harnack affirmed,[49] frequently imposed a terrible burden upon the gospel, but it never succeeded in suppressing its power. However, the most momentuous conformity which, he thought, ecclesiastical authority has been wont to require and still requires of Christians, is the doctrinal one. This is detrimental to the gospel, not because of doctrine as such (though the gospel is not a doctrine!), but because of the fact that, from the beginning, Christian dogmatic thought was combined with Greek philosophy of religion and with the intellectualism characteristic of this philosophy. The result was not only that the Christian faith came to be dependent upon metaphysics but also—and this was an observation Harnack thought was amazing and shocking—that a "fancied Christ was put in the place of the real one."[50]

IV

These several points are an indication of the program Harnack advocated (explicity and implicitly) for Christianity in the modern world. In conclusion, we now direct our attention to his major programmatic convictions and recommendations.

We must give priority to a concern that runs through his entire theological work, namely, that Christians should be freed from the requirement of holding certain rigidly defined doctrines and of maintaining other traditions only because they are regarded as authoritative in connection with a dogma whose absolute validity is simply taken for granted or affirmed without question. During the negotiations about his call to the University of Berlin, he addressed a memorandum to the Minister of Education[51] in which he made the following declaration: "Neither exegesis nor dogmatics but the results of church historical research will break the power of the traditions which are now burdening the consciences of men. Cardinal Manning once made the following frivolous statement: 'One must overcome history by dogma'—we say just the opposite; dogma must be purified by history. As Protestants we are confident that by doing this we do not break down but build up."

Harnack's whole theological work can be regarded as a commentary on this statement. He wanted to see authoritarian dogmatic thinking replaced by historical thinking. He knew how difficult it would be to achieve this goal. For he was aware of the fact that "there is nothing more conservative and unyielding than ordered religion."[52] Indeed, he had the greatest respect for the Roman Catholic Church because it had succeeded in maintaining itself throughout many ages by means of this conservatism. "The Roman Church," he said, "is the most comprehensive and powerful, the most complex and yet most uniform structure which known history has produced."[53]

In order to liberate the gospel from the connection with this powerful institution, Harnack believed that the reformers had to renounce in some way the Roman Catholic ideal of building a visible Kingdom of God on earth and of penetrating the realm of nature with the power of grace and holiness; but in order to return the Christian religion to its spiritual core, they had no choice but to effect a tremendous reduction.[54] The result was that the gospel was once more clearly seen in distinction from Roman ecclesiasticism. However, the reformers did not go far enough. They abolished Roman ecclesiasticism in the name of the Word of God and they assailed its foundations, but they left the dogma intact. Luther had a certain historical sense and, to some extent, was able to apply historical criticism to purely dogmatic authority. For example, he rejected the notion of the infallible authority of the Papacy by pointing out that it was the product of changing history. But his thinking was not really determined by historical sense.[55] Hence he was unable to recognize the Scripture as a historical product. For the same reason, he argued that the dogma declared by the ancient councils of the church was valid inasmuch as it agreed with the Word of God. The other reformers, with the exception of a few humanistic representatives of the left wing of the Reformation, followed in Luther's train. Hence, so Harnack concluded, "Protestantism was unable, from the beginning to develop fully, consistently, and strongly. It continued to be heavily burdened with Catholic remnants. When the Enlightenment finally came to its assistance, it brought with it a certain unproductive self-sufficiency which spoiled everything. Because of this, it failed to recognize the historical element through which faith in God the father is linked with Jesus Christ."[56]

Modern historical theology must complete what the Reformation began—this was Harnack's program. The application of historical thinking to all parts and phases of the Christian religion would make it possible, he believed, for the gospel of Jesus Christ to run a free, unhindered course in the world. "It must become possible," he wrote, "that one may openly say that such and such teachings and affirmations of the creeds are incorrect and that nobody is forced to confess in the Divine Service what once he is outside he does not need to confess."[57]

He hoped that the time would come when traditional dogmatic Christianity would be replaced by an undogmatic Christianity.[58] At the end of his life, he stated that he felt a certain kinship with the Congregationalists and the Quakers.[59] There can be no doubt that his whole theological outlook was similar to that of the "theologians" of the American denominations that represent the so-called free-church tradition.

There are three great themes to which he returned again and again in connection with his advocacy of the undogmatic, historical thinking in religion and theology: (1) the canonical authority of the Old Testament; (2) the doctrine of Christ; and (3) the unity of Christendom.[60]

(1) In order to release Protestantism from the shackles of literalistic Biblicism and the dogmatics connected therewith, and in order to be consistent with the historical interpretation of the Bible, indeed, in order just to "honor the truth," Harnack felt that the Protestant churches should break with the tradition of treating the Old Testament as a book of *canonical authority*. In his work on Marcion, he wrote (and he was then at the end of his career): "In the second century, the rejection of the Old Testament would have been a mistake and the Great Church rightly refused to make this mistake; its retention in the sixteenth century was due to the power of a fateful heritage from which the reformers were not yet able to withdraw; but its conservation as a canonical book in modern Protestantism is the result of a paralysis of religion and the church." Harnack did not mean, of course, to suggest that Christians, and particularly the historians and theologians among them, should no longer study the Old Testament. On the contrary, he thought that from the historical point of view it would always not only be good and useful but also *necessary* to read it in relation to the New Testament. But he was convinced that the New Testament was the basic Christian book and that it alone therefore should be held as Holy Scripture.

This view called forth a storm of protest, and it still does. Harnack's critics felt that he was assailing the very foundation of

Christianity. Barth, for example, responded to Harnack's insistence that Protestantism should "clearly decide" against the canonicity of the Old Testament by saying: "In respect of this we merely remark that if the Evangelical Church were to do this, it would lose its identity with the Church of the first seventeen centuries."[61] It is difficult to imagine that this point would have greatly impressed Harnack, for his whole proposal was inspired by the realization that, in terms of historical reality, modern Protestantism is not and cannot be "identical" with the church of former ages.[62]

(2) Of much greater importance to Harnack was his hope that modern Christians would free themselves from the burden of the dogma about the person of Jesus. Even as late as 1925,[63] he said: "By combining all the various affirmations about Christ in the one confession and witness that he is the mirror of God's paternal heart,[64] one can get free from the entire ancient dogma and, at the same time, hold fast to the root of faith." He was sure that it was not possible for any man, on the basis of faith or knowledge, to make any valid statements about Christ's nature and particularly his "divine nature." Christians must be content with the New Testament and leave room for the same diversity of thought and speech the early Christians displayed in relation to their understanding of the lordship of Christ.

Harnack looked forward with keen anticipation to the Lausanne Conference on Faith and Order in 1927. He hoped that there the churches would achieve some clarity about Christology. In a memorandum,[65] he expressed the opinion that the deliberations of the conference were "a fateful hour of decision for the Christian church," insofar as they would either make a contribution to clarification and unification of a sort the churches had not experienced for centuries or increase the division of Christendom. Then he went on to say:

There is a significant consensus in Christology. No one denies either the uniqueness of the unity of the person of the Redeemer; nor does anyone deny that the Christian faith is faith in the Father, the Son, and the Holy Spirit and that its universal confession is that in Jesus Christ the Word became flesh. . . . Should we not be satisfied with this consensus as it is expressed in the confessional affirmations that Christ is the "Son of God," the "God-Man," the "Image of God," "Our Lord"? In my judgment, this should be sufficient, and the churches would leave it to every Christian how he might further conceive the person of Christ. But, as a matter of fact, this consensus is not sufficient in our day; we need a formal decision, for, at the great ancient councils, the churches have ordained that one must believe in the *two natures* of Christ and that any statement about him in which this speculation about his two natures is rejected must be considered heretical. . . . But, in the course of the last two centuries, numerous Christians have found it impossible to express the faith in Christ through the speculation about the two natures, etc. . . . The Conference on Faith and Order will have to decide whether it shall demand that the dogmatic affirmation: Christ had two natures, shall continue to be an affirmation of faith or whether it is prepared to reaffirm the faith in the Father, the Son, and the Holy Spirit and, therefore, also in the God-man Christ, but, as far as the churches are concerned, to make no binding rules about any further speculation.

This expectation of Harnack was not fulfilled and has not been fulfilled to this day. No church body has ever officially renounced or given up or modified any dogmatic decision made by the official bodies of the ancient church.

(3) Harnack ardently believed in Christian unity. He was convinced that the Christian religion was the greatest force for the reconciliation of men with one another. He experienced with gratification the awakening of the ecumenical movement and entertained great hopes for it. But he felt strongly that such unity could be brought about only if all intolerance based on dogmatism and doctrinal authoritarianism were banished from the life of the churches.

V

After World War I, the fashion of theological thinking changed radically. The leadership of Harnack, the historian, was replaced by that of Karl Barth, the dogmatist. The difference between them as to theological method was so great that Harnack, who was one of Barth's teachers, found himself utterly unable to follow Barth. "He was ready to acknowledge Barth's deep seriousness, but his theology made him shudder."[66]

Barth has explained the difference between his own outlook and that of Harnack by pointing to the fact that, following

Schleiermacher, all "modern" Protestant theologians pursued their work by proceeding *von unten nach oben* (from man to God), whereas he advocates a method which goes *von oben nach unten* (from God to man). There is much truth in this distinction. And saying this does not necessarily mean that truth is on Barth's side. He begins his theological interpretation with revelation, and God's revelation remains his theme throughout. But the question is, by what right he can begin and proceed in this way. For he is a man and as such he is bound to history; he should therefore be ready (but he is not!) to admit that like all other knowledge also the knowledge of God can be available to him only historically.

Harnack, by contrast, started with the assumption that, together with everything else that belongs to man's realm, the Christian religion is something historical, a heritage with which every generation has to deal with respect to the past as well as to the future. Is then truth not on his side insofar as he insisted that the only adequate method of dealing with Christianity is the historical one? The discussion of this question will occupy theology for many years to come, and in this discussion Harnack's views will continue to be important.

NOTES

1. Hans Lietzmann writes in a commemorative article in *Theologische Literaturzeitung* 76 (1951): "When as a young student I became acquainted with Harnack in Venice, he told me one evening during an unforgettable conversation about his upbringing. As if he were telling a fairy-tale he said: 'We were four brothers, and when we left home, our father gave each of us one thousand dollars and told us that we should make good. All four of us did make good—and I still have the thousand dollars.'" On Harnack's relation with his father, see C. Wayne Glick, *The Reality of Christianity: A Study of A. von Harnack as Historian and Theologian* (New York: Harper & Bros., 1967), pp. 23–28. Glick also stresses Harnack's dependence on his main academic teacher in Dorpat, Moritz von Engelhardt (ibid., pp. 29–34).

2. In 1876 he founded (with his friend Emil Schürer) the *Theologische Literaturzeitung*, which is still one of the foremost critical reviews of theological scholarship. (Harnack was its sole editor from 1881 on and held this post for many years.) During 1881–82 he began (in cooperation with his friend O. von Gebhardt) the publication of the series *Texte und Untersuchungen*, which, in the course of time, became a mine of information on the history of the ancient church.

3. As an example of his students' gratitude for Harnack's teaching, I quote here a passage from a letter of Karl Holl, which he addressed to Harnack after Holl had attended Harnack's seminar in the winter semester of 1889–90. (Harnack later decisively determined Holl's career: in 1891 he made him his

collaborator in the edition of the Greek Fathers, which he prepared under the auspices of the Berlin Academy of Sciences; and, in 1906, he was instrumental in having Holl appointed as his special colleague to the second chair of church history in the University of Berlin. In this position, Holl gradually achieved great scholarly fame.) Holl wrote (on 18 April 1890): "It may be a rather one-sided way of looking at things . . . yet as highly as I certainly appreciate what you showed us about the grave tasks and the strict methods of scholarship, I count it a higher gain that . . . you awakened in me a joyful eagerness for serving our church. . . . In extending to you my special thanks, I want to give expression to my actual experience and my deepest conviction that through you I have become aware of the extent to which every service we render to our church, either of a scholarly or a practical kind, is a holy service which must be rendered by serious work without fear of or surrender to human authorities. I hope that I may demonstrate in the course of my life that in these respects I have not for nothing been your pupil" (Heinrich Karpp, ed. *Karl Holl: Briefwechsel mit Adolf von Harnack* [Tübingen: Mohr, 1966], pp. 11f.).

This particular correspondence shows very impressively with what deep human understanding Harnack was able to relate himself to his students and colleagues as a scholar and as a friend. Holl was often inclined to take life as a grave task and even as a heavy burden and he therefore often tended toward pessimism. Harnack tried again and again to give him courage and to cut him free from his depressions. He once wrote to Holl: "May you learn to rid yourself of the virtuosity of condemning each fruit-tree which God has planted for your benefit as a weeping willow" (Karpp, *K. Holl*, p. 18).

4. The only opportunity he had to satisfy this wish was given to him through his membership in the "Evangelical-Social Congress" (one of the voluntary associations so distinctive of modern Protestantism), whose purpose it was, outside the official church but through a membership recruited from the ranks of church members, to give concrete expression to the Christian responsibility for the social-political order. Harnack was its president from 1903 to 1912.

5. Cf. Friedrich Smend, *A. von Harnack: Verzeichnis seiner Schriften* (Leipzig: Heinsius, 1931), which lists 1611 titles.

6. One of Harnack's admirers, the French Jesuit scholar J. de Ghellinck, wrote about it *("En marge de l'oeuvre de Harnack," Gregorianum* 11 [1930], pp. 513 f.): "Everyone knows the three volumes of his *Dogmengeschichte*, though it is perhaps correct to say that more people talk about them than read them." *(Chacun les connait bien qu'il soit peut-etre exact de dire que les trois volumes de sa Dogmengeschichte ont trouvé moins d'hommes pour les lire que pour en parler.)*

7. Cf. Ernst Troeltsch, "Was heisst 'Wesen des Christentums?,'" *Gesammelte Schriften*, II (Tübingen: Mohr, 1913), p. 387: *Harnack's Schrift ist gewissermassen das symbolische Buch für die historisierende Richtung der Theologie.*

8. Adolf Von Harnack, *Marcion: Das Evangelium von fremden Gott* (Berlin: W. de Gruyter, 1921; 2d ed., Leipzig, 1924).

9. There was a certain time when the rumor was current that he would be appointed Minister of Education.

10. He raised him to the dignity of hereditary nobility. Harnack was the last scholar so honored in royal Prussia.

11. After World War I, it was called the Prussian State Library.

12. Agnes von Zahn-Harnack, *Adolf von Harnack*, 2d ed. (Berlin: W. de Gruyter, 1951), p. 325. See the very interesting and informative article by Felix E. Hirsch, "The Scholar as Librarian. To the Memory of Adolf von Harnack," in

The Library Quarterly IX (1939), pp. 299–320. Hirsch describes in detail how imaginatively and effectively Harnack administered his new post, finding willing collaborators among the professional librarians, especially in the person of his first director, Paul Schwenke. He also reports with admiration as follows (p. 307): "The sums he was able to procure were astounding. The Prussian bureaucracy made concessions to him which would have seemed unbelievable [under his predecessor] and which they would have denied to any librarian not invested with Harnack's authority as a scholar. . . . Although there was a strong upward trend in the financial resources of all the great libraries in the country, so rapid an increase in the budget figures as took place in the Royal Library was unparalleled. Shortly after Harnack had taken office, he persuaded the ministry to grant an extraordinary sum of 350.000 marks for the purchase of Prince Chigi's book collection and when that project had miscarried, he was permitted to spend the whole amount in filling gaps in the collections of the Royal Library. . . . Harnack did not rest until he had increased the ordinary book budget from about 150.000 marks in 1905 to 316.000 marks in 1913." From the time of his appointment until his retirement at the age of 68, he paid a daily visit to the library. He came gennerally at noon and spent one and a half or two hours there!

13. Now called *Max Planck Gesellschaft.*

14. In the fall of 1921, the German government offered him the post of ambassador to the United States, but he regretfully declined the honor.

15. Eduard Spranger, "Die Friedrich-Wilhelm-Universität in Berlin," in *Berliner Geist* (Tübingen: Mohr, 1966), p. 49. Harnack was a person of great charm. This is the impression one obtains from reading the biography his daughter Agnes wrote with a rare and congenial understanding of her father (see note 12). It is also the testimony of all who knew him well. At the memorial service held at the University of Berlin, Professor Erich Seeberg spoke of "his dutiful discipline in so ordering his daily life and dividing his time that he was able to accomplish so much—coupled as this discipline was with a chivalrous and objective formality in his dealings with men and in the management of his relations with them" (Erich Seeberg, *Adolf von Harnack* [Tübingen: Mohr, 1930], p. 25). At the same occasion the rector of the university, Professor Erhard Schmidt, a mathematician, characterized him as follows: "Harnack was of a noble, aristocratic character; his outward distinction was softened by a generous, considerate, and kind disposition. In conversation, he never let one feel his superiority; on the contrary, he enhanced the self-confidence of the one who was speaking with him by rearranging in a most agreeable way whatever was being said to him and putting it in such a form that the other took great delight in the thought he had expressed" (ibid., p. 6). From 1919 until 1930, the last year of his life, Harnack used to spend part of his vacations at Elmau in the Bavarian Alps, a famous "retreat" founded and led by Johannes Müller, a former theologian and a charismatic religious leader, who at that time exercised a profound influence upon German intellectuals by his fresh but utterly antitheological and undogmatic interpretation of Jesus. (It was characteristic of Harnack that he felt at home in the community which this man inspired.) In a long essay written in memory of Harnack, Müller describes the latter's relation with others as follows: "He deeply enjoyed the rare opportunity to be able to talk with old and young as if he were one of them and undisturbed by his extraordinary position and his fame in the world. He felt himself particularly attracted to the feminine element, in view of the fact that generally he had to deal mainly with men. There he demonstrated the full nobility of an old

culture and of Baltic aristrocracy. But whether they were men, women, or girls, he entranced all who came in contact with him by the rare charm of his personality and he delighted them again and again by his captivating conversation. He was full of humor and he had an unlimited memory" *(Grüne Blätter* XXXLI [1930], p. 141).

16. Harnack's brother-in-law, H. Rassow, writes *(Christliche Welt* 44 (1930), p. 728): "I asked him once: 'How much time would you need in order to memorize one page of Greek that you had never seen before?' He replied: 'If I read the page slowly, I would know it by heart.' " The church historian Ernst Benz reports that when as a student he consulted Harnack, the latter readily recited from memory entire passages from the writings of the Fathers and then confirmed his quotations by taking the relevant volumes from his shelves and finding the correct page at the first try. Cf. Ernst Benz, *Adolf v. Harnack zum 100. Geburtstag, Jahrbuch der Akademie der Wissenschaften und der Literatur in Mainz* (Wiesbaden: Franz Steiner Verlag, 1952), p. 212.

17. *Christliche Welt* 35 (1921), p. 315. The writer was Professor W. Bornemann.

18. Bonhoeffer was executed because he opposed the Nazi dictatorship. Harnack's eldest son, Ernst, experienced the same fate.

19. Adolf von Harnack, *Ausgewählte Reden und Aufsätze* (Berlin: W. de Gruyter, 1951), p. 210.

20. Cf. W. Pauck, "Harnack's Interpretation of Church History," *The Heritage of the Reformation* (Boston: The Free Press, 1961), pp. 337 ff.

21. Cf. Hans Lietzmann, *Gedächtnisrede auf Harnack. Sitzungsberichte der Akademie der Wissenschaften in Berlin* (Wiesbaden: Steiner, 1931), p. lviii.

22. In "Sokrates und die Alte Kirche," Adolf von Harnack, *Ausgewählte Reden und Aufsätze* (1951) p. 25.

23. Cf. Adolf von Harnack, *Wesen des Christentums*, (Leipzig: Hinrichs, 1900) p. xvii, and Adolf von Harnack, *Reden und Aufsätze*, IV (Berlin: W. de Gruyter, 1923), p. 5.

24. Harnack, "Über die Sicherheit und Grenzen geschichtlicher Erkenntnis," *Reden und Aufsätze, IV, p. 7.*

25. The remark is reported by Walter Koehler; cf. *Theologische Blätter* 7 (1930), p. 168. Harnack wrote to K. Holl: "There is always the danger that one loses touch with general scholarship *(mit der Wissenschaft im Grossen)* when one works intensively on one point, but it is of greater import to lose touch with special scholarship *(mit der Wissenschaft im Kleinen)."*

26. Cf. his lecture on "Die Religion Goethes in der Epoche seiner Vollendung," *Reden und Aufsätze*, IV, 157. It is important to note here that, throughout his life, but particularly in his later years, Harnack had a deep spiritual attachment to Goethe. In him and his work, he saw the embodiment of the humanism of Western Christian civilization.

27. Cf. his lecture entitled: "Was hat die Historie an fester Erkenntnis zur Deutung des Weltgeschehens zu bieten?" in *Ausgewählte Reden und Aufsätze*, p. 192.

28. Cf. Adolf von Harnack, *Grundriss der Dogmengeschichte*, 9th ed. (Berlin: W. de Gruyter, 1921), p. 5.

29. Harnack, *Wesen des Christentums*, p. 160.

30. Harnack, *Dogmengeschichte*, 4th ed., III, p. 896 f.

31. Ibid., p. 898.

32. Harnack, *Wesen des Christentums*, p. xix. Cf. Harnack, *Dogmengeschichte*, 4th ed., I, p. 85: "The church historian is duty-bound not to be satisfied with the establishment of the fact that the Christian religion underwent changes but to

examine to what extent new forms of it were able to protect, to implant, and to instill the gospel. In all probability the gospel would have perished if the form of 'early Christianity' had been preserved in the church; but, as a matter of fact, early Christianity perished in order that the gospel might prevail."

33. Cf. the recent and highly informative books: Philip Hefner, *Faith and the Vitalities of History: A Theological Study Based on the Work of Albrecht Ritschl* (New York: Harper & Bros., 1965); and Peter C. Hodgson, *The Formation of Historical Theology: a Study of Fredinand Ch. Baur* (New York: Harper & Bros., 1966).

34. Harnack, *Wesen des Christentums*, p. xix.

35. *Wesen des Christentums*, p. 113: "The gospel did not enter the world as a statutory religion and it can therefore have no classical and permanent manifestation in any form of intellectual or social expression, not even in the first one."

36. Ibid., p. xviii.

37. Harnack, *Dogmengeschichte*, 4th ed., I, p. 70.

38. Ibid., pp. 65 ff.

39. Harnack, *Wesen des Christentums*, p. 31.

40. Ibid., p. 86.

41. Ibid.

42. Cf. ibid., p. 122: "For most of us this identification [of the Messiah with the Logos] is unacceptable because our thinking about the world and about ethics does not lead us to conclude upon a logos as being *(einen wesenhaften Logos)*. To be sure, the affirmation 'the Logos has appeared among us' had an exciting effect, but the enthusiasm and the rapture of soul which it evoked did not lead with certainty to the God whom Jesus proclaimed."

43. Ibid., p. 87.

44. Ibid.

45. *"Die Aufgabe der theologischen Fakultäten und die allgemeine Religionsgeschichte,"* Harnack *Reden und Aufsätze*, II (Giessen, 1910), p. 172 f.

46. Harnack, *Wesen des Christentums*, p. 5.

47. Ibid., pp. 38, 71.

48. Ibid., p. 141.

49. Ibid., p. 158; Harnack, *Dogmengeschichte*, 4th ed., I, p. 82.

50. Harnack, *Wesen des Christentums*, p. 140.

51. 27 November 1888. Agnes von Zahn-Harnack, *Adolf von Harnack*, p. 130f.

52. Harnack, *Wesen des Christentums*, p. 104.

53. Ibid., p. 166.

54. Harnack, *Reden und Aufsätze*, IV, p. 338 (in an address in commemoration of A. Ritschl).

55. Harnack, *Dogmengeschichte*, 4th ed., III, p. 867.

56. Ibid., p. 906.

57. Agnes von Zahn-Harnack, *Adolf von Harnack*, p. 315.

58. In this connection, it is interesting to note that throughout his career, Harnack found himself unable to regard systematic or dogmatic theology with the same seriousness the "dogmatists" were accustomed to demand for it from themselves and others. For example, Theophil Wurm, later bishop of Württemberg and widely known as a prominent opponent of Hitler, reports that Harnack said in the course of a seminar which Wurm, then a student, attended in 1894 (cf. *Theologische Blätter* 9 [1930], p. 273), that he would propose the following outline to anyone wishing to write a dogmatic theology: "Part I: The teachings of Jesus and the apostolic interpretation of them. Part II: Mysteries; in this part, he added, one could proceed to speculate as much as one liked." And Karl Barth writes *(Kirchliche Dogmatik* I; II (Stutt-

gart: Ev. Verlag, 1938, pp. 403f.) that in the last conversation they had together, Harnack told him that if he had to write a "dogmatics," he would entitle it: "The Life of God's Children." Barth goes on to explain that Harnack intended by this suggestion to propose the substitution of the traditional kind of dogmatic theology by the personal confession of a Christian who had achieved maturity by letting his thinking be centrally determined by the history of Christianity.

59. Cf. his correspondence with Professor Erik Peterson, reprinted in the latter's *Theologische Traktate* (München: Kösel Verlag, 1951), p. 285.
60. Adolf on Harnack, *Marcion*, p. 217.
61. Barth, *Kirchliche Dogmatik* I; II, p. 82.
62. Agnes von Zahn-Harnack cites *(Adolf von Harnack*, pp. 244f.) a letter which her father wrote to Karl Holl with reference to the discussion his book on Marcion had elicited: "Is it not so that the Ancient Church was not aware of the fact that truth too develops? . . . I did not find it difficult to cause my children to accept the teaching that the Old Testament is now antiquated and only in certain parts still appealing and valuable. It is the law and history of the Jews; *our* book is the New Testament."
63. Ibid., p. 161, in an address to the Evangelical-Social Congress.
64. This was a phrase of Luther's making (cf. his *Larger Catechism*). Harnack was very fond of it and used it frequently.
65. Agnes von Zahn-Harnack, *Adolf von Harnack*, pp. 420 ff.
66. Agnes von Zahn-Harnack, *Adolf von Harnack*, p. 415.

7. Ernst Troeltsch

It is more than fifty-five years since Troeltsch died at the height of his career, but his influence is still strong and his powerful personality remains unforgotten. Despite the fact that his work as a theologian was greatly neglected under the impact of Karl Barth and his neo-orthodox followers, students and thinkers still turn to Troeltsch. In recent years, this has been happening more and more frequently. His books are again read, especially by those who want to understand the origin and character of modern civilization and the place of religion in it.

Paul Tillich was aware of the great intellectual debt he owed to Troeltsch. He remembered particularly what he had learned from him about the nature of history and about the problems of the theology of culture. Both Reinhold and H. Richard Niebuhr have often acknowledged that their ways of handling theological problems were deeply determined by their study of Troeltsch's writings. Reinhold Niebuhr has been a Troeltschian from the time when he published his first book, *Does Civilization Need Religion?* until his latter days, when he wrote an addendum to all his studies on man's historical nature and destiny in the little book on *Man's Nature and His Communities.* His brother H. Richard, who was such an effective and influential teacher of theological ethics, wrote his doctoral dissertation on Ernst Troeltsch. All his books, but expecially *The Social Sources of Denominationalism, Christ and Culture,* and *The Meaning of Revelation,* plainly show how his mind was shaped by Troelthsch's preoccupation with problems of ethics and society in Christian civilization. This is especially to be noted in view of the fact that, for a considerable time, he let his thinking be determined also by the theology of Karl Barth. Indeed, his thought was constituted by a kind of synthesis between Troeltsch and Barth, almost an "impossible possibility," because Troeltsch lacked an aerial for the Barthian methods of theological thinking just as Harnack did; and Barth, on his part, has frequently declared that, because, like Schleiermacher, Troeltsch saw in Christianity not a divine revelation but only a manifestation of religion, he was unable to do justice to the meaning of the gospel of Jesus Christ.

Many of the students of Reinhold and Richard Niebuhr probably do not know what they owe through their teachers to Troeltsch. However, all who have gone through the classrooms and seminars of James Luther Adams certainly have been made conscious of the high esteem in which this sociologist and historian of theology has held Troeltsch. He has absorbed the thought of Paul Tillich with more thoroughness than anyone else has done in this country. When his translations and interpretations of Troeltsch are published, it will be seen to what extent he has appropriated for himself the latter's social and historical ethics; we shall also be able to note how he has responded to Troeltsch in contrast to Paul Tillich.

In recent years, a considerable number of doctoral theses about the work of Troeltsch have been written and published both in this country and abroad. What their final significance for theological and historical scholarship will be, remains to be seen. But one may safely assume that Troeltsch will not remain ineffective upon the minds of those who have studied him closely.

II

It was my good fortune to be a student in several of Troeltsch's courses at the University of Berlin in the years 1920 and 1921. Troeltsch lectured on the history of philosophy, on ethics in the context of cultural history, and on similar topics. These lectures will remain unforgettable to me, not only because of the ideas and insights they communicated to me and not only because they gave me the impetus to turn to theology as a full-time student, but chiefly because of the impression upon me of the professor's personality. I am sure that most of the other students in these courses (there were in each nearly one thousand) were as deeply affected as I was.

Troeltsch was then a man in his middle fifties, of middle height, stocky and broad-shouldered. His hair and his handlebar moustache were gray. As he spoke, his gray eyes shone brightly, and when he laughed, which was often, he showed a set of beautifully regular teeth. He spoke with great animation and he threw his whole person into the act of speaking. He waved his arms and pointed with his hands and stamped his feet. His hair, which at the beginning of the lecture was carefully combed, became quickly messed up. His eyeglasses, a pair of pince-nez, which he needed in order to consult his notes from time to time, continually fell from his nose and then dangled from his vest, to which they were fastened by a black band. All the while, words fell from his lips like a torrent, and they were powerfully effective. Troeltsch's eloquence held us fascinated and spellbound. It was irresistible. We hung on every word. He spoke with a strong baritone voice in a curious rhythm. He seldom repeated the same word, and his sentences were quite long and involved. What he said was synthetic rather than analytical or critical. He placed many observations next to one another, referring all the while to other thinkers and quoting them, and he pointed to historical events, movements, and ideas. When he was done with any part of his lecture, one saw clearly what he had intended to convey.

There are similar testimonies to Troeltsch's oratorical power. One of the most impressive is that of the poet and novelist Gertrud von le Fort. She was a student of Troeltsch's in Heidelberg shortly before World War I. She later converted to Roman Catholicism but remained a friend of her teacher. In 1925 she published her lecture notes on Troeltsch's "Dogmatics." In one of her post-World War II novels, she set a moving monument to Troeltsch: He was the model of one of the main figures in her book *Der Kranz der Engel*.[1] She describes her reaction to Troeltsch's lecturing as follows:

It is impossible for me to report on the impressions this lecture made upon me, for it went above my head. Intellectually, I understood only very little. And yet the impact as such was overwhelming. For the first time in my life, I found myself exposed to and under the disturbing sway of the power of an enormous eloquence, the power of something elemental—say the power of the sea or of a storm—but yet very clearly with the distinctive awareness that this elemental power was the bearer or wing of something spiritual.[2]

Professor Georg Wünsch, who also was a student of Troeltsch in Heidelberg, says something similar: "He lectured in such a colorful, captivating way that one's breath stood still. Only the sound of the bell recalled one to the consciousness of one's own self."[3]

His manner of writing was similar to that of his speaking. His books therefore have an effect upon the readers which is very similar to that which his lectures had upon those who heard them.

At the time when I sat in his courses (and this was in the years immediately after the First World War), he was much too busy to be able to enter into a personal relationship with his students. He was then active in politics as one of the founders of the new Democratic Party. He served for a time as an Undersecretary of State in the Ministry of Education and Public Worship, and in this capacity, he exercised considerable influence upon the definitions of the rights and functions of schools and churches which were ultimately included in the constitution of the Weimar Republic. He was then also at the height of his academic fame and much sought after as a lecturer and commentator on public events. He was thus not easily accessible to us.

Perhaps this corresponded to his character. He certainly was outgoing, communicative, and friendly. But, at the same time, he gave the impression of one who preferred not to become very personal in his relations with others. There was something about him that betrayed reserve and even shyness.

Here are two remarkable descriptions of his personal character. Professor Heinrich Hofmann, one of Troeltsch's pupils and later for many years a professor in the University of Bern, Switzerland, wrote about him as follows:

He was of an effervescent temperament and his speech poured forth like a cataract. How impetuous could he be and what drastically direct words could he form when he was engaged in polemics; how heartily he could laugh when, because of his views, a certain number of wigs again became wobbly. Yet in this powerful nature there lived an inward tenderness; his explosive power was inwardly checked by a deep ethos, by measured restraint and human considerateness. It was this combination of power and moderation which constituted the charm of his personality.[4]

In the later years of his life, one of Troeltsch's closest friends was the historian Friedrich Meinecke. They were both intensely interested in the problems of the philosophy of history and they were of the same mind in their judgment of political affairs. Meinecke wrote several highly informative and deeply sympathetic essays about his friend. In one of them he speaks of him as follows:

One had to hear him talk in order to understand him fully. Then the lively and bold but energetically conceived abstract thought-complexes, which he liked quite cyclopedically to heap up in enormous sentence-structures, assumed at once an inner vitality and a fascinating clearness; then there appeared behind the great thinker a great human being for whom all knowledge was transformed into personal-spiritual vitality. He was a God-seeker of the grand manner who impetuously questioned and criticized the great God-seekers of world-history while, at the same time, he revered them. In every moment, he was both a skeptic and a believer; simultaneously analytical and constructive; in need of faith and thirsty for life.[5]

It is not easy to say much about him that is biographical. In his numerous writings, the references to his personal life and career are sparse. He certainly was no autobiographical thinker like Paul Tillich, although he could from time to time be quite frank in expressing his feelings and judgments about himself and others among his friends and critics. Moreover, he certainly was gifted with a remarkable skill of describing the character of men and movements. But he said very little about himself that is biographically substantial. The only self-description we have of him is an essay characteristically entitled "My Books," which he furnished to a symposium and which contains brief autobiographies written by distinguished professors of philosophy.[6] Only very few of his letters have ever been published. His literary remains, I understand, were destroyed in the bombing attacks upon Germany during World War II. What others have said or reported about him, particularly his friends at the time of his death, is, though generally brief, often quite revealing and informative. The following biographical sketch is based upon these incomplete sources.

III

Ernst Troeltsch was born near Augsburg as the oldest son of a physician on 17 February 1865. He was the descendant of South German burghers of Swabian and Bavarian stock, and the "mild," that is, unaggressive, nationalism which he displayed in his political activities throughout his life was determined by this heritage. He was educated at the Anna-Gymnasium in Augsburg. There he received a thorough humanistic education in a cultural setting that was strongly determined through family, school, and pulpit by what was then called neo-orthodox Lutheranism, a form of Lutheran churchmanship that permitted an orthodox confessionalism to enter into an alliance with Pietism and Romanticism.[7] He remained always grateful that he was given this training "in wonderfully few prescribed courses and hours of instruction."[8]

Troeltsch himself later wrote that "his drive for knowledge was directed from the beginning toward the world of history,"[9] but his mind was always open for the natural sciences, and thus he came to see at an early time all problems of history and of the philosophy of culture in the framework of a scientific world view. His father hoped that, at the proper time, he would take up the study of medicine, and he constantly stimulated his son's scientific interests. Troeltsch later remembered that in his parental house he always had the opportunity of observing and consulting "skeletons, anatomic charts, electrical machines, and botanical and geological collections and books." This was at the time when Darwinism first became popular among the educated throughout the Western world.

When, in 1884, Troeltsch entered the University of Erlangen, he found it difficult to decide what studies he should take up. The law attracted him only in connection with history insofar as it seemed to him to determine the great institutions that form the historical development. He was fascinated also by classical philology, but he thought that his teachers had demonstrated to him by their demeanor and outlook that the Greek ideals of life were no longer realizable. Philosophy did not appeal to him because it was not creative; and medicine interested him only theoretically. "Hence," he said, "I became a theologian."[10] He believed that theology furnished the most interesting themes for study because it appeared to him to raise fruitful metaphysical problems and at the same time get one involved in intense historical questions.

Yet, the theological faculty of Erlangen did not impress him. To be sure, several of its members—F. H. R. Frank, K. A. G. von Zezschwitz, Th. Zahn—were influential and even famous scholars, but their theological outlook was that of Lutheran neo-orthodoxy. Troeltsch and his friends treated them with cool respect, feeling in their hearts that they were antiques.[11] The only teacher in Erlangen who made an impression upon them was the philosopher Gustav Class, a man who, on the basis of later German Idealism and through dependence upon Leibniz, endeavored to secure room for religion in the life of the human intellect. He was sympathetic toward R. H. Lotze who, just like R. Eucken at a later time, defended, in idealist fashion, the freeedom of the spirit against a positivism determined by the natural sciences.

One of Troeltsch's best friends was Wilhelm Bousset, who later became one of the most prominent and influential interpreters of the New Testament on the basis of the history of religion. They were in almost constant contact with one another for eight years, first as students in Erlangen and in Göttingen, and then as young instructors in Göttingen. Troeltsch reports[12] that because of the shape of his face and his curly hair, Bousset was called the "Moor," and Troeltsch invented and spread the legend that Bousset's grandfather had been a moor who, as a member of the band at the ducal court of Mecklenburg, beat the drums. Bousset in turn told all sorts of tales about Troeltsch, some of which the latter had to deny until the end of his life.

One of these is the story of Troeltsch's arrival in Heidelberg where, not yet thirty years old, he assumed the chair of systematic theology. According to custom, he presented himself to all his colleagues in the university by paying them a personal visit. So Troeltsch went to see the most distinguished among them, the famous historian of philosophy Kuno Fischer who for many years was enthroned at Heidelberg as a prince of scholars and who was notorious for his immense professorial vanity. As Troeltsch entered Fischer's room, he walked up to him and said in his outgoing, exuberant way: "My dear colleague, I am so glad finally to make your personal acquaintance!" Fischer assumed a distant air and replied: "Address me as 'Your Excellency,' please!" Then there followed a cool conversation which lasted no longer than the prescribed seven minutes. Immediately thereafter, Troeltsch went to the railroad station, assembled all available porters, paid each a handsome tip and then, having ascertained that the men knew Professor Fischer and where he lived and which route he took on his way from his house to the university and at what time of day, he instructed them that, on the following day, they were to take up posts at different street lamps. As Fischer passed, each of them was to lift his cap, bow deeply, and say, "Good morning, Your Excellency!" It is said that this was actually done and that Professor Fischer acknowledged the salutation as though everything were in proper order.

Troeltsch and Bousset decided to complete their studies in Göttingen. There they came immediately under the influence of Albrecht Ritschl, and theology became for them an exciting branch of learning. They were Ritschl's last pupils. He impressed them by the power of his personality and his utterly unromantic and bourgeois but deeply moral integrity, and they were captivated by the grand conception and design of his theology. They read the New Testament after his fashion and let him inspire them to undertake a close historical study of the Reformation and especially the theology of Luther. They also made it their concern to understand religion independently from naturalism. Troeltsch read H. Lotze who, for many years, had been an influential teacher in Göttingen but who had left there just as Troeltsch arrived. His personalism remained always attractive to Troeltsch. He must have found it reconcilable with Ritschl's teachings, even though Ritschl endeavored to separate religion from philosophy and especially metaphysics. But both Lotze and Ritschl wanted nothing so much as to affirm the supremacy of the human spirit over nature.

Gradually, another influence made itself felt upon Troeltsch's thinking. History became more and more important for him as he began more fully to appreciate the use of the historical method for the proper interpretation of Christianity and its sources. Historical studies promised to revolutionize theological work. Men like Wellhausen and Harnack were just then opening new horizons in studies of the Bible and of the history of Christian doctrine. In this connection, it proved decisive for Troeltsch's entire career that he and his friends came under the influence of Paul de Lagarde who, as a historian of religion and as a philological expert in languages, was Ritschl's antipode. He taught them to see Christianity in the context of the history of religion and he demanded that strict historical and philological methods be employed in the interpretation of religious texts. Troeltsch recognized increasingly Ritschl's onesidedness; first of all, his use of the Bible, which could not be justified in terms of an historical interpretation, and then his modernization of the Reformation and especially of Luther's theology. He also came to suspect that there was not that continuity between the Reformation and the modern era which was commonly assumed everywhere and which only a few, among them Lagarde, denied.

He then conceived the plan of describing historically the process by which Western civilization was formed in order to assign to the Christian religion its proper place in this process. In other words, he felt that the Christian religion should be interpreted in the context of cultural history. He realized fully how radically such a program differed from the traditional theological studies, including ecclesiastical history and the history of doctrine.

When in 1890, after a brief period of church work as a vicar, he began his career as an academic teacher by becoming a *Privatdozent* in Göttingen, he had the vocational sense that he would revolutionize theology through historical studies. He believed himself supported in this by the enthusiasm of other young men who at the same time acquired the *venia legendi* and who also were engaged primarily in historical investigations. They all referred to themselves as "the little theological faculty of Göttingen," and they were in intimate personal contact with one another and eagerly learned from each other: Wilhelm Bousset, William Wrede, Hermann Gunkel, and Albert Eichhorn, who were later joined by Johannes Weiss, Wilhelm Heitmüller, and Paul Wernle. Most of them were biblical scholars and as such historians of religion. Troeltsch alone was engaged in systematic theological work, but his chief interest lay in intellectual and cultural history. Troeltsch later wrote about this collaboration as follows: "We had a wonderful time; we were marvelously easy-going and utterly indifferent about the future but the present meant everything to us, for it was full of mutual stimulation and it teemed with new discoveries."[13]

Troeltsch was lucky: as early as 1892, he was appointed an associate professor in Bonn and, two years later, he was called to the chair of systematic theology in Heidelberg. He stayed there until 1915. From 1909 on he taught also philosophical courses.

IV

Troeltsch brought into his career two big problems which he hoped to solve by scholarly investigations.[14] The first, which was to occupy him during the earlier part of his lifework, was the problem of the nature of religion in the context of man's intellectual development. The second, which kept him engaged throughout his life, was the problem of the historical development of the religious spirit in connection with its imbeddedness in the universal life process.

Realizing that this program could not possibly be executed, because it was much too inclusive, he decided to concentrate on a part of it for work on which he would be able to acquire competence in not too long a time. Without losing sight of the larger question, he set himself the task of analyzing the development of religion in the context of universal life by concentrating his attention upon Christianity and its connection with Western cultural history.

He made a beginning with his doctoral dissertation on *Reason and Revelation in Melanchthon and Johann Gerhard* (1891). He analyzed first the thought of Melanchthon in relation to that of Luther and then the teaching of Gerhard, the foremost representative of Lutheran Orthodoxy, in relation to that of Melanchthon. Apart from demonstrating how Orthodoxy had arisen from the Reformation by way of Melanchthon's interpretation of Luther's doctrines by means of Aristotelianism and humanistic rhetorical methods, the result of this study was the conclusion that the thinking of the German Lutherans had remained basically medieval but that, in comparison with medieval scholasticism, they had achieved under the influence of Luther's fresh discovery of the Gospel a simplification of Christian theological thought which they combined with certain Stoic ideas, particularly those relating to natural law. These had been part of Christianity for a long time, and, like other ancient materials absorbed by Christian thinkers, they had been periodically revived. This was happening also in the aftermath of the Reformation.

From here Troeltsch was led to raise the question when and under what circumstances so-called modern civilization had arisen, that is, how it had come about that an autonomous secular culture had come to affirm itself over against a tradition that was bound to the churches and saturated with ecclesiastical dogmas and doctrines. In contrast to the answer commonly given that the Protestant Reformation had laid the foundations of modern civilization, he pointed to the Enlightenment of the eighteenth century. This movement, he argued, had transformed to social-political and economic secularization of life, begun in the age of the Renaissance and in part continued under the auspices of the Protestant Reformation, into a new educational system with the help of the philosophies of the eighteenth century, and had pushed the supranatural powers of church and theology into the background.[15] Specific studies[16] of the Enlightenment, Deism, the English Moralists of the eighteenth century, and German Idealism confirmed him in this view. Moreover, he felt that he had the support of Wilhelm Dilthey, with whose historical studies he now became acquainted.

In 1906 Troeltsch published a large work entitled *Protestant Christianity and Ecclesiasticism in the Modern Age,*[17] an analytical survey of the development of Protestantism in its relation to the cultural life. It is a marvelous piece of work, indeed unique, because no ecclesiastical or secular historian has had knowledge and courage enough to undertake the same task. It is really the story of the steady and continual emancipation of Western civilization from the church or the story of the gradual secularization of Western culture with special attention to the relations between Protestantism and civilization. Troeltsch showed, on the one hand, the great difference between the order of Roman Catholicism and the tenets of the Protestant reformers and, on the other hand, the deep divergence between Old Protestantism and New Protestantism.

At a meeting of German historians in 1906, he presented the same argument in a paper entitled "The Significance of the Reformation for the Rise of the Modern World."[18] He did not deny that the Protestant reformers had inaugurated a new age in the history of Christianity, and he gave full recognition to the fact that they had destroyed the ecclesiastical unity of European culture; but he reaffirmed his conviction that the forms of life that were fostered by the reformers and their successors, the founders of the Protestant churches, were more closely related to the Middle Ages than to the modern world.

At the time, his thesis was generally rejected. One still adhered to the view which, strangely enough, had first been expressed by the Enlighteners and then became common among historians, that the Reformation marked the beginning of modern civilization, because Martin Luther and his followers had defied, and by their defiance had undone, the heteronomous authoritarianism of the Roman Church. Today, Troeltsch's interpretation is generally regarded as correct because it is widely recognized that, in this age, the churches no longer determine the decisions that shape the character of civilization and public life; and that Protestantism and Roman Catholicism, insofar as they are represented by ecclesiastical organizations, have more in common than they share together or singly with the men and powers that mould modern civilization.

What disturbed Troeltsch especially about traditional Christianity was the persistence with which representative ecclesiastical bodies and spokesmen adhered to supernaturalism in some form or other. For him Christianity was a religion among religions. He believed that concerning its nature it must be interpreted epistemologically or psychologically and concerning its historical forms it must be regarded as subject to an analysis by methods that are applied to all historical phenomena.

During the first decade of this century, he was a very active participant of discussions on the philosophy of religion, and he published numerous papers of his own. In most of them, he pursued arguments that were in line with what had been begun by Schleiermacher, though his own philosophical preferences at the time were formed by his attachment to such neo-Kantians as Heinrich Rickert and Wilhelm Windelband. But his deeply passionate interest belonged to historical studies. All his thinking was filled with the awareness that the omnipresence in modern cultural life of the sense of history or of the historical consciousness constituted the most important difference from other ages.

He therefore became preoccupied with questions about the nature of history and of historical knowledge and their importance for the right understanding of religion and its place in human life. He also steeped himself in historical studies as such chiefly because he wanted to know as fully as possible the perils and possibilities of his own age. His reading was very wide. Indeed, his friends always marveled at the rate at which he absorbed book after book.

Thus it is not surprising that he acquired a scholarly reputation chiefly as a historian and as a philosopher of history. Nevertheless, the judgment widely prevailed (and sometimes is expressed even today) that he was the systematic or constructive theologian of the so-called *"religionsgeschichtliche Schule."* Though he held a chair of systematic theology and therefore regularly lectured on subjects of this discipline, he did not attribute too much importance to it. For he believed that the days of theological summas and systems had passed forever. The individualism that determined the practice of religion everywhere in the Western world and the diversity of religious forms that followed from this made it impossible in his opinion to rally a school of students or a congregation of believers around a system of doctrines. Troeltsch taught courses in systematic theology because he wanted to demonstrate how a person who had acquired the modern world view based on science, history, and philosophy would relate himself to the heritage of Christian thought. Moreover, he wanted to prepare his students for the work of spiritual leadership in churches whose members they would have to treat as modern men and women. In his view, books on systematic theology, for example, those of Wilhelm Herrmann, were not works of scholarship, but devotional books.[19]

It is understandable that Troeltsch was no friend of ecclesiastical governments. They impressed him not only as too conservative, but also as too authoritarian. He disliked their alliances with political authorities, especially in monarchical Germany and most particularly in Prussia. He was deeply aroused when these church bureaucracies interfered with theological scholarship by trying to influence appointments to academic positions, or when they staged heresy trials against ministers who held liberal opinions about liturgy or doctrine, or when they stirred up bitter public controversies by insisting on conformity with creeds and confessions of faith. During the first years of Troeltsch's professional career, Harnack was frequently the center and victim of such troubles, especially in connection with his historical interpretation of the Apostles' Creed (1892) and the publication of his lectures on the "Nature of Christianity" (1901).

V

The most representative journal of religious and theological liberalism in Germany was *Die Christliche Welt,* a biweekly founded in 1886 by Martin Rade (1857–1940), one of the earliest pupils of Adolf Harnack and a Ritschlian, like his teacher. He edited it throughout his long life and from 1900 on in Marburg where, in 1903, he became a professor of theology. Around this journal, Rade gathered many loyal readers and supporters and among them also the most influential liberal theological teachers, including Harnack and Troeltsch.[20] They not only contributed frequently to its columns, but they also were active in a loose organization called *Freunde der Christlichen Welt,* which met regularly every year for the discussion of common, mainly theological, problems. Troeltsch was intimately connected with this group and eagerly participated in its life, especially in his earlier years. He remained loyal to Rade and *Die Christliche Welt* until the end of his life.

About one of Troeltsch's earliest appearances in this circle, Walter Koehler (1870–1947), one of his first students who in 1940 published a large interpretative work about his teacher, reports as follows:

It was in 1896, at a gathering of theologians in Eisenach, that Ernst Troeltsch dramatically burst upon the intellectual scene. One of the most respected of Germany's theological scholars, Julius Kaftan, had just completed a learned, somewhat scholastic lecture on the meaning of the logos-doctrine. With the opening of general discussion, there leaped with youthful élan to the rostrum a young professor who began his statement with the words: "Gentlemen, everything is tottering." Then he went on to outline with large, firm strokes a picture of the situation which was to confirm his judgment. The older scholars were appalled. When their spokesman [Ferdinand Kattenbusch] in turn took the floor, he rejected Troeltsch's line of reasoning as "paltry theology"—at which Troeltsch got up and left, slamming the door behind him.[21]

Troeltsch insisted that everything had evolved and developed —also man and religion. Hence he demanded that Christianity, including Jesus its founder, be interpreted in the context of the history of religion. This was unacceptable to the older Ritschlians, and especially to Kattenbusch, who wrote to Rade early in 1898 that he did not want to be identified with Troeltsch, though he said that personally he liked this "son of nature."[22] But he did not want even to seem to be cooperative with him, for he regarded Troeltsch's position as diametrically different from his own. In an article published in *Die Christliche Welt,* he disclosed this salient point: "We older Ritschlians," he wrote "see in Christianity a factor at work that has entered history from without."[23] In agreement with Ritschl himself, he believed this factor, namely, the revelation in Jesus, to be supernatural or at least superhistorical. Troeltsch replied to this by saying that the Ritschlians, in order to maintain the autonomy and independence of the Christian religion and theology, had the tendency to push aside difficulties that arose from history just as they were avoiding coming to terms theologically with the methods and findings of the natural sciences.[24] Instead he felt that it was necessary to acknowledge in principle the historization of theology. Hence the historical method would have to replace the dogmatic method in theology, that is, the procedure that permitted the interpretation of religious data, particularly those pertaining to Christianity, to be dictated by purely dogmatic ideas or teachings. Thus Troeltsch envisaged a nondogmatic or undogmatic Christianity. "Religion as such can get along without dogmatics," he observed.[25]

In 1902 he drew the consequences from this position by publishing a long essay on "The Absoluteness of Christianity and the History of Religions." He rejected all arguments for the absoluteness of Christianity that were based either on the affirmation of external or internal miracles, as Orthodox and Pietist theologians, and even the Ritschlians, were doing or on the Hegelian assertion that the development of religion had reached its climax in Christianity, the embodiment of religion itself. Instead he argued that all high religions "naively" advance claims for absoluteness which cannot effectively be refuted. He was prepared to ascribe a certain superiority to Christianity because he believed that because of its ethics it exercised a universal appeal upon all men, an appeal for which he saw no parallel in any other faith. He realized that if this view were correct, foreign missions as carried out traditionally could no longer be defended, and he did not hesitate to draw this conclusion, especially in the light of the fact he regarded as insurmountable, namely, that all high religions have entered, in the course of their development, into a union with historical cultures which no effort to displace the religious faith with the intent to substitute for it another one can effectively or justifiably dissolve.

Many problems arose for Troeltsch from this position. The foremost ones were the following: (1) the philosophical question: how can the truth of religion be ascertained? and (2) the historical question: how is the correlation between religion and culture to be explained?

Troeltsch gave full attention to both, always in the context of an animated discussion with other thinkers and researchers. Though he continued to be active and productive as a philosopher of religion, his major interest was now more and more directed to the problems of the theology of culture.

The richness and diversity of the historical world fascinated him. With ever greater force the question of the nature and direction of modern Western civilization impressed itself upon his mind. He became involved in political action (for several years, he represented the University of Heidelberg in the upper house of parliament in the Grand Duchy of Baden) and in discussions of social policy. All this called forth the question of how he could find a grounding for truth and value in the flow of all things human.[26] In his thinking on the philosophy of history, he had let his outlook be determined chiefly by Hegel and Dilthey. Now they no longer satisfied him fully. The problems of intellectual history seemed to him much more complicated than they made them appear, especially in view of the hard practical realities in which the intellectual and spiritual concerns of men are imbedded. He plunged into sociological studies and learned a new way of seeing things.[27] At the same time, he came under the spell of the overwhelmingly powerful person of Max Weber.

VI

Thus began a highly fruitful association of two scholars, each of whom was occasionally described by others as a genius. Neither of them, though an expert in his own field, was a mere specialist. The interest of both ranged far over the realm of human civilization, and both were passionate contemporaries of their own era.

When they became acquainted with one another, Max Weber, who had started out as a legal scholar and had then taken up the teaching of economics and political science, had turned to sociological investigations. He was already at work on his famous essay on "Protestant Ethics and the Spirit of Capitalism" and on the manifold problems of economic ethics which he was to analyze and discuss in the large works he later published. He was "a man of enormous intellectual power and versatility who barely held together by force of an iron resolve the desperate contradictions that threatened his sanity."[28] Troeltsch wrote later: "For years I experienced in daily contact with him the infinitely stimulating power of this man, and I am aware of owing him a great part of my knowledge and ability."[29]

The two men were of different temperaments. Weber was a man of stubborn persistency who could grow ferocious when he felt it necessary to oppose political actions he thought stupid or irresponsible (he despised William II!), or when he believed his personal honor to be attacked. Troeltsch was much more conciliatory, ever prepared to settle differences with others and to adjust himself to their weaknesses. In referring to this friendship in the biography of her husband, Marianne Weber characterizes Troeltsch in the following way: "Freedom and comprehensiveness of mind; an outgoing vivaciousness; a plastic and concrete way of thinking; broad humor and an immediate personal warmth made him a companion with whom scholarly and personal relations became enjoyable and fruitful."[30]

In 1905 Professor and Mrs. Weber and Troeltsch made a trip

to the United States. They had been invited to address the "Scientific World-Congress" which Professor Hugo Münsterberg had orgnanized in connection with the World's Fair in St. Louis.[31] Troeltsch delivered a lecture on "Psychology and Epistemology in the Science of Religion." Together and separately, they traveled through the eastern and southern states. Troeltsch's humor and peeling laughter enlivened the party, and Weber's curiosity and power of close and discriminating observation gave the journey the character of a scientific exploration. Weber gathered material for his theory concerning the interrelations between Puritan asceticism and the capitalistic mentality.[32] They must have talked and debated about these issues as they moved about in this country.

In support of this, I can tell the following amusing story: Many years ago, I became acquainted with a minister named Hans Haupt. He was the son of a theological professor in the University of Halle in Germany and he was married to the daughter of a professor of economics in the same institution. He came to this country around 1900 and settled in Tonawanda, New York, where he became the minister of a German-Evangelical Church. Because of his family connections he was often visited and consulted by Germany academic persons who desired information about American religious and ecclesiastical developments. He also published occasional articles about the United States in German journals. Troeltsch and Weber informed him of their impending voyage and of their intention to visit him. Telling him about their research project, they asked him to collect as much material as possible about American denominations and their moral teachings and attitudes, especially in relation to economic practices. Haupt immediately went to work and, with considerable difficulty, laid hold of the desired information. When his distinguished visitors arrived, they spent several days with him. In between an inspection of the town of Tonawanda and visits to nearby Niagara Falls, they talked and argued all the time. They hardly asked for Haupt's opinion and failed to inspect the material he had gathered, but they took it with them. Haupt had the impression that the professors knew all that could be known without having to weigh empirical evidence. In fairness to them, one must say that, though Haupt may have had reasons for complaint about their behavior, they (and particularly Max Weber) made extensive use of factual data and statistics when they explicated their thesis about the nature of Calvinist economic ethics.

The friendship between Weber and Troeltsch deepened during the following years. In the fall of 1909, they moved into a big old house situated on the river Neckar, Weber taking the lower and Troeltsch taking the upper floor. The closest relationship prevailed between them. They enjoyed and relaxed in the natural beauty of Old Heidelberg, and their house became the intellectual center of the academic community. But all this came to an unhappy end. It is tragic that the bonds of this friendship were broken because of weakness.

When World War I broke out, several of the hospitals and clinics of Heidelberg were transformed into military hospitals.[33] Weber, who was a reserve officer, was put in charge of them. In this capacity, he permitted a few German civilians (who had family ties with Frenchmen) to visit French prisoners of war who were placed in these hospitals. It so happened that Troeltsch had accepted the assignment to serve as the civilian administrator of one of these military hospitals. When he learned that public opinion was becoming aroused because of the visits that were being paid to the French and that the visitors were being accused of treason, he decided to permit the visits only if the visitors were accompanied by a military person. When Weber was informed of this, he became greatly agitated and accused his friend of cowardice and lack of courage in view of the invalid and inhumane public rumors. To be sure, he apologized afterwards for his vehemence, but at the same time expected Troeltsch to see the error of his ways. But no excuses came forth from him and so the break remained. Only five years later, their wives succeeded in bringing about a reconciliation of sorts.[34] By that time, Troeltsch was in Berlin and Weber in Munich. Close association was no longer possible anyway.

In 1917 Troeltsch wrote to a friend about this as follows:

In the course of the war, Max Weber has assumed such radical attitudes and he views the whole situation so pessimistically and with so much hostility that he has become totally isolated; he has fallen out with most people, including me. Older differences concerning politics and general principles came to the fore in him, and he broke off relations with me in the most violent fashion for no special reason. In the last resort, his life is a continuous duel with everything that he regards as corruptive, and in particular with the person of the Emperor whom he holds responsible for practically everything. It is impossible to argue with him. You can imagine that I am sorry about this. I certainly did not want this to happen.[35]

What was in the background of this unfortunate episode was, of course, the war situation. It forced men like Troeltsch and Weber to make political judgments that were very difficult, not only objectively, but also subjectively. H. Stuart Hughes is quite correct when he writes:

Both of them, Weber the earliest and most decisively . . . Troeltsch not until the war years—were to cross the invisible barricade that separated the opponents from the supporters of the regime. And they did it with the deepest sorrow, driven against their will by the irresponsible behavior of the Emperor, the calamitous mistakes in foreign policy, the unyielding resistance to the democratization of the constitution of Prussia and of the Reich. . . . With each year of the postponed reform, they felt the chances growing dimmer of saving their country from a major catastrophe.[36]

Undoubtedly, Troeltsch became politically active, especially in relation to foreign affairs, under the influence of Weber, and he remained so until the end of his life. But the major lesson which he learned from him at the beginning of their association and which he developed fully as an interpreter of Christian history was that the Christian faith like any other high religion is and has been a powerful formative factor in social relations. He learned not only that there exists an interconnection between Protestantism and modern economic attitudes and practices, but also that the origin, development, and the modern containment of Christianity have been sociologically conditioned. Moreover, he came to see, again under the impact of Weber's views, that the Marxist interpretation of history, and particularly the doctrine of economic substructures and ideological superstructures, was largely true. He wrote later that all this took hold of him "with greatest force."[37]

There existed then no historical or systematic studies on the interconnection between Christianity and society. When Troeltsch was asked to review what he thought was a "miserable" book by M. von Nathusius on *The Social Responsibility of the Evangelical Church,* he became forcefully aware of his own as well as the general ignorance about the social aspects of the religion. Without taking time first to outline carefully a program of study, he went to work, and instead of a book review he wrote a volume comprising nearly a thousand pages entitled *The Social Teachings of the Christian Churches and Denominations.*[38] "This was," to use his own words, "a history of the ecclesiastical culture of Christianity, a full parallel to Harnack's *History of Dogma,* in which all religious, dogmatic, and theological factors were seen as the basis of social-ethical effects or as the reflection or retroaction of social conditions."

He concentrated his attention upon the social teachings of the Christian groups in order to illuminate the relation between the impetus for action that issued from the faith of Christians throughout the generations and the actual state of things prevailing at different times and places. The result was that he gave a much more complex and dynamic picture of the development of Christianity than that which is offered by church historians who see this development primarily in relation to its environmental background or by historians of doctrine who tend to deal only with Christian intellectual history. Surveying Christian social history from the beginning to the eighteenth century, focusing his attention mainly upon Roman Catholicism and Protestantism, and omitting a full treatment either of Eastern Orthodoxy or of Anglicanism, he showed how what he called the eschatological ethical utopianism of the early Christians emitted from itself an impetus that broke into the orders of ancient society and changed them, being at the same time affected by them—like a giant spring that as it rises breaks the rock formation in which it originates and then, becoming a torrent and river, makes its way to the sea, being channeled by the formation of the earth through which it passes, but carrying with it masses of rock and soil which it absorbs.

He clarified many things, of which I mention here only a few: (1) He showed that Christian moral and social doctrines have never been expressions of a pure religious spirit or of an absolute ethic, but have always been compromises,[39] that is, results of a mediating synthesis by which Christian individuals and groups have come to terms with their environments, even with elements alien to their spirit. Troeltsch used this concept of compromise throughout his career. In one of his last pieces of writing, he said:

The fact remains that all intransigeance breaks down in practice and can only end in disaster. The history of Christianity itself is most instructive in this connection. It is, in the long run, a tremendous, continuous compromise between the utopian demands of the Kingdom of God and the permanent conditions of the actual human life. It was indeed a sound instinct which led its founders to look for a speedy dissolution of the present world order.

(2) He demonstrated the importance of his observation chiefly by pointing to the place which since ancient times was given in Christian social affairs to natural law as defined by the Stoics and Aristotelians. This made possible, in medieval Catholicism, the remarkable synthesis between nature and grace, Aristotelianism and Biblicism, world and church, indeed shaped the ethics of all Western Christianity, including that of major Protestant churches.

(3) In describing the major forms of Christian social organization, Troeltsch distinguished between churches and sects. In doing so he followed Weber, who had used this distinction in his studies of Calvinism. For him the terms "church" and "sect" referred to sociological models or ideal types as they must be used in all sociological or historical analyses for purposes of clarification and classification.[40] Actual social orders or organizations do not necessarily represent what these models as genetic concepts symbolize. Perhaps Troeltsch used them too rigidly or mechanically,[41] as if the basic definition of "church" and "sect" could be regarded as the description of empirical reality. For this he has been much criticized. But it is undeniable that as he analyzed the relevance of these concepts to the historical development of Christian social groups and their orders and works, he made possible a clear and suggestive understanding of the sociological processes that have molded the Christian encounter with the world. The suggestiveness of his analysis is expressed in the definition of the

basic concepts he offers in the "conclusion" of *The Social Teachings:*

The *Church* is the holy institution and the institution of grace, endowed with the effect and result of the work of redemption. It can absorb the masses and adapt itself to the world, since, up to a certain point, it can neglect subjective holiness in exchange for the objective treasures of grace and redemption. The *Sect* is the free association of Christians who are stronger and more conscious of their faith. They join together as the truly reborn, separate themselves from the world, remain limited to a small circle, emphasize the law instead of grace, and in their ranks set up love as the Christian order of life with greater or lesser radicalism. All of this is regarded as the preparation for and the expectation of the coming Kingdom of God. *Mysticism* is the intensification and the subjectivization of the thoughts and ideas that have become solidified in cult and doctrine so that they are a purely personal and inner possession of the heart. Under its auspices only fluid and completely personally limited groups can assemble. What remains in them of cult, dogma, and connection with history tends to become so fluid that it disappears.[42]

Troeltsch laid special emphasis upon Roman Catholicism and Calvinism. They appeared to him as the most effective social orders in Christendom. "The Roman Catholic or Papal church type," he wrote,[43] "is undoubtedly the most unified and most effective church type, practically as well as logically most completely formed. The Calvinist church type closely approached the sect-type, in the course of its history, and in connection with legal, political, social, and economic developments incorporated its pharisaic-democratic characteristics in huge mass-movements.[44]

Troeltsch said once: "I have carried my *Social Teachings* only to the eighteenth century and this is for a good reason. From that time on, European Civilization can no longer be called Christian. *(Die offizielle Christlichkeit Europas ist mit ihm zu Ende.)*"[45] He was deeply convinced that beginning with the period of the Enlightenment, and particularly since the rise of High Capitalism and the formation of the big political powers, Western civilization has become emancipated from the shaping and unifying influence of the old Christian institutions, with the result that it is being exposed more and more to secularization and secularism.

He became increasingly involved in the effort to understand "modern civilization" or "the modern era of Western civilization" and to achieve the vision of a cultural synthesis, as he called it, in which the values of the Christian cultural heritage would be preserved and incorporated in the common life. So he turned more and more to the studies on ethics and the philosophy of history.

To some extent, he had outgrown the faculty of theology. When he received a call to the University of Berlin in order to teach philosophy with special attention to the philosophy of history and the philosophy of religion, he accepted.[46]

VII

It was the spring of 1915 and World War I was still in its first undecisive stages. Heidelberg seemed to him a little provincial; some of his closest friends (for example, the jurist George Jellinek) had died; he was estranged from Max Weber; his relations with the circle of friends of *Die Christliche Welt* were no longer as warm as they had been earlier. He also felt that the philosophy of religion rather than systematic theology was his field of specialization. It is not true as it is frequently stated that he forsook the theological faculty because he believed that his own theological work had ended in failure. In the autobiographical sketch of his literary production, he says specifically:

I have at all times fulfilled the practical educational tasks assigned to the theological faculty with warmest respect for the great subject and with personal love for my students. I considered dogmatics as a practical concern in which lack of clarity and the insecurity of human knowledge play an essentially important role but which nevertheless permits the main value of practical religion to be communicated to the hearts of the students as a burning and propulsive power.[47]

And in another context of the same paper he wrote: "If I stay healthy and alive, I should like to return to the study of religion in order to complete my philosophy of religion. This is my first love."[48]

At the beginning of this essay, I described Troeltsch's great influence and success as a teacher and lecturer in Berlin. It is not necessary to elaborate this theme further. But what I must stress is that in Berlin he rapidly assumed the stature of a great public figure. During the period when the form and constitution of the new German Republic took shape, his name was sometimes mentioned as that of a possible and worthy candidate for the post of president.

He had occasion to observe closely the setting, complexity, and agony in which political decisions are made when he became intimately acquainted with the Chancellor von Bethmann Hollweg, that rather tragic figure who, despite his faults and failures, deserves high human respect. He also assumed responsibility in the molding of public opinion as a public speaker and as an author of articles. He joined the still small circles of professors and members of the upper middle classes who opposed the war aims of the militarists and annexationists in the conservative parties. He identified himself with men like Harnack, Hans Delbrück, and Friedrich Meinecke,[49] who advocated inner political and social reforms and who warned their countrymen of the dangers of an excessive nationalism. When the war was lost, he joined those who undertook the tasks of cultural and political reconstruction. "In these bitter years of national discouragement and civil conflict," says H. Stuart Hughes, who is inclined to be rather critical of Troeltsch's philosophical thought,

Troeltsch at last found his authentic voice. The monthly articles he contributed to the review *Der Kunstwart* under the signature *Spektator*[50] rank as the most judicious and at the same time the most moving commentary on the new Republic's struggle for existence. Where in his theological and philosophical writings Troeltsch had been dense, wordy, and confused, in this new journalistic and polemical vein, he went directly to the point. . . . The "Spectator Letters" belong in that rare category of occasional pieces that have won immortality. The frightful demagoguery and provocation from the right, which Troeltsch very clearly recognized as the symptoms of a new barbarism that might arise in the future, made, he felt, the task of a responsible German government almost impossible. Only if leading citizens should acquiesce in democracy . . . "with inner warmth" would it be possible to build the future. And then alone would it be possible to salvage and restore those broader values of humanism and rationality that Troeltsch . . . had most at heart.[51]

VIII

In 1922 there appeared what was to be Troeltsch's last publication, a large volume entitled *Der Historismus und seine Probleme*.[52]

It contained a series of learned articles in which the work of modern historians and philosophers of history was reviewed in considerable detail, with special attention to the concepts of historical individuality, historical norms, and historical development. The book differs from most works on the nature and meaning of history because its pages are filled with a profound passion. On the one hand, there is the affirmation which is reiterated again and again that in the modern world all human life has become historicized, that is, that all human decisions, undertakings, and conditions are determined by historical factors so that everything human appears to be set in changing historical relations. On the other hand, there is expressed a deep concern about the possibility that this relativism may lead to an anarchy of values and to skepticism and nihilism.[53] Hence he makes a great effort to show how "history can be overcome by history,"[54] that is, how by live historical decisions one can avoid becoming entangled in historicism. These live historical decisions, which must be made by individuals as well as by groups, relate to the cultural heritage insofar as it is apprehended in any given present. It must be understood, evaluated, and judged. Thus it becomes transformed, that is, reduced or enlarged. That in it which is judged to be valid only for the past out of which it has come is relegated to the past or, as Schleiermacher said in a memorable passage of his *Glaubenslehre*,[55] entrusted to history for safekeeping. And that in it which is recognized as of value for the present is incorporated in present action by way of a renaissance or a reformation. These historical assessments and actions undertaken in the present thus appropriate a legacy of past generations for the use of generations to come. This responsibility is carried out everywhere in human society in great cultural enterprises undertaken on vast public platforms as well as in the execution of small programs which remain confined to privacy. The historical sense expressed in this is often unconscious, but from time to time, and according to the requirement of the circumstances in which it is brought into play, it needs to be refined and sharpened by historical scholarship and the assistance of historical experts.

In this sense, the interest in history was for Troeltsch something eminently practical. "The merely contemplative view of history is something unnatural and senseless," he wrote.

It leads to a bad historism insofar as in it there is displayed an unlimited relativism, a playful occupation with the historical materials, and a paralysis of the will to live one's own life. The personal interest of the spectator then turns into the enjoyment of the play of the phenomena and the diversity of happenings; into the readiness of comprehending and excusing everything; into a mere interest in knowledge or even into a skepticism that may issue in sophisticated irony or, in the case of people of hard temperaments, in sarcasm, or, in the case of the kind-hearted, in humor.[56]

For him a practical historicism or an "activist philosophy of history"[57] consisted of the proposition of a cultural synthesis or program based on an historical analysis or interpretation of Europeanism or Western civilization. He intended to outline this synthesis in a second volume devoted to the theme of historicism. But he died before he could write it. It would have been a summary of the results of his entire work. In lectures which he intended to deliver in England in March of 1923, he offered a moving outline of this. Fortunately, he had prepared these lectures far in advance. And so they could be published. The English translation was given the rather innocuous title of *Christian Thought: Its History and Applications*.[58] The German version was more adequately if somewhat presumptuously entitled *Die Überwindung des Historismus (The Triumph over Historicism)*. Troeltsch really did not believe that historicism in the good and true sense of the term could be overcome. He was persuaded that it could be made the platform for responsible and constructive action.

Thus he said at the conclusion of his lecture on "Mankind's Common Spirit":

The task of the damming and controlling of the stream of historical life is . . . on all sides complicated. It involves a combination of the various fundamental tendencies of the ethical consciousness and the only evidence which can ever be deduced for the decisive combinations is but a conviction of faith based on conscience and conditioned by individuality. The solution thus gained . . . can only be spread from individual centers, and made into a spirit of self-communication and love which will as far as possible spread itself over the widest circles, but will always be at war with other forms of belief . . .

With these complex forces it is possible to dam and control the stream of life. But every such control is always . . . a struggle; it is ever chang-

ing; it develops ethical public spirit along various lines, and only excep-
tionally and in a narrower circle is it of centrally binding force. Inasmuch as no unified church any longer exercises this binding force, the
task has devolved upon a number of churches and also, along with
them, upon personal associations and leagues which are a substitute for
the churches, and will themselves have to strive to become a kind of
church.

The task of damming and controlling is therefore essentially incapa-
ble of completion and essentially unending; and yet it is always soluble
and practicable in each new case. A radical and absolute solution does
not exist. . . . History within itself cannot be transcended. . . . In history
itself there are only relative victories.[59]

In expressing his deepest conviction in this manner, Troeltsch
did not speak as a skeptic, as some have surmised, or as one who
because of his relativism was uncertain of the truth. He felt that
he was testifying to the truth.

A truth which, in the first instance, is *a truth for us* does not cease, because of this, to be very truth and life. What we learn daily through our
love for our fellow men, namely, that they are independent beings with
standards of their own, we ought also to be able to learn through our
love for mankind as a whole—that here too there exist autonomous
civilizations with standards of their own. . . . In our earthly experience
the Divine Life in not One but Many. But to apprehend the One in the
Many constitutes the special character of love.[60]

What lies behind these sentences represents Troeltsch's religious faith. In 1907 he expressed it in these words: "Truth is
always polymorph, never monomorph; it manifests itself in different forms and kinds, not in different degrees."[61] All these
many finite forms of truth, he believed, are part of the one infinite
divine life and are suspended in it. "All historical religions," he
wrote at the end of his lecture of 1923 on 'Christianity among the
World Religions,' "are tending in the same direction and . . . seem
impelled by an inner force to strive upward towards some unknown final height where alone the ultimate unity and the final
validity can lie. And, as all religion has thus a common goal in the
Unknown, the Future, perchance in the Beyond, so too it has a
common ground in the Divine Spirit ever pressing the finite mind
onward towards further light and fuller consciousness, a Spirit

which indwells the finite Spirit and whose ultimate union with it is the purpose of the whole many-sided process.[62]

IX

On 13 January 1923 he fell ill with heart trouble and on 1 February he died. A friend of his, the wife of a former Heidelberg professor, who visited him in the last days of his life, writes about him as follows:

Now we have lost also Troeltsch, who was always so full of vitality. . . . It seems that, for some time, his heart gave him quiet warnings, but he was not wont to save himself. He had never been ill. He stated sometime ago that he could not be stingy with his strength and that he would rather have a short life filled to the brim. There was an unceasing heightening of his life in the last months. Foreign institutions recognized and honored him in many ways, then came his election as dean [of the philosophical faculty in Berlin], then his appointment to full membership in the Academy of Sciences[63]—in his personal and public life he was reaping a rich, fruitful harvest. Then suddenly, with a tremendous pain, sickness befell him—an embolism of the lung caused by the heart itself.[64]

Adolf von Harnack delivered the final oration and in giving moving utterance to his own personal loss of one who had been his friend, he characterized Troeltsch beautifully. He called him the representative German philosopher of his own era. He expressed his astonishment at Troeltsch's enormous power of absorption and at his incredible industry. "It is unbelieveable," he said, "how much he read day after day," always taking in knowledge in order to produce knowledge. He also remarked on Troeltsch's wonderful power of combination and on the fact that, while he read, he readily thought of something that was better, more important, and more comprehensive. He praised Troeltsch's thoughtfulness and his tolerant spirit. But, he said, Troeltsch despised the distortions of the rationalists and the extravagance of the systematicians. Then he went on to describe Troeltsch's person and character:

How he spoke when he lectured was very peculiar and, at the same time, fascinating. He did not aim at giving sharp and precise formulations but with ever fresh efforts and with an overflowing eloquence which was always abundantly at his command, he tossed an observation or an idea to and fro, attacking it from all sides and placing it in ever different relations, until it seemed to be purified and clear. His mind acted like a powerful centrifugal machine or like a rotating drum which shakes the object and pushes it around until it is cleansed from all foreign elements and until it lights up its own distinctiveness.

He was a splendid man and a good fellow in the best sense of this word. There was in him an elemental power and abundance of light and life. He was at all times upright and sincere, honest and frank. There was nothing about him that was contrived or petty. But in this powerful person of elemental naturalness there lived a quiet, noble, and pure soul and this was what was best and deepest about him. At the core of his disposition, there was a tenderness and a chaste love.

Few creative men who have become famous have been[65] praised by their peers as Troeltsch was by Harnack!

NOTES

1. See the remark of A. Dietrich at the conclusion of his brief biography of Troeltsch in *Biographisches Jahrbuch*, 1923 (Berlin, 1930), pp. 349–68.
2. Gertrud von le Fort, *Der Kranz der Engel*, 6th ed. (Munich: Ehrenwirth Verlag, 1953), p. 80.
3. George Wünsch, "Ernst Troeltsch zum Gedächtnis," *Christliche Welt* 37 (1923), p. 105.
4. Heinrich Hofmann, "Ernst Troeltsch zum Gedächtnis," *Theologische Blätter* 2 (1923), p. 77.
5. Friedrich Meinecke, "Zur Theorie und Philosophie der Geschichte" in *Werke*, IV (Stuttgart: Koehler, 1959), p. 364.
6. Reprinted in the 4th volume of Ernst Troeltsch, *Collected Works (Gesammelte Schriften*, IV [Berlin: W. de Gruyter 1925], p. 3–20).
7. Wünsch, "Ernst Troeltsch zum Gedächtnis," p. 106.
8. Troeltsch, *Gesammelte Schriften*, IV, 3.
9. Ibid.
10. Ibid., p. 4.
11. Cf. Ernst Troeltsch, "Die kleine Göttinger Fakultät von 1890," *Christliche Welt* 34 (1920), p. 281.
12. Ibid.
13. Ibid., p. 282.
14. Troeltsch, *Gesammelte Schriften*, IV, 6.
15. Troeltsch, *Gesammelte Schriften*, IV, 7.
16. These were published in the form of long articles in *Protestantische Realenzyklopädie*, ed. A. Hauck, 3d ed. (Leipzig: Hinrichs, 1896–1913).
17. Pages 431–755 of "Geschichte der Christlichen Religion," *Die Kultur der Gegenwart*, ed. P. Hinneberg, vol. I; IV, 1 (Leipzig, 1906; 2d ed., 1909, 1922).
18. Curiously enough, this work was published in an English translation under the title *Protestantism and Progress* (New York, 1912; Boston: Beacon Press, 1958).

19. See Walther Koehler, *Ernst Troeltsch* (Tübingen: Mohr, 1941), p. 339.
20. Johannes Rathje, *Die Welt des freien Protestantismus. Ein Beitrag zur deutsch-evangelischen Geistesgeschichte, dargestellt am Leben und Werk von Martin Rade* (Stuttgart: Klotz, 1952).
21. Cf. W. Koehler, *Ernst Troeltsch*, p. 1; also H. Stuart Hughes, *Consciousness and Society: The Reorientation of European Social Thought, 1890–1930* (New York: Knopf, 1958), pp. 229 f.
22. Cf. Rathje, *Die Welt des freien Protestantismus*, p. 94. Letter to Rade (17 January 1898): *"ich mag den Naturburschen leiden."*
23. Ibid., p. 106; *Christliche Welt* 3 (1898) nos. 3 and 4.
24. Cf. Ibid., p. 106; *Christliche Welt* 3 (98) nos. 27–28.
25. Cf. Ibid., p. 109.
26. Cf. Hughes, *Consciousness and Society*, p. 231.
27. Cf. *Gesammelte Schriften*, IV, 11.
28. Hughes, *Consciousness and Society*, p. 19.
29. Ernst Troeltsch, *Deutscher Geist und Westeuropa*, ed. H. Baron (Tübingen: Mohr, 1925), p. 249.
30. Marianne Weber, *Max Weber: Ein Lebensbild* (Tübingen: Mohr, 1926), p. 240.
31. Harnack also came to the United States on this occasion.
32. See the chapter on "The Asceticism of the Puritan Sects in Calvinist Ethics," Max Weber, *The Spirit of Capitalism and the Ethics of Protestantism* (New York: Scribners, 1930), pp. 95–154.
33. On the following, see Eduard Baumgarten, *Max Weber: Werk und Person* (Tübingen: Mohr, 1964), p. 624.
34. Weber, *Ein Lebensbild*, p. 532.
35. To Paul Honigsheim. Cf. Baumgarten, *Max Weber*, p. 489.
36. Hughes, *Consciousness and Society*, p. 49.
37. Troeltsch, *Gesammelte Schriften*, IV, 11.
38. First published in the form of long articles between 1908 and 1910, then as Vol. I of Troeltsch's *Gesammelte Schriften* in 1912. In 1931, an English translation (by Olive Wyon) appeared.
39. Cf. John R. Hanson, "Ernst Troeltsch's Concept of Compromise," *Lutheran Quarterly*, XVIII (1966), pp. 351–61. Also James L. Adams, "Ernst Troeltsch as Analyst of Religion," in *Journal for the Scientific Study of Religion*, I (1961), p. 105.
40. Cf. Benjamin A. Reist, *Toward a Theology of Involvement: The Thought of Ernst Troeltsch* (Philadelphia: Westminster Press, 1966), pp. 106 ff.
41. Cf. Hughes, *Consciousness and Society*, p. 235.
42. Troeltsch, *Gesammelte Schriften*, I, 967. Cf. Reist, *Toward a Theology of Involvement*, p. 116.
43. Ernst Troeltsch, *In Zeitschrift für Theologie und Kirche* (Tübingen: Mohr, 1920), p. 119.
44. Here Troeltsch probably had in mind the rise of American denominationalism on the Frontier, i.e., the Methodists and Baptists and evangelical movements.
45. Cf. Dietrich, *Biographisches Jahrbuch* (1923), p. 355.
46. Cf. the article by Ulrich Pretzel, "E. Troeltsch's Berufung an die Berliner Universität," in *Studium Berolinense* (Berlin, 1960), pp. 507–14.
47. Troeltsch, *Gesammelte Schriften*, IV, 12.
48. Ibid., p. 15.
49. In his autobiography, F. Meinecke describes in detail his and his friend's involvement in these struggles. He pays special attention to E. Troeltsch. See *Erlebtes, 1862–1891* (Stuttgart: Ev. Verlag, 1964), pp. 258 ff. and 266 ff.

50. After Troeltsch's death Meinecke collected and published these articles in one volume: *Spektatorbriefe* (Tübingen: Mohr 1924).
51. Hughes, *Consciousness and Society*, p. 379.
52. Troeltsch, *Gesammelte Schriften*, III.
53. F. Meinecke recalled ("E. Troeltsch und das Problem des Historismus," in *Werke*, IV: *Zur Theorie und Philosophie der Geschichte* [Stuttgart: Koehler Verlag, 1959], p. 369) that Troeltsch once referred "with some horror to the remark of the master of the art of historical empathy, Dilthey, when in the evening of his life he spoke of the anarchy of convictions' *(die Anarchie der Uberzeugungen); (*Cf. W. Dilthey, *Gesammelte Schriften*, V, [Leipzig & Berlin, B. G. Teubner: 1929], which would in the end be the consequence of modern historical thought."
54. Troeltsch, *Gesammelte Schriften*, III, 772.
55. F. Schleiermacher, *The Christian Faith*, trans. H. R. Mackintosh and J. S. Stewart (Edinburgh: T. & T. Clark, 1928), p. 475.
56. Troeltsch, *Gesammelte Schriften*, III, 61.
57. This is his own phrase: Troeltsch, *Gesammelte Schriften*, III, 13.
58. The editor and chief translator of this volume was Baron Friedrich von Hügel. It was he on whose initiative Troeltsch had been invited to lecture in England. Indeed, von Hügel himself had made the engagements for Troeltsch's prospective visits to Oxford, London, and Edinburgh in March 1923. As he himself writes in his introduction and in an appreciative, yet not uncritical essay on Troeltsch which is included in the first volume of his *Essays and Addresses on the Philosophy of Religion* (London, J. M. Dent 1921), he had concerned himself with Troeltsch's published writings since 1896. He was attracted to Troeltsch because he believed that Troeltsch was interested in the same problems that engaged his own attention. Moreover, he was persuaded that he could learn much from Troeltsch's vast scholarship. It is interesting to hear from him that he, the Roman Catholic layman, believed to have received from Troeltsch a true understanding of Thomas Aquinas (he referred, in this connection, to the *Social Teachings*). In April of 1901 he spent a week with Troeltsch in Heidelberg. This was the only time when the two met each other personally. They remained in touch with one another by correspondence. World War I interrupted the correspondence but it was resumed, on von Hügels initiative, in 1920.

After Troeltsch's death, von Hügel published part of the correspondence in *Die Christliche Welt* (1923; pp. 312 ff.). We can obtain from these letters some information about Troeltsch's private life. Thus we learn, for example, that Troeltsch got married in 1901 and that his marriage, to his own great sorrow, remained childless until 1913 when (in July) a son was born to him. This event caused Troeltsch (as others of his friends have also written) to be overjoyed.

In the first letter Troeltsch sent to von Hügel after World War I, he wrote: "All of us are grieving over the death of loved ones. When war broke out, my mother suffered a stroke and she died soon after. After her death, my father had a complete breakdown; he remained alive for two more years without knowing that we were at war. My sister lost her only son; he was killed after only fourteen days of war-service. The health of my brother-in-law was so much upset by this that he died a year later" (p. 312). It is no wonder that in another letter, written somewhat later, Troeltsch was moved to write to his friend: "That man must be considered happy whom death has freed from the madness of this world! Whoever must stay on this earth a while longer, must strain the love for his fellow men not a little in order to endure them. But, fortunately, the love for men is in the last resort and properly speaking, not love for men but love for God which loves that in man which is divine and not the poor confused creature as such" (p. 314).

One can understand that von Hügel was led to remark that Troeltsch lacked lighheartedness and a sense of humor. But this characterization is undoubtedly not correct. What Heinrich Hoffmann says *(Theologische Blätter* [1923], p. 77) is much more appropriate: "Despite a gaiety which occasionally even overflowed, he was deeply sensitive of the dark sides of existence, its enigmatic character, and the pain and guilt with which it is filled."

59. Ernst Troeltsch, *Christian Thought* (New York: Meridian, 1957), p. 144.
60. Ibid., p. 23.
61. Cf. Koehler, *Ernst Troeltsch,* p. 1.
62. Troeltsch, *Christian Thought,* p. 61. At the end of his life, Troeltsch was clearly filled with a certain pessimism. He was not sure whether Western civilization could still bring forth creative, reconstructive forces. His mind was filled with dark forebodings: He feared the outbreak of a new world conflict, and the behavior of certain radical nationalist groups in Germany led him to conclude that possibly Germany might fall victim to a new barbarism (cf. his *Spektatorbriefe).* He was greatly impressed by Oswald Spengler's *Decline of the West.*

In her novel already quoted, Gertrud von le Fort describes Troeltsch's dark outlook in the following moving passages: "He said that the professors had no keys with which to open the mystical door of metaphysics. Nobody can unlock this door, he said, all one can do is to explode it, so to speak. We cannot assure ourselves of the ultimate mysteries except by a bold leap into their depth. This leap is an enormous daring; it is an entirely personal decision, but we can act on it despite the dangers and the apparent uncertainty that are involved in it, because it is no blind accident that we entertain such and such ideas about the ultimate mysteries, for these ideas are effected in us by the divine life itself. (He did not say "effected by God" but "by the divine life"). In our own civilization all essential ideas of the ultimate mysteries are determined and maintained by Christianity" *(Der Kranz der Engel,* p. 210).

A little later, there follows this passage: "I expressed gratitude for his lectures and the inward strengthening I had derived from them.

He replied: 'Oh, all I have been able to do for you is that I showed you the sunset of Christianity. When the sun has set, it still glows for a long time.'

'Does not the sunset promise a new dawn?' I quickly asked. 'You too believe, don't you, that the sun will rise again?'

'I do not know,' he said, honestly. 'No, I really do not know that; but then, we do not need to know everything. What I do know is that it is possible to stay alive with a great sunset.'

'But can the sunset last long?' I asked."

63. It was mainly on the initiative of Harnack that Troeltsch was elected a full member of the Berlin Academy. In earlier elections he had been turned down, in all probability because of his political views. Cf. F. Meinecke, *Erlebtes,* p. 282.
64. The letter is printed in Marianne Weber's memoirs, *Lebenserinnerungen* (Bremen: Johs. Storm, 1948), p. 351.
65. Cf. W. Pauck, *Harnack & Troeltsch: Two Historical Theologians* (New York: Oxford University Press, 1968), p. 125. Pauck was present on this occasion.—Ed.

8. Karl Holl

Karl Holl (1866–1926), author of "The Cultural Significance of the Reformation," was Professor of church history in the University of Berlin from 1906 to 1926. As such he was the immediate colleague of Adolf von Harnack. Although the two men were different in temperament (Harnack was open and versatile, diplomatic and tolerant, while Holl was very strict in the demands he made of himself and of others, hence tending to be diffident and severe), they were close friends who cooperated beautifully with one another. Harnack, fifteen years older than Holl, was at the height of worldwide influence and fame when Holl came from the University of Tübingen to Berlin, and for some years Harnack overshadowed his colleague and friend. But in the years immediately after the First World War, when Harnack had reached retirement age, Holl suddenly began to exercise a deep impact upon Christian thought. An ever-growing number of students flocked to his lectures and he was hailed as a widely influential thinker. The immediate cause of this was the fact that, in 1921, he had begun to publish his collected essays. They were all scholarly articles, research papers, or academic orations, dealing with a wide range of church-historical subjects. Although not easily accessible (some were published in the Proceedings of the Berlin Academy of Sciences, of which Holl had become a member in 1915), these writings were already famous in academic circles, for almost without exception they were highly original and executed with an amazing scholarly skill. Holl was a master of languages; wherever possible, he used the primary sources and studied and interpreted them according to the strictest rules of philological criticism. It was characteristic of him that, as a man of mature years, he insisted on learning Russian in order to be able to read original texts pertaining to the Eastern Orthodox Church. Two volumes (one dealing with Eastern Christianity from Paul to Tolstoy and the other with Western Christianity from Tertullian to

Mary Baker Eddy) were published only in 1928, two years after Holl's death, but according to his plans. They had been preceded by a large volume, first published in 1921 and reissued with revisions in 1923, devoted entirely to a study of various phases of the thought and teaching of Martin Luther. Here were thorough and extended treatments of such themes as the following: Luther's understanding of the nature and meaning of religion; Luther's reconstruction of Christian ethics; Luther's judgments of himself; Luther's significance for the history and development of exegesis and hermeneutics; the cultural significance of the Reformation.

This volume made Holl famous almost overnight. Its influence was and still is very great, despite the fact that it was never intended to make a ready and wide appeal. It contained intricate discussions on difficult theological themes like justification and predestination. The writing was clear and direct in style, but it was also filled with innumerable complicated footnotes in small print, in which the German and Latin words of Luther and his interpreters were reproduced exactly as they had been written or spoken in the sixteenth century. The author plainly wished his writing to be read as that of a historian engaged in the effort to understand Luther's thought and work in the context of the sixteenth century; but, at the same time, he conveyed to his readers a sense of urgency about the validity of Luther's thought that made them regard his exposition as being of utmost importance for contemporary religion and theology.

Holl's Luther essays affected the theological discussion of our times at three points: (1) they steadied the thinking of many who had been thrown off balance by the violent criticisms that Barth and his friends leveled against liberal theology; (2) they came quickly to be regarded as the climax of a fresh interest in the theological thought of Martin Luther, which had been developing for several years, inaugurating the so-called Luther renaissance in contemporary Protestantism; (3) they were addressed to historical problems that Max Weber and Ernst Troeltsch in particular had raised about the interrelations between religion and culture and about the significance of the Reformation for the rise of modern civilization.

Holl's essay "The Cultural Significance of the Reformation" is of special interest because of its relevance to the third point, and this we must therefore discuss in more detail. But in view of the fact that it presupposes Holl's basic conception of Luther's theological thought, a few words about the other two points will not be out of place.

(1) Karl Barth's *The Epistle to the Romans* and other writings that came from his pen between 1918 and 1925 had dealt such a blow to the anthropocentric and humanistic side of liberal theology and to the historical method on which it relied that there was considerable consternation in the camp of its adherents. Harnack called Barth a despiser of scientific (i.e., historically critical) theology and expressed his utter surprise at the fact that he who in his historical work had found himself able to understand or to make sense out of many types of theological thought appeared to lack an aerial that would enable him to receive the Barthian ideas. He and his friends (and also many of his followers and students) feared that Barth would do great harm to the Christian gospel in the modern world if his apparent attempt to free Protestant theology from the method of historical criticism should prove successful. In this situation Holl's work on Luther showed to many a way out of the difficulty.* It was the ripe fruit of strict historical studies and as such a product of modern Protestant historical theology. At the same time it presented a plea (entirely by the weight and power of its argument) for the renewal of Luther's faith in modern Protestantism. And this faith was shown to be theocentric and thus utterly different from any form of humanism. Moreover, it was defined as directed solely to the gospel of the forgiveness of sin and as such utterly different from all religions and religious practices that live by the notion that only people who have proved themselves worthy of God's holiness are acceptable in his sight. In other words, Holl's method and argument seemed to constitute an important medium between Barthianism and liberal theology. On this account it was warmly welcomed by many who could not swallow Barth's neo-orthodoxy but were critical of the liberals because they seemed to them to lack religious depth and were therefore unable to understand the gospel as the divine promise of forgiveness to the sinner. It was therefore not surprising that

---

*Pauck was one of the many. He wrote his doctoral dissertation under Holl's tutelage.—Ed.

Holl was criticized alike by Barth and unrepentant liberals. However, these very criticisms kept his book alive. (The German text is now in its seventh edition, published in 1948.)

(2) A very important phase of contemporary Protestantism is the deep interest shown by many in the thought of the Reformers. This interest is not merely historical. The Reformers, and especially Luther and Calvin, are being studied passionately with the expectation that they will be able to to say a creative and saving word to Christians of today. Many excellent and profound books have been written about Luther's teaching in recent years and they have made his thought so relevant to the needs of our day that this concern for him represents a veritable Luther-renaissance. It was stimulated chiefly by two factors: the modern custom of celebrating anniversaries of great men of the past, and the discovery and publication of important writings of the *young* Luther.

Luther became an exceedingly prominent beneficiary of the modern passion to commemorate great men and their achievements by the celebration of anniversaries. Since October 31, 1917, when, despite the war, the whole Protestant world commemorated the beginning of the Reformation through Luther's publication of the Ninety-five Theses on Indulgences, until February 18, 1946, when the four hundredth anniversary of Luther's death was observed, all important events in the Reformer's life and every achievement of his labors have been interpreted to modern men in hundreds of books and commentaries. Our generation is better informed about him and the course of the Protestant Reformation than any other of former ages, including that of the Reformation itself. Holl's Luther essays played an important role in all this. They defined the problems for many other students of Luther and set the tone for their studies. Moreover, they were so original and at the same time so powerful that they remained unmatched; indeed, they are still fresh today and will not be outdated for a long time. Holl concentrated his attention on the young Luther, and he succeeded in showing clearly from the sources what Luther's motivations were and what they remained throughout his career. Futhermore, in his interpretation of Luther, he disregarded or bypassed many of the scenes and events that confined the Reformer to his own time and place, and he chose to illuminate those aspects of his thought and life which set off his particular comprehension of the gospel from that of other Christian thinkers.

(3) In *The Cultural Significance of the Reformation* Holl makes frequent reference to the works of Weber and Troeltsch. The very theme of this study seems to have been suggested by Max Weber's investigation of the relation between "the Protestant ethic and the spirit of capitalism" and by Ernst Troeltsch's treatment of the connection between Protestantism and modern civilization in his book on "the significance of the Reformation for the development of modern civilization" (which in the English translation is called *Protestantism and Progress*) and particularly in his large work *The Social Teaching of the Christian Churches.*

These epoch-making studies, which are still the subject of many fruitful discussions, must be seen against the background of two characteristically modern interests. In the first place, they represent the reaction of two famous thinkers to the Marxist view of history. Although not partisan works, they were designed to show that a good case can be made for the shaping influence of religious ideas upon political, social, and economic factors of life. Indeed they were nothing else than detailed historical investigations of the interrelations between religion and civilization. In the second place, these books—and particularly those by Troeltsch—must be appreciated in connection with the inquiry that has been carried on since the Enlightenment and is still the explicit or implicit preoccupation of all thinkers concerned with the philosophical or cultural interpretation of history: the inquiry about the importance of the Reformation and of Protestantism for the rise and development of modern civilization.

The concern of the men of the Enlightenment for human freedom and autonomy developed the notion that the Reformation of Martin Luther marked the beginning of the "modern era," because one felt that Luther's so-called rediscovery of the gospel and his assaults upon the papacy had brought about the breakup of the authoritarianism of the papacy and of the Roman Catholic Church. During the American and French revolutions it was frequently asserted that the struggle for liberty in which men were engaged was somehow a continuation of the protest of Martin Luther against the authority of the papacy. The historians of the nineteenth century took it for granted that the "modern age" began with the Reformation, and in the twentieth century this idea became so universal that even Roman Catholic historians felt compelled to undertake the proof that the so-called crises of "modern civilization" were the end result of the revolt of Luther and the Protestant Reformers against the faith and order of the papal Church. However, it was never easy to support general judgments of this kind by convincing historical evidence. Hence it was of highest significance that when, in 1906, Ernst Troeltsch was asked to substitute for Max Weber (who was ill) to deliver a lecture before a congress of historians on Protestantism and the spirit of the modern age, he chose to point out as objectively as possible that although the rise of the modern world must be understood in terms of the attitudes engendered by the Renaissance and the Reformation and that although Protestantism produced and continues to shape the religious spirit of modern Western civilization, the factors that really determine modern civilization—secularized political power and technological economic power, made possible by the historical sense and by the discoveries and investigations of the natural sciences—must be interpreted as being in opposition to the Reformation and to Protestantism. In other words, Troeltsch argued that modern civilization had *two* special beginnings—in the Reformation, which effected the emancipation of powerful cultural forces from the papacy; and in the spirit of the nineteenth century which, formed by the Enlightenment, emancipated common life from the authority of organized religion, including that of Protestantism.

Anyone who wishes fully to understand the setting of Holl's inquiry about the cultural significance of the Reformation must consult Troeltsch's lecture. He will find that Holl—who covers practically the same ground as Troeltsch—gives different judgments and comes to different conclusions. Holl does not choose to deal with the general historical problem of the extent to which the modern world still is dependent upon Protestantism, but he undertakes the task to specify as concretely as possible where and how the Reformation formed cultural attitudes. He does so under the auspices of a somewhat indefinite title: *The Cultural Significance [Kulturbedeutung] of the Reformation.* He does not appear to share Troeltsch's negative and critical judgment about the secularization of modern life, although he does not directly and specifically reject it, but he leaves the overall impression that he would not mind being counted among those early moderns who were sure that Luther inaugurated the modern world.

Moreover, Holl seems to be concerned to demonstrate the cultural effects of the Reformation by proofs or interpretations that are specific. The scope of his knowledge and the thoroughness of his acquaintance with widely spread literary sources certainly are most impressive. One can see how many fruitful investigations in the field of religion and culture can be undertaken and should still be made. Yet one will also notice how precarious such an inquiry is. Even a master like Holl can frequently be observed in the commission of two basic faults that beset many a historian: he often does not appear to have taken into consideration all the concrete environmental factors to which the ideas and attitudes he discusses were related. Furthermore, he discloses very sharply the biased opinions and prejudices that informed his thinking. This is made especially evident in the discussion of political matters. There he shows himself as a German patriot who tended to idealize his own people; and as a nationalist who seems not to have sensed that many of his judgments, which he regarded as historically correct and morally sound, were inspired by a provincial conviction that his country could do no wrong.

It is because even the noblest historians commit such errors of judgment that history must be rewritten again and again. Today many people are eager to learn more about the interrelations between religion and culture and specifically between Protestant Christianity and modern civilization. Perhaps the publication of Holl's essays in an English translation will stimulate such investigations. Undertaken from a competence comparable to his, they will demonstrate how deeply and searchingly he probed.

May 1959

9. A Brief Criticism of Barth's *Dogmatics*

In the summer of 1938, Peter Barth, the editor of the *Opera Selecta* of Calvin, told some of us who were his colleagues on the faculty of Adolph Keller's Ecumenical Seminar in Geneva the following story about his brother Karl: "Our family used to spend the summer vacations in the country. One day after breakfast, our father decided that we should all go on a hike or a picnic. All members of the family were rounded up, but Karl, who was then nine or ten years old, was nowhere to be found. We finally went off without him. When we came back in the late afternoon, there was still no sign of him. At last, we located him in a barn. He was seated on a three-legged stool in front of a barrel, the top of which served him as a desk. He had been writing all day. When we asked him what he was up to, he replied: "I am writing my 'Collected Works.' "

What he thus began, Karl Barth has apparently been continuing to do to this day. His "Collected Works" now fill large bookshelves. Now past seventy years of age,* he is still busy and preoccupied with writing. And what a skillful writer he is! Words flow incessantly from his pen. It seems that he must do his thinking while he is writing. He is as productive as a journalist who must finish a story every day and as creative as a novelist with great imagination who cannot but give form to his ideas in words. Indeed, in his pronouncements on the church- and world-situation, Barth appears to be a theological journalist. And in his dogmatic works, he writes, if I may say so, like a theological novelist. He resembles a Thomas Mann or a Thomas Wolfe. Like them, he draws upon an inexhaustible font of imagination and, like them, he is a master, nay, a wizard of the written word.

The volumes of his *Church Dogmatics* are written in a sober,

---

*This essay was written in 1957. Karl Barth was born in 1886 and died in 1968.

didactic, but flourishing style that flows steadily along like a broad, swift river. (The English translators have reproduced it with admirable competence.) Its sentences are long and involved and repetitive. An idea which can be captured in a few words is expressed in an ever new series of sentences. Different words and varying phrases articulate it over and over again. It imprints itself upon the mind of the reader in the same way that a musical theme, developed in the movement of a sonata or symphony, lays hold of the mind of the listener.

Of course, Barth's basic ideas are of such a sort that they cannot be communicated by any other method. For example, his doctrine of the knowledge of God is grounded in the thesis that "God is known by God and by God alone" (II, 1, p. 47). In order to explain what he means by this, Barth fills dozens of pages. But when he is done, he has stated and restated only this one idea.

Only this one idea, I say. What a strange idea it is, what a disturbing idea to be entertained and explained by a human mind! One can deal with it only in one of two ways of explanation: either state it and then say no more about it (for, if only God can know God, a man cannot possibly say anything about knowing him!); or state it and then deal with it laboriously and in many twists and contortions of thought in terms of an impossible human possibility (for if, when God is knowable only to God, a man nevertheless finds that he is capable of this knowledge of God, he has indeed a lot of explaining to do!).

Barth is this kind of a man! He can and dares to speak of God's communion with man and of man's communion with God on the basis of the thesis that God can be known only by God himself. And he has found it necessary to fill not dozens but thousands of pages in order to explain how this can be. He can do this because he knows what God's counsels are. If I may be allowed to say so, he writes as if he had looked into God's cards.

This doctrine of the knowledge of God has been his theme from the beginning of his career as a theological author. His commentary on the Epistle to the Romans was a turbulent exposition of the idea that God is in heaven and man on earth; and that man deceives himself if he thinks that he can reach heaven from earth; indeed, that men, particularly Christian men, have been deceiving themselves throughout the ages, but never more thoroughly than in modern times when they believed that by religion and religiousness they could obtain a relation with God. Barth still thinks so. In Volume I, 2, of the *Church Dogmatics*, he presents a long chapter on religion as unbelief and superstition. Throughout the whole work, he declares himself a sworn enemy of all so-called natural knowledge of God, all "natural theology," all paths toward God *"von unten nach oben."* Like the Roman Catholic conception of the *analogia entis,* all this appears to him as the invention of Antichrist.

However, he has never been only a critic. He was and is (and now more fully than ever) a constructive, or rather, an expository thinker. From the beginning he has pointed to the availability of an access to God: by the way that leads *"von oben nach unten,"* in God's revelation of himself in Jesus Christ to which the Bible bears witness. In the Word in which God knows himself he can be known also by man, not in the sense that human godlessness and atheism are transformed into godliness and faith or in the sense that man's incapacity for God is replaced by an openness for the divine, but in the sense that God draws man into his own divine life and makes him a participant of his own divine self-knowledge. In this way, Barth has stated the matter from the beginning, and he finds ever new ways of saying it again. Only he speaks now of the objective factuality of this event in unparadoxical terms. He has banished from his thought Kierkegaardian existential dialectics that he employed in his earlier works and the vocabulary by means of which he expressed it.

In volume IV, 2, of the *Dogmatics,* one can read sentences (p. 136) that I translate as follows: "The Incarnation is in itself a fact produced by an act of God's majesty and as such it has not only the character of an actual happening but also that of revelation. Because it has this character, it reveals, opens, and discloses itself and makes itself knowable by creating the possibility of being seen, heard, and understood, or rather: it creates the eyes that see it, the ears that hear it, the thoughts that understand it. Because it has this character, it is a light that can be and is actually seen—'in thy light we shall see the light' (Ps. 36, 10), i.e., it renders itself knowable as a fact. It removes the bar and opens the door toward its givenness (objectivity); it enlarges itself in the direction of a subject; it comprehends and embraces this subject;

it becomes the known object of this subject. By the action of the object the subject that is not capable of knowing it is thus enabled to know it." In other words, revelation produces its own possibility of being known, or: by disclosing himself, God creates the possibility of being known. (This is one of those long involved statements that represents one of the aforementioned variations of Barth's theological-symphonic themes.)

Along these lines Barth's thought has remained steady and identical. But, as the work on the *Dogmatics* has progressed, he has seen fit to modify his basic theme. In connection with the extremely elaborate development of the doctrines of Creation and Reconciliation, he was led to put an ever-increasing weight upon Christology. His theology is now "concentrated upon Christ" to such an extent that all doctrines on the nature and life of God and on the nature and destiny of man are explained on the basis of the second article of the Creed: the faith in Jesus Christ, very God of very God and very man of very man. The man Christ Jesus, the incarnate Son of God, born of the Virgin, crucified under Pontius Pilate, raised from the dead and (after forty days) ascended into heaven, is the Alpha and the Omega, God in action as Savior and Creator. Christ, the Reconciler, is the actual ground of all being and of all knowing. From, in, and to him are all things. He is the *summum esse* and the *summum bonum*. In him, all reality is disclosed as upheld and surrounded by the triumphant grace of God. God is love.

The doctrine of the Trinity and the Chalcedonian dogma of the two natures of Christ, regarded as implicit in the biblical Kerygma of Christ, serve Barth as the basis of a grand speculation on God, Man, and Nature. The Bible as well as the cosmological, soteriological, and anthropological doctrines of historical theology furnish him the individual parts of his system of a Christological metaphysics. It is amazing to see how he handles these parts as his thought ranges over the whole Bible and the entire tradition of Christian theology down to its remote and obscure corners. (Here one can learn much!)

Barth's theology has thus become a system of speculative biblical metaphysics. It has been characterized, not ineptly, as "Christomonism." He is not far removed from the world of German Idealism. Indeed, we must rank Barth next to the great speculative theologians of Christian history: Origen, Thomas Aquinas, Schleiermacher. In the light of the faith of the prophets and apostles and the Protestant Reformers, particularly Luther but also Calvin, he is as great a seducer as these "systematic theologians" were. If they are heretical because of their service to the harlot Reason, he is too. If it can be said that Schelling has made a Plotinian gnostic out of Tillich, then it is not inappropriate to say that Plato has tempted Barth to develop a biblical-Christological theosophy or gnosis.

All who love dogmatic thinking will be fascinated, thrilled, and enriched by the reading of the volumes of the *Church Dogmatics*— in company with the Roman Catholic Thomists who, despite Barth's strictures on the *analogia entis,* seem to be able to appropriate his system best of all. But anyone who likes to have his imagination excited by the thrill of theological metaphysics will have a rousing experience by reading Barth.

What influence will this *Church Dogmatics* have upon the churches? Will it profoundly affect the course of Protestantism? I am so bold as to believe that it will not change the course of thought and action either of Old or New Protestantism. Despite its great depth and range, Barth's thinking is too willful and unrealistic. A theology based on the principle that man cannot know God but which, in dependence on a revelation in which God knows himself, presumes to explain what God is in himself, what his inner life is, and even what his purposes are for time and eternity, must prove in the end to be irrelevant to the human situation.

Today the human situation, including that of the churches, must be handled by critical anthropological thinking and by means of decisions derived from clear, judicious historical thinking. Barth says that church history is merely an auxiliary theological discipline, because he believes that the church must be guided by dogmatic theology oriented to the Bible. But dogmatic speculation, even if this is based on the Bible, cannot help us. What we need most is historical understanding and not theosophy. The churches have more need of a Harnack than of a Barth.

In the volume *Antwort,* which a number of Barth's friends published in honor of his seventieth birthday, Eduard Thurneysen, his old-time friend, presents (under the title "The Beginnings") a series of letters he received from Barth during the time when they were neighboring pastors in the Swiss Aargau. One of the letters (written on April 20, 1920) reads as follows: "In Basel, I took heart and went to Eberhard Vischer and inquired for Harnack. I burst into an important party, where (as I later heard in a roundabout way) they had been talking mostly about me. Harnack sat enthroned on a sofa; they addressed him 'Your Excellency,' and he distributed *bon mots* ('two things are international,' he said, 'money and intellect.'). Afterwards, I had a private conversation with him and Eberhard Vischer, for an hour or so. I asked him what he meant by 'profane' and was told that he had in mind the onesidedness of my thinking . . . because it intruded upon God's mystery. He could not reply quite so readily to my question whether he would not admit that I was at least historically correct in my understanding of the New Testament. In seeking to answer this, the two gentlemen became very much involved, and the sum of what they said amounted to this, that the forgiveness of sins is something very simple and a part of the love of the neighbor, and Harnack said that he practiced it constantly. They were willing to concede that a little disturbance of the church might be desirable but insisted that I should keep my conception of God to myself and not turn it into an 'article of export.' Finally they called me a Calvinist and an intellectualist and then dismissed me with the prediction that according to all the evidence of church history, I would probably found a sect and become the recipient of inspirations."

This is a very nice story, very characteristic of all persons concerned. And the judgments expressed in it are all correct, I think, that of Barth on Harnack as well as that of Harnack on Barth.

May 1957

10. Paul Tillich: Heir of the Nineteenth Century

Paul Tillich's mind was formed by his upbringing in the manse of a Prussian Evangelical Lutheran minister in small towns of the Province of Brandenburg and in the city of Berlin. The customs and traditions that surrounded him and which he gradually made his own were German and Lutheran. He absorbed them at home and in school. Even as a child he consciously regarded himself as a member of the church as a spiritual community. This consciousness was never extinguished despite the fact that, in time, he found much to criticize in church doctrine and practice. Even though, in his later days, he did not regard himself as an active churchman, he could say with conviction that the church had "always been his home."[1] He found moving words to describe what this meant to him:

My love for church-buildings and their mystic atmosphere, for liturgy and music and sermons, and for the great Christian festivals that molded the life of the town for days and even weeks of the year left an indelible feeling in me for the ecclesiastical and sacramental. To these must be added the mysteries of Christian doctrine and their impact on the inner life of a child, the language of the Scriptures, and the exciting experiences of holiness, guilt, and forgiveness.[2]

These words assume additional significance through Tillich's forthright statement: "I am a Lutheran by birth, education, religious experience, and theological reflection."[3] In other words, he knew himself as a Lutheran and wanted to be known as such.[4]

When Tillich was ordained, he became a minister in the Evangelical Union Church of Prussia (i.e., not a "Lutheran" pastor); and when, after his emigration from Germany to the United States, he sought ministerial standing in accordance with his background, he received it not from a Lutheran body but from the "Evangelical-Reformed Synod," a denomination that exhibited close kinship with Tillich's German home church. Later (in 1957) it merged with the "Congregational Christian Churches" to form "the United Church of Christ," in which not only German and American but also Lutheran and Calvinist traditions were united. Thus Tillich had ministerial standing in a church body of which some congregations loyally maintained forms of Lutheran Pietism, while others were faithful descendants of New England Puritanism. Tillich was not linked by education to either of these traditions. Had he been aware of this and more conscious than he was of the internal and external development of the church in which he was baptized, confirmed, and ordained, he would perhaps not have written as definitively as he did that the substance of his religion was and would remain Lutheran.

Yet his spiritual mood and disposition certainly *were* Lutheran. This meant not only that his theological thought was based on the Bible and directed to the doctrine of justification by grace through faith, as indeed it was throughout his career, but also that his outlook upon the world was marked by an awareness of the corruption of existence and even of its irrational and demonic nature. Consequently he "repudiated every kind of social Utopia (including the metaphysics of progressivism)" and rejected "Puritan legalism in private and corporate life."[5] One may even go so far as to say that he harbored a prejudice against Calvinism and Puritanism. Over against the Calvinist emphasis on divine transcendence he frequently invoked the Lutheran principle *finitum capax infiniti* (the finite is capable of comprehending the infinite), and on this basis he explained and defended his propensities toward mysticism and in particular what he called his "mystical participation in nature."[6] As a Lutheran he loved and enjoyed nature and all its gifts. At the same time, he was pessimistic about the possibility of improving the life of men by moral education. Thus he could write the sentence: "However changeable human nature may be, it is not amenable to fundamental moral correction."[7]

How centrally important the doctrine of justification became for his entire thought will be made clear as we interpret his development, especially during the years of his theological studies. But a word must here be said about his relation to the Bible, for he was never a Biblicist. This fact is important for the assessment of his systematic theology, especially if one reads it (as many have done following Tillich's own example) in comparison with Karl Barth's dogmatics. Each volume of Barth's *Church Dogmatics* contains a lengthy and extensive index of biblical quotations (and some of these quotations are veritable commentaries on biblical passages). The editors of Tillich's writings decided to supply a similar index; the third volume of his *Systematische Theologie* contains one (though the American edition, which Tillich himself authorized for publication, lacks it), and another is provided for the thirteen volumes of his *Gesammelte Werke*. These indexes are surprisingly slight. One learns from them, for example, that in the three volumes of the *Systematic Theology* the Old Testament is quoted less than twenty times.

The Bible was for him not authority or norm but source and document. As such it requires, he believed, a historical interpretation in terms of its origin and its transmission from generation to generation in the life of the church. Tillich preferred to say that his theology had a biblical foundation rather than that it was based on the authority of the Bible as the Word of God. He believed that his own system of theology was "dependent on Paul's constructive doctrine of the New Creation in Christ"[8] and he therefore wished to be considered a "Paulinist." The opinion, however, that this is another evidence of the Lutheran strain in his thought cannot be entirely sustained, for he connected his dependence on Paul not primarily with the doctrine of justification, but with that of the mystical presence of the Spirit. The eighth chapter of the Epistle to the Romans and the First Letter to the Corinthians were his favorite passages.

Tillich's Christian training was significantly supplemented by the humanistic education he received at the Gymnasium. He developed a love for classical languages and literature. The Greeks fascinated him. As an adolescent, he read the works of the Greek dramatists and philosophers.

He was an avid reader who became personally involved in the subjects and themes of his reading.[9] He liked to subject ideas to critical analysis and derived satisfaction from ordering his thoughts in logically coherent outlines. As a young man, he used every free hour in order to study philosophical books. He reports that he found a copy of Albert Schwegler's text book on the history of philosophy on a country preacher's bookshelf and a volume of J. G. Fichte's *Theory of Science (Wissenschaftslehre)* on a cart of secondhand books upon which he happened in a street in Berlin. He also remembered throughout his life that, "in a state of boyish excitement,"[10] he bought Kant's *Critique of Pure Reason* for a few pennies in a bookstore.

It was fortunate for him that his father had a deep interest in philosophy, for father and son often engaged in philosophical conversations. Thus a close bond was formed between them which underlay Tillich's thinking and personal outlook on life throughout his career. This was of particular importance to him during his university years, for he kept his father informed about his studies and ideas, about his teachers and fellow students, and about his hopes and disappointments. Indeed, he let his parent fully participate in his own progress. It is therefore not surprising that, when the time came for him to decide on a field of study at the university, he chose theology and philosophy. He was intellectually well prepared for this and began his studies with confidence. He had heard a philosophical lecture for the first time when he was about sixteen years old and he never forgot it. He had chanced into a course by Julius Kaftan, who held the chair of systematic theology at the University of Berlin. Tillich was intrigued by the generalizations the professor produced when he argued that the three major Christian denominational groups had developed theological sytems that were shaped by the ideas of three great philosophers: Eastern Orthodoxy by Plato, Roman Catholicism by Aristotle, and Protestantism by Kant.

In the autumn of 1904, Tillich completed his secondary education. He then followed in his father's footsteps not only by registering as a theological student in the universities of Berlin (1904), Tübingen (1905), Halle (1905–07), and again Berlin (1907–08), but also by joining the student association Wingolf.

His life was now shaped by three influences: his studies, his friendships, and his relations with his father.

These relations assumed a special character because, on becoming a student, Tillich, though financially dependent upon his father, enjoyed personal freedom for the first time in his life. Within the limits of the university traditions and customs, he made the most of his freedom. He spent the long university vacations either at home or in a resort (Misdroy) on the shore of the Baltic Sea, which his father frequented with regularity every year. He then engaged in special studies for which he had no time during the regular academic year, partly because it was often interrupted by special observances and festivities, private and official, and by hikes, excursions, and visits to other academic centers.

Tillich was an industrious student, faithful in class attendance and conforming to the prescribed curriculum. He was almost entirely absorbed in intellectual pursuits and he quickly won the respect of his fellow students as a clear thinker and a formidable debater. He loved philosophical and theological discussions. He developed a special attachment to a few of his professors and, on the whole, was well satisfied with his teachers. But occasionally he was quite critical of them. He was then barely twenty years old. In Halle, he reacted to his classes not without some haughtiness, like an overconfident student. About a course taught by F. Loofs, a learned and highly esteemed church historian, to whose teaching he remained permanently indebted, he wrote,

I have given up the "History of Dogma." Loofs says not more but rather less than one can read in his textbook. I have now bought it for nine marks, but I am saving six marks of course fees.[11]

Another evaluation of the teaching of his professors reads as follows:

So far Lütgert has not said anything new but he presents the old stuff in a nice way. Kautzsch is relatively bearable, but his introduction to the introduction to the history of the history of his discipline (the Old Testament) is not exactly of great interest. Kattenbusch is a good historian but a poor rhetorician.[12]

The divinity faculty of Halle occupied a position between theological orthodoxy and liberalism. This was, on the whole, also young Tillich's point of view. In discussions with his fellow students he often said that he wanted to avoid both an unalterable dogmatism and an arbitrary subjectivism. His major concern was to achieve an understanding of Christianity that rested on an objective foundation and not on subjective experience. But when he explained this to himself by asserting, on the one hand, that faith is the product and gift of revelation and, on the other hand, that what is given in revelation is known only to faith, he saw that he was moving in a circle. He was much disturbed about this, especially because the two systematic theologians among his teachers, Martin Kähler and Wilhelm Lütgert, whom he greatly admired, did not show him a way out of his difficulty. He turned to his father and explained his doubt. An interesting correspondence ensued.[13] Tillich began it as follows:

Kähler's apologetics is a stumbling block for me. I find its systematic structure infinitely difficult so that only very intensive study and a comprehensive knowledge of the relevant materials derived from all disciplines of theology and philosophy can lead to a penetrating comprehension of it. Of course I benefit greatly from his ingenious and strong explanation of individual details and his outstanding personality.

Furthermore, I do not understand the basis of his system. He moves with intent and purpose in the circle of faith and what he has thus apprehended but he does not explain how one gets inside the circle. Consequently I suffer from "tremendous blockage," if I may use Windelband's term.[14]

Kähler recognizes only with qualifications, either the tradition of the church or the Bible as the source of Christian truth and he regards the religious consciousness only as the presupposition but never as the source of faith. On the contrary, only faith can decide what is important in the two sources referred to. . . . On the other hand, it must be recognized that faith is based on a proclamation which is truthful. Thus we have here a circular argument: ultimately only faith can decide about its own presupposition, namely the validity of what is given historically. This is the consequence of the equally paradoxical assertion that eternal truth can become accessible to us only in the historical (*historisch*) flow of historic (*geschichtlich*) Christianity.[15] (*im historisch fliessenden, dem geschichtlichen Christentum*) He rejects all attempts to demonstrate the necessity of Christian truth and even of religion otherwise than historically (*historisch*) but not psychologically as Schleiermacher does, or metaphysically by ideas.

His father replied (on 26 May 1906):

I understand what offends you in Kähler's views but he is right in saying that one can get into the circle of Christian knowledge only through an act of faith or through rebirth. It is no paradox that faith is, on the one hand, produced by the word of God in Scripture and that, on the other hand, it is independent from Scripture in so far as it is a new organ of knowledge. . . . There is no knowledge without presupposition or bias.

But Tillich persisted in his doubt. In further notes to his father, he repeated his earlier questions:

I am on a rather serious war-footing with the problems of theology, with the fundamental issues of apologetics as well as with certain special problems. It seems to me that there is a contradiction between the objective truth which Christianity is supposed to offer and its historical mediation. And the entire history of theology shows that this contradiction cannot be resolved. Moreover, I do not understand the relation between truth and value judgments *(Wertschätzung)* on the basis of experience.

He (Kähler) assigns the basic and central doctrines of justification and Christology to the introduction of Apologetics, and naturally he tries to prove historically that they are the center of Christianity, but this is impossible without a prior judgment of faith. This, however, is the final step towards a theology of consciousness. The contrast to Lütgert is very clear, because, in his course on ethics, the latter proposes the principle that the Christian requirements *(Forderungen)* are established in their truth-value only if it can be shown by simple psychological observation and analysis that only this ethics is in accordance with what men ought to be *(Wesen des Menschen)* and, in accordance with this he makes many fine observations. But there is always the question whether in the last resort it is not his own point of view from which the world appears to him as it does. But I like this approach very much. To be sure, his *Ethics* is not at all systematic. It is a summary of significant points rather than an organism.

Now the father felt obliged to give an extended reply, dated 16 June 1906:

Your scientific *(wissenschaftliche)* development has now taken a certain one-sided turn. Its starting point was a theoretical-philosophical interest which became steadily stronger. I have a part in this because, being greatly interested in systematic problems, I have talked much with you about these things and thus I have perhaps furthered this tendency in you—perhaps too much. Then there was your participation in the efforts to settle Wingolf problems by theoretical discussion[16] and your possibly premature preoccupation with dogmatics and apologetics. All this can produce a purely rational understanding and conception of Christianity. You may be in danger of becoming an intellectualist. And this is a real danger. But if you see it in time and overcome it, you can only profit by it. And for you this time is now. For the present, therefore, give up the attempt to prove to yourself by means of intellectual speculation the truth of Christianity theoretically and then to construct it systematically. There are theological methods which are no less scientific, especially exegesis. Most of all, do not forget that Christianity is a matter of conscience. Hence nobody reads the Bible with profit except he does so with a seeking heart and with ... prayer.... Remember your confirmation text[17] and act in accordance with John 14:21. "He who has my commandments and keeps them, he it is who loves me and he who loves me will be loved by my Father, and I will love him and manifest myself to him." Think also of Matt. 11:25–30 "Come unto me, all who labor and are heavy laden and I will give you rest ..." Then you will understand better what Christian experience is: *Gnosis* (knowledge) comes with *Pistis* (faith) and not conversely. God and his revelation cannot be rationally comprehended.... He alone is the light and not human wisdom which can prosper only under his light. May God reveal himself ever more fully to you, my dear son, and may he enlighten you from above by his spirit who far exceeds the spirit of logic.... This is what your father implores for you with my prayers; he too is acquainted with spiritual struggles and wrestlings but through God's help and grace he can say: I know in whom I believe ...

Then the elder Tillich added an afterthought which he dictated and appended to the letter. It reads as follows: "when a philosophical system does not prove to be useful for the classification of the basic truth of Christianity, one must maintain the latter and give up the former—in other words: one's system must be corrected under God's guidance."

This letter elicited the following detailed reply from Paul Tillich:

My heartiest thanks for your letter. Aside from the positive motives and ideas which it presents to me, its chief value consists in this that it has caused me once again to think through my present position. In so far as I have achieved clarity about this, I want to explain it to you.

You are entirely right in thinking that my interest in theology was mediated to me purely intellectually. This was sufficient to arouse in me joy and enthusiasm for my studies only as long as I could maintain it, i.e., this interest, over against all objections to the basic assumptions of Christianity; and, until a short time ago, this was the case. It is due to three motives that a change has now come about.

First, my work in dogmatics has led me to great inner contradictions.

Second, my own philosophical thought has produced in me a steady opposition to church-dogmatics until finally it too became intrinsically almost untenable.

Third, I encountered the exciting power of Fichte's idea of autonomy in matters of world view, even in contrast to his own history, and I was thus liberated to a certain degree from the strong influence of the educational experience that has determined my thinking and I became critical of it. Thus I was led to affirm the autonomy of thinking. But this just now proved itself to be quite inadequate, partly because of its intrinsic dissolution and partly because of its relation to action which must be suspended, of course, until knowledge can be achieved—which in my case means until the system can be constructed. This is tantamount to an absolute criticism of autonomous intellectualism.

At the same time, I studied Herrmann (Marburg) more closely. His rejection of speculation became now quite attractive to me and I appreciated especially his emphasis upon the person of Jesus and God's revelation in his personal life whose effects call forth in us religious and moral dedication. He keeps aloof from the foolish irrelevancies of radical criticism as well as from orthodox intellectualism. Instead he puts the emphasis upon the positive personal relation to the Bible and the person of Christ. I am confident that I shall find all this to be of great positive value for myself and my theology as I follow his direction and also your insistence on a searching reading of the Bible. I realize that the transition to these views will not be without difficulties for me in so far as I must detach myself from my present opinions and turn to the new method of thought which, I realize, is in complete contrast to what I have held until now. But I believe that there is a great blessing in all this so that you do not need to be apprehensive, especially in view of the fact that the aim I pursue is quite firm and clear.

Faithfully yours,
Paul

The father's response to this self-disclosure was brief but positive:

We shall see each other in a week or so but you will probably be glad to know already today that what you have shared with me does not disturb me. Crises of the kind through which you are passing today can be a great blessing if they are overcome in the good fight of faith. What I regret is that you are engaged in such a radical change of thought. . . . As you break with intellectualism you will probably throw much overboard that should never be rejected . . ."[18]

This correspondence is most revealing. It gives a vivid impression of the nature of Tillich's relation to his father. It was clearly marked by openness and mutual confidence. There was apparently nothing that hindered Tillich from communicating to his father what his experience meant to him. He freely disclosed, although not with full clarity, the intellectual and spiritual difficulties which he encountered in connection with his studies. In his later writings, especially in his autobiographical essays, he says repeatedly how difficult it was for him to achieve independence from parental authority. He describes his father as a strict conservative Lutheran who, in the presence of doubt, sometimes grew angry as he defended his point of view. Tillich even goes so far as to say that he identified his father's authority with the religious authority of revelation. This, he says, "made every attempt at autonomous thinking an act of religious daring" and "connected criticism with a sense of guilt."[19]

These views and feelings do not seem to be supported by the letters we have cited. To be sure, Tillich mentions the long philosophical discussions with his father and describes them as "the most agreeable instances of a positive relation" to him. But then he continues, "Nevertheless, in these discussions the breakthrough occurred. From an independent philosophical position a state of general independence spread out in all directions, at first theoretically, later practically."[20]

It is, of course, conceivable that, in writing all this, Tillich had in mind not only all the freedom from parental authority he had achieved but also the unorthodox position he assumed in theology and the radical opinions he advocated, and the unconventional lifestyle he adopted when he returned from the First World War and began his professional career.

But his emancipation from the authoritarianism his father personified never led to a breakdown of cordial personal relations. A year before his death, (30 July 1937: he was 80 years of age) the father wrote to his son that he was reading the book *On the Boundary* and that he had begun to dictate his opinion of it. Tillich on his part felt the presence of his father for some time after the latter's death. He wrote to his friend and brother-in-law Alfred Fritz that he still often dreamt of his father.

The letters we have quoted are interesting also for further reasons. They show that the theological student Paul Tillich, twenty years of age, was already occupied with problems and themes of thought which later became the structure and substance of his entire theological work. He thought of "the system" he would have to construct; he was aware of what was implied in his discovery of the idea of autonomy while he was under the influence of Kant and Fichte; he began to correlate philosophy and theology; he wrestled with "the theological circle," realizing that revelation and faith belong together, that revelation is objectively given only in so far as it is subjectively received.[21]

Next to the relationship with his father (and, of course, his family) friendships were the formative factors in Tillich's development. He found them in the student association Wingolf, a national corporation which united student groups that had been organized at most German universities. In becoming a Wingolfite Tillich followed the example of his father. By joining the fellowship first in Berlin, then in Tübingen, and finally in Halle, in 1905, he became a life-member of the *Wingolfsbund.* From the beginning he took this membershp very seriously, not only because it put him into close association with fellow students but also because it required of him and his friends the observance of a Christian principle of fellowship. For most Wingolfites it was sufficient that they were mindful of the slogan around which they were united: *Di henos panta* ("all through one," namely Christ). Indeed, for most of them the principles and requirements implied in this slogan presented no particular difficulties because they came from Christian homes and many of them were sons or descendants of ministers. But when Tillich came to Halle, the fellowship there was troubled by the question of what the Christian principle meant spiritually and practically for the common life. In the course of time, he became the leader of the often difficult discussions about the definition of Christianity and the significance of Christian principles for individual and social action. At the end of his third semester of study at Halle, his fellows elected him formally as their presiding officer, an honor and responsibility that he remembered with pride and a sense of accomplishment until his dying day.

His skill in formulating definitions and distinctions and his passion for clear and coherent thinking were now put to the test.

The results of his efforts never ceased to be vividly remembered by him. "The question of the principles of a Christian community," he wrote later,

was so thoroughly argued out in the group that all who were active in the struggle profited a great deal by it. At that time, I came to understand the value of objective statements like denominational creeds. When a community gives general recognition to a confessional basis whose meaning transcends subjective belief or doubt, it will hold together even while allowing room for tendencies toward doubt, criticism, and uncertainty.[22]

When the long debates had led to a consensus, Tillich was asked to formulate a summary of the major points agreed upon in a statement. This statement was to be presented at a national meeting of representatives chosen from the local Wingolf groups. Tillich reported to his father, "I am about to construct the first 'dogmatics' of my life. . . . It is to be a brief but substantial exposition of the Wingolfite ideal."[23] Tillich's statement affirmed that the basis of Christian community must be the message of the Bible, objectively understood and kept independent from subjectivistic arbitrariness. He rejected a selective as well as a literal interpretation of the Bible and suggested that the content of the Bible should be comprehensively expressed in a few brief biblical terms, in effect, in the form of a creed saying that the biblical witness presents to men Jesus Christ as their only Lord and Redeemer. Moreover, he recommended that personal doubt or indecision should be tolerated. He was persuaded that one could not require a member of the fellowship to accept the creed for himself personally; one could only expect of him that he would be willing to live in a community that was based on this creed.

Much later he recalled[24] that, at the national Wingolf convention, he defended the view that the basis of their community was not dependent on individual experiences, but on the Christian principle and that, if a person had doubts or inner difficulties about this principle, he must be recognized as a member of the fellowship as long as he remained seriously concerned about his doubt. In this context, Tillich formulated for the first time the thesis which he included in many of his later theological teachings, namely, "that faith embraces itself as well as doubt about itself."[25]

His activities on behalf of the Wingolf fellowship provided Tillich also with the key for the understanding of the nature of the church. "I question," he later testified, "whether without it, I would have understood the meaning of the church existentially and theoretically."[26]

In the long and explicit interpretation of the nature of the church, which is presented in the third volume of his *Systematic Theology*, Tillich offers the following definitions[27] which, though he does not say so explicitly, appear to be directly derived from the student debates about the nature of a Christian community:

... a church is a community of those who affirm that Jesus is the Christ. ... For the individual, this means the decision—*not* as to whether he, personally, can accept the assertion that Jesus is the Christ, *but* the decision as to whether he wishes to belong or not to belong to a group that asserts that Jesus is the Christ. If he decides against this, he has left the church, even if ... he does not formalize this denial ...

In the opposite situation, there are some who consciously or unconsciously want to belong to the church. ... and who are in a state of doubt about the basic assertion that Jesus is the Christ. ... For them it must be said that the criterion of one's belonging to the church is the serious desire ... to participate in the life of a group which is based on the New Being as it has appeared in Jesus as the Christ. ... They can be assured that they fully belong to the church ...

Still another idea which Tillich probably conceived in connection with his membership in the Wingolf and which he advanced again and again throughout his career was that of a "Bund" or voluntary association or "fellowship" or "league" whose members should be associated with one another in a bond of common spiritual and social concerns. Occasionally, he also used the term *Orden*, or "order," implying that its members were to realize a special purpose, like members of a religious or monastic order. The most succinct definition of this can be found in the following passage contained in his first autobiography:

I desire and always have desired a fellowship *(Bund)* that is bound to no party. ... This group should be the vanguard for a more righteous social order, established in the prophetic spirit and in accord with the demand of the Kairos.[28]

The circle of the Religious Socialists in Berlin and the loosely organized followers who adopted their views represented such a *Bund,* and Tillich was their chief spokesman. Indeed, one can say that the group of his religious-socialist friends was for him the successor of the Wingolf fellowship, in spirit at least. Of course, it is also possible that the German Youth movement had some influence upon Tillich's idea of a *Bund.* The many small groups that constituted this movement applied this term to themselves.[29] During the First World War many *Bünde* were formed throughout Germany as a protest against the bourgeois establishment, and many of them regarded themselves as forerunners of a new social order. It is noteworthy that the student corporations stayed aloof from this youth movement, probably in most part because the informal and often spontaneously romantic ways of the new groups could not be blended or combined with the traditionalist rules and statutes of the student organizations. At any rate, there is no indication of Tillich's interest in joining the youth movement while he was a student and, later, a young minister, although its purposes certainly were congenial to him. In 1913 (12 and 13 October), thousands of young people held a festival at the *Hoher Meissner* in Thuringia. As the *Freideutsche Jugend* (Free German Youth) they issued a proclamation in which, among other things, they declared that:[30]

The Free German Young People want to shape their lives according to their own determination, out of their own responsibility and with inner truthfulness. United they stand for this freedom under all circumstances.[31]

In his own use of the term "Bund" Tillich may have combined what he himself had experienced in the Wingolf, what he had observed in the behavior of the Free German Youth, and what he was involved in when, after 1918, be became one of the organizers of Religious Socialism.

In 1936 and 1937, when in the face of the rise and progress of National Socialism he began to think of the possible end of the Protestant era and, in connection with his participation in the work of the Ecumenical Movement, to consider new ways by which a Christian social program could be actualized, he resorted again to the proposal of forming an "order" for this purpose. "The post-Protestant actualization of Christianity," he wrote, "must be brought about by a group which in the sociological form of a voluntary association *(Bund)* or "order" *(Orden)*, prepares the structure of what is to come. . . ."[33] He did not think that Christianity could be rendered more effective by the formation of a great, all-inclusive church; nor did he believe that the existing churches should retreat into a reservation or into the catacombs, as some people said; but he was convinced that a renewal could be brought about by the formation of "an order or a fellowship" which would aim to realize in itself the needed transformation, not as a sect but as the bearer of the Spirit.

When Tillich was in England in 1936, helping to prepare the Oxford Conference on Life and Work, he advocated this proposal everywhere with great fervor and urgency and he spoke about it also to J. H. Oldham, who was the organizer of the conference and its executive secretary. It was with an exaggeration that was typical of him that in his diary Tillich recorded Oldham's response in these words: "He says that he finds my idea of a religious order a thousand times more important than the whole Oxford Conference for which he is working day and night."[34]

Several years later, just after the Second World War had begun, he expressed again "the idea of an esoteric group which must prepare for the future."[35]

All this shows how deeply his thinking had been formed by membership in the fellowship of the *Wingolfsbund.* It was important for him for still another reason. It provided him with friendships that lasted until death put an end to them. One of them was of decisive significance for the development of Tillich's thought: that with Herman Schafft (1883–1959).

Tillich first met Schafft in the autumn of 1904 at a meeting of the Berlin Wingolf. They became close friends during the years that followed, particularly when they made common cause in the debates in the Halle Wingolf about the meaning and validity of the Christian principle for a student fellowship. They had much in common: both were ministers' sons and both were ardent and dedicated students of theology. Each of them was of a deeply romantic turn of mind. From the beginning Schafft, three years older than Tillich, assumed a position of authority in their relationship. Tillich thought of him as his "spiritual father,"[36] and Schafft readily assumed the role of guide and counselor. Tillich gladly followed his advice, especially when Schafft corrected him in his tendency to formulate exaggerated or extreme theological distinctions. Schafft liked to take the position of a mediator. When someone contrasted certain points too sharply and exclusively, he was wont to remark "*et . . . et*" (both . . . and). Yet he was open to new ideas and, being endowed with a warm and contagious pedagogic talent, he shared his enthusiasm for new discoveries with others.

The old Tillich remembered that he and his student friends were introduced by Schafft to Kierkegaard.[37] He recalled the deep impression Kierkegaard made upon his thinking, but unfortunately, he never indicated which one of Kierkegaard's books they read and discussed. In 1910, Tillich, Schafft, and others debated the problem of the Jesus of history on the basis of a paper by Tillich in which he summed up the results of his study of the works of Kierkegaard and Kähler and of the modern research in the life of Jesus. Schafft was unwilling to accept Tillich's findings because they were too critical of the teachings and practices of the church.

Schafft was not a conservative, but he wanted to preserve old traditions and he did so by interpreting them in such a way that they would make sense to people. He was a reformer who desired to revitalize old customs and conventions. For this reason, he took a deep interest in the German youth movement (he was one of the new Wingolfites who did so). In the course of time, he became an enthusiastic participant, particularly after the meeting of the Free German Youth at the *Hoher Meissner* in 1913. He adopted the ideals and customs that were characteristic of the youth movement. He loved and rediscovered folk songs and folk dances and was enthusiastic about the revitalized social life of the young people with their songfests, group discussions, and hikes through the countryside, especially when these culminated in the exploration of nature and the rediscovery of long-forgotten historical places.

Tillich did not fully share his friend's fervor. He hesitated to break with the conventions in which he had been brought up, but Schafft could easily arouse in him a romanticism about nature and an enthusiasm for a free, unbound life under the sky and in the open air. Tillich felt that Schafft knew how to combine spirit and vitality. He wrote about this in the manner so characteristic of him:

When we wandered through the hills and dales and came to some point from which he could show me the landscape at our feet and when I then exclaimed "You have led me to a seat of the absolute," a unity of spirit and vitality was manifest.[38]

When the First World War broke out, Schafft, unlike Tillich, volunteered for military service as an army chaplain. After the war he was active in the ministry, assuming special responsibility for the handicapped (deafmutes), for church social work, and for the religious education of the young. He also took on responsibilities for the reconciliation of the social classes. In particular he aimed to overcome the alienation of the industrial workers from the church. He became a religious socialist and aligned himself with the group around his friend Tillich. He adopted Tillich's analysis of the religious and social crisis of Western civilization and made good use of Tillich's slogans and central ideas concerning the kairos, the demonic, and the triad of autonomy, heteronomy, and theonomy. But he always spoke from within the church and on its behalf, whereas Tillich assumed a position on the boundary of the church. Both were theologically preoccupied with the problem of the justification of the doubter, and in this both probably were aware of their indebtedness to their teacher, Martin Kähler in Halle. Tillich learned a great deal from Schafft, particularly a fresh appreciation of the doctrine of the Holy Spirit. Indeed, one can say that Schafft stands behind Tillich's extensive discussion of the Spiritual Presence in the third volume of the *Systematic Theology*. Schafft probably was more concerned than Tillich with giving expression to the spontaneity of life under the Spirit, but both were agreed in the conviction that the life of a Christian must be marked neither by formlessness nor by legalism. In all this, Tillich remained the theoretician and analyst who displayed great skill in the use of abstract terms; while Schafft spoke as a practical theologian who relied on his experiences among the common people, but particularly on his membership in the one community to which he was specially attached. It was a settlement called *Neuwerk*, situated in Schlüchtern in Hesse. It was a product of the youth movement, an experimental socialist commune, which had come into being shortly after the First World War. Schafft was one of its founders and leaders and he edited a journal which reflected its ideals and practices.[39] He believed that, in time, this group and others like it would bring about a revitalization of the church and to this task he lent all his spiritual gifts and talents.[40]

Like Tillich, he was dismissed from his posts when the Nazis came to power. After their downfall, he was appointed to a high position in the Hessian ministry of education at Kassel. Tillich remained in warm touch with him and saw him regularly during his visits to Germany in 1948 and after. He felt that his lifelong friendship with Schafft was one of his main sources of strength.

A word must now be said about Tillich's university teachers, especially in view of the fact that he was very conscious of the importance of the teacher-pupil relationship in his own development. He himself regarded as his teacher anyone from whom he had learned something, even if he had never received direct instruction from him. Students who had taken a course from him and remarked on this to him in some fashion, became his "pupils," even if they could not recall specifically what they had heard in his classes. It is, of course, natural that men and women remember their teachers and how, directly or indirectly, they formed their minds. But Tillich regarded his relation to those of his teachers to whom he felt especially indebted as a personal bond.

The professor who, in the course of time, assumed the most direct responsibility for his studies was Wilhelm Lütgert (1867–1938), first professor of the New Testament and, from 1912 on, professor of systematic theology at Halle. He supervised Tillich's work for the degree of Licentiate in theology,[41] and he was his sponsor when Tillich applied for admission to the theological faculty as a teacher (with the title of *Privatdozent*). Thus Tillich was in a special sense Lütgert's student, but he did not enter into a close relationship with him. When he thought of himself as an alumnus of the University of Halle, he remembered first of all what he owed to Martin Kähler, who at Tillich's time was the senior of the theological faculty and about to retire, and to Fritz Medicus (1876–1956), a young instructor in philosophy who was beginning his academic career. One can say that Kähler was the one among his professors whom Tillich most admired and Medicus the one by whom he felt most encouraged, especially in philosophical thinking.

Kähler (1835–1912) was a systematic theologian who set himself apart from authoritarian orthodoxy as well as from liberal modernism. He regarded himself as a Bible theologian. As such he developed ideas in line with the teachings of the Protestant reformers, particularly Luther.

The basic theme of Kähler's theology was the doctrine of justification through faith by grace. His chief work was entitled "The Science of Christian doctrine presented on the basis of justification" (1883). It consisted of three parts: Christian Apologetics; Evangelical Dogmatics; and Theological Ethics. Kähler was an independent thinker. In his youth he had identified himself with the spirit of German classical and romantic philosophy and literature, especially Goethe. Later he was affected by the German evangelical revival movement of the mid-nineteenth century. Indeed, "he was converted in the literal sense of being turned around."[42] Under the influence of this awakening he advocated a strong Christocentrism in connection with personal piety, but he rejected all individualistic tendencies that were indifferent to or hostile to the church. At the end of his career, he won fame as the author of a lecture entitled "The So-Called Historical Jesus and the Biblical Christ of History" (1892).

The view he presented was as follows: The historical-critical interpretation of the gospels can provide no certain or absolutely dependable knowledge of Jesus of Nazareth. Therefore faith cannot be founded on so-called historical facts. It is impossible to establish relations with the historical Jesus as he was in himself; the biblical writings are not biographies but testimonies of faith. They cannot serve as sources for a "life of Jesus." They represent Jesus as the Christ or savior as the apostles saw him in faith. What the evangelists affirm to have experienced with and in Jesus can be understood only by faith, and this faith is a response to Jesus Christ as Peter and the other disciples proclaimed him.

As we shall see, this argument made a profound impression upon Paul Tillich; at first not in and by itself, but in connection with and through the force of Kähler's personality. Kähler was accustomed to lecture from a prepared manuscript; occasionally he dictated lessons to the students. He did not exactly captivate them when he proceeded in this way. But he overpowered them when he put his manuscript aside and spontaneously expounded the point he wished to impress upon their memory. By these digressions[43] Kähler obtained a lively response from his students.

Kähler was a faithful and convinced member of the Wingolf, and as such he frequently joined the Wingolf fraternity of Halle at their get-togethers. In 1905 Tillich was present at a specially memorable meeting with Kähler. He wrote his father a letter about it that breathes the excitement the old gentleman aroused in the minds of the young students:

Last Saturday we had a special evening meeting in order to observe Kähler's one hundredth semester.[44] Lütgert[45] and other professors were also present. Kähler delivered two powerful speeches. In the first one, he spoke of himself and his relation to the Wingolf. Among other things, he told the story of his conversion and we all were deeply moved. I have never heard anyone speak so intimately and inwardly. In the second speech, he dealt with the Wingolf and its nature. The following theme ran through it: *verbum stat, homo socors praeterfluit.* (The word stands firm and man merely passes by.)[46] Finally, he said that the meeting we were all attending was perhaps the last one he could spend with the Wingolf and that therefore he would leave that saying to us as his testament. Until now, I have not experienced anything greater in the Wingolf. All the other professors, even including those of Berlin, appeared to me as dwarfs and children in comparison with this great man.

It is not easy to specify Kähler's impact upon Tillich's thinking, chiefly because it was Tillich's habit to content himself with general expressions of gratitude toward anyone who had stimulated his thought. He hardly ever referred to a specific passage in the work of another.

On reading Kähler's books with the purpose of finding the connections between his ideas and those of Tillich, one comes upon certain uncommon phrases and formulations Tillich also frequently used. Thus the suspicion arises that Tillich took them over from Kähler, but this cannot be proved.

For example, one of Tillich's favorite terms was *Gehalt.* He used it often in his early writings in the sense of "import" as distinguished from *Inhalt* (content). We encounter the same distinction in Kähler's writings.[47] A similar observation can be made concerning the use of the phrase "unconditioned" or "unconditional." It is not as prominent in Kähler's writings as in Tillich's, but it appears in contexts which suggest that Tillich's use of the word which, by the way, was frequently employed by Kant and the Idealists, may be due to Kähler's influence upon him. For example, in discussing "the living God" in contrast to "the absolute" of Schelling's idealism, Kähler writes:

if one conceives the universal as the precondition *(Voraussetzung)* of everything determined, it appears as the unconditioned which conditions everything else. This translation of the presupposition of thought into the ground of being *(Daseinsgrund)* implies the identification of the indetermined and indeterminable unconditioned or, in other words, the simple, with "the supreme being." Thus everything determined is regarded (or signified) as something less, as something that in the last resort is not or ought not to be, while that which transcends everything real is considered as that which truly has being *(das wahrhaft Seiende)*.[48]

This terminology was certainly not the special property of Kähler, but one will not go wrong in thinking that the very fact that he used it must have been of importance to Tillich, who employed it throughout his life. In this connection, it should be noted that Kähler warned again and again that one should not think of God as a being among beings, as if he were an object,[49] and that particularly one should not speak of him as "the supreme being," a phrase Kähler called meaningless *(inhaltsleer)*.[50]

Late in life, Tillich once stated that what he had learned from Kähler "went deep into his subconscious." As he said this, he had in mind Kähler's definition of sin as "contradiction to essence" *(Wesenswidrigkeit)*,[51] but Kähler's subtle influence can be discerned also in many other ideas.

We refer especially to Kähler's Biblicism. What Tillich has to say about the character and authority of the Bible as God's word appears to be a reproduction of his teacher's interpretation. According to Kähler the Bible *"documents"* the preaching about Jesus as the Christ which called the apostolic church into being.[52] Tillich, like Kähler, regards the Bible as "the basic source of systematic theology because it is the original *document* about the events on which the Christian church is founded"; and its "documentary character is identical with the fact that it contains the original witness of those, i.e., the apostles, who participated in the revealing events."[53] The Bible exhibits "theologically inter- preted facts," which are not properly understood if they are treat- ed either in terms of sheer historical givenness or on the assump- tion of a miraculous literal inspiration. The biblical theologian must use all available exegetical tools in order to let the Bible speak for itself; at the same time, he must let it speak to him and his situation in such a way that the biblical message becomes a matter of ultimate concern to him. He thus "unites philology and devo- tion in dealing with the biblical texts."[54] As Tillich goes on to characterize that biblical theology which systematic theology needs as "historical-critical" without any restrictions and, at the same time, as devotional-interpretative, taking account of the fact that it deals with matters of ultimate concern, he appears to have in mind the work of Martin Kähler. For Kähler intended first of all to be nothing but a Bible theologian. It is remarkable that his pupil Paul Tillich strove mightily to preserve this kind of theology even while he constructed a theological system along philosophical (on- tological) lines.

Tillich himself had chiefly two things in mind[55] when he ex- plained what he had learned from Kähler, namely justification and Christology. His upbringing in the Lutheran tradition readily enabled him to understand Kähler's interpretation of justification which stressed on the one hand, the assertion that all human claims before God and every identification with God must be denied and, on the other hand, the idea that man's estrangement from God, his guilt and despair, are overcome through the para- doxical judgment that before God the sinner is just,[56] that he is accepted despite the fact that he is unacceptable. What impressed Tillich most, and became a significant part of his own teaching, was Kähler's extension of this doctrine so that it applied also to human thought generally and particularly to the situation of mod- ern man between faith and doubt: Not only human acts but also human thoughts stand under the divine "No." To boast of possess- ing the truth is just as sinful as to lay claim to moral perfection. An insistence on orthodoxy which rules out doubt or uncertainty is intellectual pharisaism. It makes faith dependent upon an intel- lectual "work,"[57] just as moral pharisaism regards moral achieve- ments as a precondition of faith. No one can say of himself without being assailed by doubt that he is in the situation of faith. Yet he is not lost, because just as forgiveness is not actualized without repentance, so having the truth is not actualized except through doubt in so far as it is a search for truth. Thus the doubter too is justified as he sees that the truth which he seeks and the meaning for which he yearns are not the aim but the precondition of his doubt.[58]

Tillich here agreed with Kähler, who made a deep impression on him (and also upon his friends, particularly Schafft): as an old man Kähler confessed that he was still plagued by doubt and uncertainty about many articles of faith,[59] but that he was certain that justification implied not only the victory over sin but also the triumph over doubt. Here Tillich went beyond Kähler by injecting into this discussion of justification in relation to doubt the philosophical argument of Augustine that "in the situation of doubt the truth from which one feels separated is present in so far as in every doubt the formal affirmation of truth as truth is presupposed."[60] In other words, there is no "No" without a preceding "Yes"[61] or, as Tillich liked to point out, there is no atheism.

This basic principle was one of Tillich's fundamental ideas. He affirmed it not only in his philosophy but also in his theology; it was impossible for him to separate theological from philosophical questions. Indeed, he dealt with theological questions as if they could best be answered by means of philosophical analysis and argument. This is demonstrated in his treatment of justification in relation to doubt. The question was originally proposed to him by Kähler as a theological one; the answer Tillich gave to it was inspired by philosophical considerations which were somewhat removed from Kähler's concerns. But the fact that Tillich returned again and again to a discussion of the problem of doubt shows how deeply Kähler had affected him[62] and how deeply he himself was involved in doubt.

In the Introduction to *The Protestant Era*, Tillich shows, by way of an autobiographical characterization of his early essays on Protestantism, what influence Kähler's treatment of the idea of justification had on him and on his friends. "The step I myself took in these years," he writes,"

was the insight that ... not only he who is in sin but also he who is in doubt, even of doubt about God, need not separate us from God. There is faith in every serious doubt, namely the faith in the truth as such, even if the only Truth we can express is our lack of truth ... So the paradox got hold of me that he who seriously denies God, affirms him. Without it I would not have remained a theologian.[63]

Tillich goes on to indicate why these ideas (and what he believed was implied by them) had "immense" consequences for him. He was led to realize "that there is no place *beside* the divine, there is no possible atheism." Then he added, "At the time of their discovery and ever since then, these ideas gave me personally a strong feeling of relief."[64]

Tillich gives one the clear impression that he wished to suggest here how the teaching on justification by faith and not by works became an existential truth for him and in what sense he became a "conscious Protestant." Addressing himself to the difficulties of faith in his own time, he spoke like Luther:

You cannot reach God by the work of right thinking or by a sacrifice of the intellect or by submission to strange authorities, such as the doctrines of the church and the Bible. You cannot and you are not even asked to try it. Neither works of piety nor works of morality nor works of the intellect establish unity with God ... But just as you are justified as a *sinner* (though unjust, you are just), so in the status of *doubt* you are in the status of truth. And if all this comes together and you are desperate about the meaning of life, the seriousness of your despair is the expression of the meaning in which you are still living.[65]

The most important evidence of Kähler's influence on Tillich, however, is his Christology. We have already mentioned the fact that Kähler wished to be regarded as a Bible theologian. His major concern as a professor of systematic theology, who as such lectured regularly also on the interpretation of the New Testament, was to achieve a comprehensive knowledge of the history of the effect *(Wirkung)* and authority *(Geltung)* of the Bible. Like those German Pietist theologians (Richard Rothe of Heidelberg, J. T. Beck of Tübingen, F. A. G. Tholuck of Halle, and also J. C. K. Hofmann of Erlangen) under whom he had studied and with whom he allied himself, he aimed at the construction of a "positive" theology that would be free, not only from the "arbitrariness" and "subjectivism" of the critical-historical exegesis of the Scriptures, but also from the "ballast" of a legalistic Biblicism based on the doctrine of verbal inspiration. He once said that he was chiefly concerned to demonstrate that the Bible could not have been invented and that, for the same reason it was impossible to replace it or find a substitute for it.[66] As a biblical theologian Kähler was opposed both to dogmatism and historicism. "Dogma," he said, "needs to be historically interpreted and, at the same time, transformed in a modern way," but it must not be "dissolved or abolished by means of historical criticism."[67]

In this context, Kähler developed and formulated his argument *against* the quest of the so-called Jesus of history and *for* the historical, biblical Christ. He denied that the gospels were written in order to serve as sources for a scientifically (i.e., historically) designed biography of Jesus. Their purpose, he said, is to arouse faith in Jesus through a vivid proclamation of his saving activity.[68] The gospels and, indeed, the entire New Testament do not present a biography of Jesus, but a "picture" of him as Christ or Savior. Jesus himself was the author of this picture in so far as he evoked in his disciples faith in his saving power. This faith does not depend on a Christological dogma nor on Jesus in so far as he is a historiographical construct,[69] but on the apostolic picture of Christ.

Kähler's argument was impressive! The so-called "Life of Jesus research" and, at the same time, a merely traditionalist dogmatism concerning the figure of Christ, were rejected, while the biblical picture of Christ was affirmed as the basis of the utterly unique character and authority of the Bible. The biblical books, Kähler said, proclaim and celebrate the historical fact of Christ as testified to in the faith of his disciples.[70]

Instead of referring to "Jesus" or "Jesus Christ" or even "Christ," Kähler preferred to point to the *"picture of Christ."* He may have done this under the influence of Martin Luther, who in the pulpit was wont to direct the attention of his hearers to the biblical picture of Christ, admonishing them to "impress" or "imprint" this picture upon their hearts in order to represent it to themselves.[71] In a similar way Kähler pointed to the picture of Christ "apprehended in faith" or "preached in faith," a picture which, he said, "conveys a confession of faith." He regarded Christ himself as the author of this picture, and even went so far as to declare that it was a "dubious undertaking to distinguish in any way the historical Christ from his biblical picture."[72]

Tillich speaks similarly of the "picture of Christ." In his view, this picture is the result of the transforming power which Jesus as the Christ exercised upon his first disciples, and it still has transforming power in those who in faith accept him as their savior or healer.[73]

It is very probable that Tillich formed this conception originally under the influence of Kähler, but it also bears the imprint of other sources.

There is, first of all, Luther's rejection of the interpretation of the figure of Jesus as a law-giver or moral teacher. Luther repeated again and again: "Christ is not another Moses," and Tillich emphatically shared this view.[74] He wrote:

Every legalistic or didactic interpretation of the figure of Jesus is dull. At this point, my idea of the New Being originated. It was at first nothing else but the attempt to think in Christological terms. If one regards Christ as a new teacher or legislator, one can accept him or reject him . . . the picture of him which has imprinted itself upon his followers and about the historical accuracy of which we neither can or must know anything, is the picture of a real personal life which draws those who participate in it into the sphere of something new.[75]

Here, so Tillich remarks, Christology began to make sense to him because the idea of the New Being furnished him a key to it. "Until then," he writes, "like most younger theologians in those years at the beginning of this century, I fluctuated between the superficiality of a theology that called itself liberal and the absurdity of an inflexible orthodoxy."[76]

A further important factor in Tillich's conception of the picture of Christ was the Platonic idea of kowledge through participation. He was persuaded that the Christian "participates" in the New Being which is manifested in the picture of Jesus the Christ. This participation is possible because of Christ's own share in God, which "has a universality in which everyone can participate."[77] Moreover, the picture of Christ symbolizes the savior. Like all symbols, it participates in what it symbolizes. Indeed, as a symbol, picture, or icon it has the same power and effectiveness as that which it represents.[78]

Tillich acknowledged his indebtedness to Kähler for his Christological views and he stated specifically that he shared Kähler's skepticism about the range and validity of historical knowledge,[79] but he never quoted Kähler directly. The earliest available evidence of his Christological thought along the lines of Kähler's ideas is a carefully outlined paper on "Christian certainty and the historical Jesus," presented in the form of 128 theses,[80] which Tillich prepared for a conference of younger theologians that had been convened by his friend Schafft in 1911. The discussion lasted for several days. Much later, Tillich recalled that his formulations had been rather "radical." He denied that historical certainty about Jesus could ever be reached, and argued that faith could therefore not be based on historical knowledge.[81] He affirmed that the basis of Christianity is the acknowledgment of Jesus as the Christ and that this faith is produced by the impact of the biblical picture of Jesus Christ upon men.[82] The whole argument culminated in the following sentence.[83] "The proposition that uncertainty about the historical Jesus is unavoidable is the ultimate consequence of the doctrine of justification, for it liberates us from the law of a double faith, namely faith in the historical Jesus and faith in God made manifest in Jesus." Tillich meant to say that because historical knowledge about Jesus can never be certain, the Christian faith cannot be based upon the person of the historical Jesus. For the same reason it is also impossible to absolutize Jesus and to see in him the personification of God. Thus an open and unrestrained acknowledgment of historical uncertainty, Tillich maintained, invalidates any faith that is based on heteronomous authority—or, as he formulated the matter: "This proposition that uncertainty about the historical Jesus is unavoidable is also the final consequence of the liberation from the pope; conversely to establish faith in the historical Jesus will inevitably bring about a return to the papacy" (i.e., to heteronomous authority.)[84]

It is obvious that Tillich here defended the teaching of Kähler. It is equally clear that he went beyond Kähler, not only by coupling the skepticism concerning historical knowledge about Jesus with the rejection of any absolutization of Jesus but also by setting the whole discussion in the context of a philosophical and theological analysis of freedom and authority or autonomy and heteronomy.

These ideas were later developed in several directions, but the structure of Tillich's Christology remained the same throughout his career. A few very important themes were added under the influence of Schelling, as we shall see.

A good statement of Tillich's basic view can be found in the following quotation from *The Dynamics of Faith,* the book that may be regarded as the best popular summary of his theology.[85]

Historical research has made it obvious that there is no way to get with more than a degree of probability at the historical events which have produced the biblical picture of the Christ . . . [but] faith can say that the reality which is manifest in the New Testament picture of Jesus as the Christ has saving power for those who are grasped by it, no matter how much or how little can be traced to the historical figure who is called Jesus of Nazareth."[86]

Taking here essentially the same position as Kähler, Tillich went beyond his teacher by stressing two fundamental points: he intensified the skepticism concerning the historical Jesus of Nazareth and he emphasized more strongly the transforming power emanating from the biblical picture of Jesus Christ. Characteristic of this is the way by which he opens the central discussion on "the reality of the Christ" in the second volume of his *Systematic Theology.*[87]

Christianity is what it is through the affirmation that Jesus of Nazareth . . . is actually the Christ, namely he who brings the new state of things, the New Being . . . Christianity was born, not with the birth of the man who is called "Jesus," but in the moment in which one of his followers was driven to say to him, "Thou art the Christ." And Christianity will live as long as there are people who repeat this assertion, for "Christ is not the Christ without those who receive him as the Christ."[88]

Tillich then goes on to present a many-sided discussion of great intricacy about the relation between faith and history. He concludes with the following statement, which clearly seems to be written in Kähler's spirit:

In all respects the New Testament is the document where the picture of Jesus as the Christ appears in its original and basic form. All other documents, from the Apostolic Fathers to the writings of present-day theologians, are dependent upon this original document. In itself, the New Testament is an integral part of the event which it documents . . . and upon which the Christian faith rests.[89]

Tillich's theological thought must thus be seen as constituting a biblical and Christocentric legacy from Kähler. This is remarkable in view of the fact that, in contrast to Kähler, it is also philosophical through and through.

Even in his boyhood Tillich had been occupied with philosophical speculations and, as a young student barely twenty years of age, he displayed philosophical skills that won him the admiration of fellow students. These gifts were further developed under the influence of his teacher in philosophy at the University of Halle.

Just as Kähler deepened Tillich's inherited Lutheran faith, so the philosopher Fritz Medicus strengthened and focused the philosophical interests Tillich had earlier begun to cultivate under the influence of his father. When he entered the university, he was acquainted with the history of philosophy, but he had a special knowledge of the writings of Kant. He also had an interest in J. G. Fichte whose "Theory of Science" he had read through and made his own. In Halle, between 1905 and 1907, he became attracted to Medicus who was then a *Privatdozent* of philosophy and engaged in research on Fichte. In 1905, Medicus published thirteen lectures on this thinker and in 1908–1912, he edited a selection of Fichte's writings in six volumes, adding a biography. When Tillich became a member of his seminar he and Medicus became personal friends, and quite naturally he identified himself with the interests of his teacher. Gradually Medicus opened up to him the whole world of German Idealism, leading him first to Fichte and then to Schelling.[90]

In the winter semester 1907–08 Tillich completed his formal education. He no longer registered for university lecture courses or seminars. Instead, he began to prepare himself for the final examinations. He decided to take the hurdle of the theological board examination before the Brandenburg Consistory of the Prussian Evangelical Church first. He passed it early in 1909. The requirements he had to fulfill consisted of an oral test in philosophy, exegesis, and dogmatics and the preparation of assigned theological assays. The subjects given to him were "Johannine Theology" and "The sources and norms of theological knowledge." In order to complete this task, Tillich undertook a thorough review of all he had learned so far. He worked through the textbooks of the major fields of theology, paying special attention to the differences between the several theological parties and schools; but like Kähler he avoided any identification with extremes of either the theological right or left. For a while he preferred to hold a mediating position between orthodoxy and liberalism especially insofar as the authority of the Bible was concerned. In this connection, he obtained a number of important insights.

At the same time, he turned to radical New Testament studies. He read Albert Schweitzer's work on the quest of the historical Jesus and found reinforcement for his own view of the historical Jesus, to which he adhered until the end of his life. Later, in the early twenties, he read with similar approval R. Bultmann's critical analysis of the literary and historical sources of the gospels (*Die Geschichte der synoptischen Tradition*, Göttingen: Vandenhoeck u. Ruprecht, 1921). He now became fully acquainted with the interpretation of the biblical books by the methods used in the study of the history of religion. He was impressed particularly by the work of Hermann Gunkel, who had recently published a commentary on the Book of Genesis in which he showed that the tales contained in that first book of the Old Testament and in the poetry of the Book of Psalms can be understood best against the background of ancient oriental myths and legends. All this fascinated Tillich. He adopted the new method and henceforth insisted that the Bible must first of all be interpreted historically and not literally or dogmatically. Gunkel remained a favorite of his throughout his career.[91]

He also plunged into other, primarily historical studies. He acquired a thorough knowledge of the history of Christian doctrine, most probably through a careful re-reading of the *History of Dogma* by Friedrich Loofs, one of the earliest pupils and friends of Adolf Harnack. Loofs was a specialist in the history of the doctrine of the Trinity, and at the same time an expert in the history of Lutheran doctrine. Tillich had taken Loofs's course at Halle without getting very excited about it, perhaps in part because Kähler rejected Harnack's and Loofs's interpretation of the Hellenistic origin and development of Christian dogma and frequently engaged in polemics against Harnack's school.

It is interesting to observe how Tillich was affected by these arguments. Although he esteemed Harnack as the foremost representative of German theological and humanistic learning, he continued to be swayed by Kähler's criticism of him. He judged that Harnack was influenced too much by the rational principles and moral attitudes of the Enlightenment of the eighteenth century.

In the course of preparing himself for the final examination, Tillich encountered the writings of Ernst Troeltsch (1865–1923) and became aware of Troeltsch's leadership in Protestant liberalism. His concern for a historical rather than a dogmatic understanding of Protestantism, and his critical assessment of the interrelations between Protestant religiousness and modern cultural life, made a deep impression upon Tillich. This impression became stronger when, in 1911 and 1912, Troeltsch began to publish his *Collected Writings,* in which he demonstrated in the form of lengthy historical essays and monographs the entanglement of Christianity in the various movements of Western civilization.

In addition to Troeltsch's philosophical and theological writings, Tillich read the latter's remarkable cultural history of Protestantism, first published in 1906 and reissued three years later in an enlarged edition.[92] We cannot say when he became acquainted with Troeltsch's *Soziallehren,* that grand analysis of the impact of Christianity upon society and conversely of the influence of social-political movements and conditions upon Christian social teachings and attitudes. We know that after he had read the work he considered himself one of Troeltsch's "students."[93] His own studies on the theology of culture and particularly his program of Religious Socialism are at least partially the result of this attachment to Troeltsch.

It was characteristic of Tillich that he did not study in order to acquire learning, but in order to achieve understanding. What mattered to him was not erudition, but comprehension. He acquired knowledge and understanding by letting ideas and persons lay hold of him or, to use a favorite term of his, letting himself "be grasped" by them. Then he formulated his own response to them and this became the basis of further inquiry and analysis.

What he liked best was to debate: he would adopt some point

or insight suggested and combine it with the basic view he had formed and thought through before he had become engaged in the inquiry. Thus his thinking was fed by various sources and became many-sided. It was in constant motion from question to answer and from answer to question.

In this setting, friends became highly significant for Tillich, for they served as partners in those debates, either in direct, personal encounters or in correspondence. Almost all friends of Tillich were such debating partners. Hermann Schafft was one of the earliest. In 1908, while Tillich crammed for the "First Examination" and worked on the required papers, Friedrich Büchsel (1883–1945),[94] who like Tillich was a pupil of Medicus but aspired to become a biblical scholar, was one of his chief companions and correspondents.[95] In 1908 or thereabouts Tillich first met Emanuel Hirsch (1888–1972), who soon became an intimate friend. He was a debater and critic of extraordinary range and acumen. At about the same time, Kurt Leese (1887–1965) entered Tillich's circle. Among Tillich's friends, he was the one who identified himself most closely, although not uncritically, with Tillich's philosophical outlook. When, in 1909, Tillich first assumed professional responsibilities as a minister and theologian, at the same time working on his theses for higher academic degrees, a young minister and educator, Richard Wegener, was at his side as his mentor and critic. The two were constantly engaged in exploratory discussion. Indeed, they finally decided to organize study groups for members of the Berlin intelligentsia, believing that through an exchange of opinion a better understanding of Christianity could be achieved.

From January 1909 until August 1912, Tillich was kept busy with practical church work and with the preparation of papers assigned to him as part of his examinations. On 27 July 1912, he passed his second church board examination and, in August of the same year, he was ordained to the ministry. In the meantime, he had also definitely decided to earn the university degree which would enable him to enter an academic career. Even as a student he had occasionally thought of becoming a professor of philosophy or theology. He continued to waver about his choice of a profession, but despite this uncertainty he fulfilled the requirements for the Doctorate in Philosophy (22 August 1910) and then proceeded to obtain the equivalent degree in theology, that of a Licentiate of Theology (16 December 1911).[96]

All this was to have momentous consequences for him because, in preparing the required dissertations, he became thoroughly steeped in the thought of the philosopher F. W. J. Schelling, to whom Medicus had first directed him and for whom he felt a deep affinity as soon as he began to study his works.[97] Much later, at the end of his life, he told his students in Chicago, "I recall the unforgettable moment when by chance I came into possession of the very rare first edition of the Collected Works of Schelling in a bookstore on my way to the University of Berlin. I had no money but I bought it anyway, and this spending of nonexistent money was probably more important than all the other nonexistent or sometime existing money that I have spent. For what I learned from Schelling became determinative of my own philosophical and theological development."[98]

Indeed, throughout Tillich's life Schelling remained for him his "great teacher in philosophy and theology."[99] At first it was the philosophy of nature, i.e., the interpretation of nature as visible spirit, which fascinated him. Later Schelling's so-called positive philosophy, its existential overtones and its "higher empiricism," assumed great importance for him. Early in 1918, when his duties as an army chaplain slackened for a while, permitting him in leisure hours to turn to philosophical studies, he wrote to his friend E. Hirsch:

I still remember, how, overwhelmed by the magic mood of spring that pervades the philosophy of nature, I was seized by the gloomy power of the "positive philosophy" and how deeply I was affected in my religious feeling by the great sentence which sets the tone of this entire philosophy, *Deitas est dominatio dei*,[100] [Deity is divine lordship]. Then reason took over and I proceeded to interpret Schelling II in terms of Schelling I; after this I left him and went to Hegel and then to Nietzsche.[101]

This statement must not be understood to mean that Tillich forsook Schelling in favor of Hegel or Nietzsche. He read Hegel avidly in order to understand on what grounds Schelling criticized Hegel's "essentialism." Many years later, as professor of philosophy in Frankfurt, Tillich again paid special attention to Hegel. He devoted the whole winter semester 1931–32 to him both in a lecture course and in seminars. Tillich's thinking was then permeated with Hegel's basic ideas; in particular the themes of love and life with which the young Hegel had dealt extensively in his theological writings attracted Tillich's attention again and again. Life is constituted, so he asserted, by knowledge and love, the "forms of union of the separated who belong to each other and want to reunite."[102] Life is marked by the rhythm of original union, separation, and reunion; by the rhythm of unity, estrangement, and reconciliation. These ideas, carried as a perennial theme in the neoplatonic tradition of philosophic thought, occur throughout Tillich's philosophy. They show to what extent he was dependent upon Hegel, despite the fact that he rejected the latter's idealism. He felt that it failed to come to terms with the destructive realities of existence and that it was unable to deal with the demonic powers of life and especially with the forces of oppression and injustice.[103] One can see here also how Tillich, in drawing the consequences from this judgment, could adopt the Marxist criticism of Hegel.

It is equally noteworthy that Tillich himself remained an idealist, at least as far as the theory of knowledge was concerned. "I am epistemologically an idealist if idealism means the assertion of the identity of thought and being," he said, " . . . Nor can I deny that there is a correspondence between reality and the human spirit which is probably expressed most adequately in the concept of 'meaning' . . . When idealism elaborates the categories that give meaning to the various realms of existence, it seeks to fulfill that task which is the only justification for philosophy."[104]

Schelling, he felt, was deeply aware of the limitation of idealistic doctrines when he reasoned that "reality is the manifestation of pure essence as well as of its contradiction" and "that human existence in particular exhibits the contradiction of essence." Tillich recognized these aspects of Schelling's thought as soon as he became fully familiar with it, and he sensed their importance for a critical evaluation of German Idealism in the context of the history of ideas; but he felt confirmed in his estimate of the existentialist elements in Schelling only when he became fully acquainted with Nietzsche (1917) and when the existentialism of modern art, especially in expressionism, began to intrigue him.[105]

From then on he tended to interpret Schelling as a fountain-head of a way of thinking he sometimes characterized as *Lebensphilosophie* and which, so he believed, represented a revolt against the objectification and reification of human value in modern civilization.[106]

At any rate, Tillich became a Schellingian. He read Schelling's works carefully and eagerly and made every effort to understand them. He patiently thought through Schelling's philosophical arguments and became steeped in his thought. He prepared for his own use a syllabus[107] of Schelling's ideas, which served him as a ready index and compendium. On this basis, he prepared his two dissertations, but he went further: throughout his life he carried in his subconsciousness the structure of Schelling's thought; he kept alive the understanding he had obtained of it and he adhered to the original estimate he had formed of it.

In a lecture he delivered in Stuttgart at the observance of the centennial of Schelling's death, Tillich declared:

He was *the* teacher for me, even though the beginning of my university studies and the year of his death are separated by exactly fifty years.[108]

At all times his basic ideas have been of help to me in many different fields. As my own thought developed I have never forgotten my dependence upon Schelling. My work on the problems of systematic theology would have been impossible without him. In the years of my intensive preoccupation with him, his picture imprinted itself so deeply on my mind, that I cannot do anything else today than to speak to you out of the structure of this picture.[109]

The effect of Tillich's first thorough reading and study of Schelling's philosophy was that it came to determine the organization and content of his own thought. He often referred to Schelling, but he seldom quoted him directly or literally. He had him in mind, however, in all he thought and taught; and his basic understanding of him remained the same throughout the years,[110] beginning with his dissertations: his philosophical thesis, "The Construction of the History of Religion in Schelling's Positive Philosophy. Its presuppositions and principles" (1910); and his theological thesis, "Mysticism and Guilt Consciousness in Schelling's Philosophical Development" (1912).[111]

Each of these writings deals with Schelling's mature philosophy or, as it is now commonly referred to in Germany, his *Spät-*

philosophie.[112] One cannot say that Tillich created the themes he chose for his dissertation with utmost clarity, but he certainly displayed comprehensive acquaintance with Schelling's thought, and this remained his principal resource throughout his life.

After his ordination on 18 August 1912, Tillich became an assistant minister in the Church of the Redeemer *(Erlöserkirche)* in Berlin north. His friend Richard Wegener had in the meantime accepted a position of *Jugendpastor* (minister of youth) in Berlin east. The two continued the friendship begun several years earlier in Lichtenrade. Wegener specialized more and more in music and educational work, while Tillich combined his ecclesiastical duties with philosophical studies.

In the course of time both were led to realize that the churches they served were in deep trouble because they did not effectively reach the people who were separated from the spiritual tradition by a vast chasm. The lower classes had given up their connection with the churches because they had come increasingly under the influence of the socialist parties and their hostility against the feudalist-capitalist ruling classes. The people of the middle classes were linked to the churches through the conventionality of pietistic religiousness and dogmatic orthodoxy, but they were unable to relate the Christian faith effectively or meaningfully to the thought-forms of modern civilization. They had first encountered these in school and most adopted them for themselves through literature and the arts, through newspapers and journals, and particularly through work in factories and offices, and not least through membership in voluntary associations of many kinds. They had become estranged from ecclesiastical traditions and conventions. They no longer spoke or understood the language of the leaders, preachers, and teachers of the church. The upper classes, closely linked to the monarchical governments and the institutions and establishments of landed privilege, inherited wealth, and elitism, regarded the churches as one of the main safeguards of their power and therefore protected them, confirming them in their conservative attitudes and their opposition to social change. They did not understand the need to build bridges between Christianity and the modern mind.

Early in his ministry Paul Tillich had come to the conclusion that the vocabulary of ecclesiastical speech had to be changed if a fruitful communication between pulpit and pew was to be achieved. On the basis of his own experience he had come to feel that certain key words and phrases of theology and religion should be banished from use in the churches for long periods of time, until their original meaning could possible be recovered for the benefit of all. Tillich advocated this strategy in his classroom throughout his career. In academic as well as popular lectures he made it a practice to explain technical terms by analysis and interpretation of their etymology. For the same reason he emphasized the symbolic nature of language and he never grew tired of saying that the language of religion is symbolical.

All this became existentially important for Tillich in the latter part of the year 1912. Having completed his formal education, he felt compelled to come to a decision about his future. Apparently, he proposed to his superiors that they give him a full ministerial appointment to the church where he was then serving as an assistant *(Hilfsprediger)*, but he withdrew this application[113] because he had finally made up his mind to choose an academic career. For this purpose, he proceeded to negotiate with the theological faculty at Halle for qualification as a university lecturer *(Privatdozent);* but, at the same time, he considered the possibility of staying in the practical ministry as an "apologist." His conversation with Harnack[114] probably concerned these alternate plans.

For sometime Tillich and Wegener had carried on discussions about doing work as church apologists. They finally resolved to secure an appointment as full time apologists assigned to the entire city of Berlin and not merely to local congregations or individual church districts. In December 1912 Tillich personally submitted such a plan to the president of the Consistory (the highest administrative office of the Evangelical Church in Berlin). Wegener spoke of founding an "order of apologists" *(einen Apologeten-Orden).* One time at least the two friends translated their plan into action: in the period from January until March 1913 they organized "theological" discussion groups in private homes, situated in private parts of Berlin. Each of these met fortnightly to consider ideas that were presented to them in a series of lectures. The meetings began around 8 P.M. and closed at about 11:30 P.M. Paul Tillich was the main speaker and discussion leader. He presented five different lectures four times each at the different meetings. The entire program consisted of the following lectures and discussions: (1) The Historical Antecedents of Present-Day Thought; (2) The Courage of seeking the Truth; (3) The Objections of Skepticism; (4) Aesthetic and Religious Mysticism; (5) Mysticism and Guilt Consciousness; (6) Redemption; (7) Religion and Art.

Wegener assumed responsibility for the lectures and discussions on doubt; and Pastor Eduard Le Seur, an assistant minister in the suburb of Lichterfelde, who later became one of Berlin's most effective preachers, dealt with the theme of artistic and religious mysticism.[115]

These *Vernunft-Abende*, as Tillich and Wegener called them, were quite successful, at least in Tillich's own estimate. He included this judgment in a report he drew up and probably submitted to his ecclesiastical superiors.[116] With the assistance of Wegener he also prepared a lengthy paper entitled "Church Apologetics," a detailed proposal and program for apologetic work.[117] Perhaps he hoped that the plan would be officially adopted; but it was not. We do not know whether it was seriously considered as a practical possibility. One can understand why it was not translated into action, for whatever apologetic work was being done in the German evangelical churches at the time was part of an exceedingly variegated but insufficiently organized activity of social work concerned primarily with relief and welfare, commonly known as home missions *(Innere Mission)*. After World War I, bold and enterprising men, who were assigned the task of reorganizing the former so-called state churches, established the "Central Committee of Home Missions." In 1921 this body founded "The Central Office for Apologetics" in Spandau, near Berlin. Several of Tillich's proposals then became reality, particularly that which concerned the communication of the gospel to educated people who were alienated from the church.

This problem was uppermost in the mind of the young Tillich shortly after he had entered the ministry. Then and later, indeed, he regarded himself as an apologist who correlated modern ideas with Christian truth seeking answers to questions that troubled the minds of people who had been raised and trained in the traditions of Western civilization, but who were no longer sure of their faith. At the end of his career he declared to American students what he had affirmed directly and indirectly in hundreds of formal and informal lectures throughout the years:

I presuppose in my theological thinking the entire history of Christian thought until now and I consider the attitude of people who are in doubt or estrangement or opposition to everything ecclesiastical and religious, including Christianity. And I must speak to them. *My work is with those who ask questions* and for them I am here.[118]

He believed that he was called to the work of a Christian apologist, in the sense that he practiced "the art of answering [questions]."[119] He consciously gave his theological system the character not of "proclamation," in the manner of Karl Barth, but of "apologetics." Because he intended to "answer theologically the question implied in the human situation," he formulated an "answering theology" using what he called the "method of correlation" as a way of uniting message and situation.[120]

The consistency with which Tillich developed his thought is certainly remarkable: ideas and plans which he first conceived and formulated as a twenty-six-year old, standing on the threshold of his professional career, remained valid for him until the last year of his long life. The goals he envisaged in his beginnings remained essentially the same throughout his career.

In his Memorandum of 1913 he distinguished between theoretical and practical apologetics:

Theoretical *[wissenschaftliche]* apologetics classifies the theological system in terms of method and content as a part of the general system of knowledge and thus establishes the right of theology to be regarded as a science. Practical apologetics, on the other hand, proceeds by way of dialectical thought from any prevailing contravention of truth to the Christian truth.[121]

Thus theoretical apologetics is a philosophical inquiry, while practical apologetics represents theological discipline.

The subject of the "system of knowledge" (or of the sciences) occupied Tillich's thinking for a long time. He chose to treat it in its entirety in his first major book, which was published in 1923 under the title *Das System der Wissenschaften nach Gegenständen und Methoden*. This work did not receive much attention and did not become influential.[122] But it was highly important for Tillich himself. It was representative of his plan to construct a theological system in the context of the whole range of the scientific pursuit of knowledge.

In order to convey a sense of what Tillich attempted to communicate to the participants of the *Vernunft-Abende,* a word must now be said about the papers he presented there. Each one of them was clearly outlined and organized and contained a wealth of material relating to historical thought and to contemporary discussion. The lecturer addressed himself to skeptics and seekers. It was his purpose to encourage them in their quest. Confidently believing that, through disciplined thinking, truth can be found, he urged his audience to formulate basic concepts and learn how to defend them as valid. He spoke eloquently of the "courage to truth" *(Mut zur Wahrheit).* The warmth and urgency of his words gave the impression that he himself was existentially involved in this. "Whoever has the courage to say there is no truth," he explained,

has obviously the courage to affirm at least one truth. And if this one truth that there is no truth, is not to be taken as an arbitrary assertion, he must give reasons for it thus indicating that he presupposed criteria for what is true or false; in other words: doubt on principle invalidates itself. . . . The awareness of being involved in a never ending opposition to the eternal spirit carries within itself the certainty of being in complete and unqualified communion with truth. The courage to accept this "nevertheless" *[den Mut zu diesem dennoch]* is the highest achievement of the courage to truth. In other words, courage to truth is the courage, despite endless doubt, to become unified with living truth itself.[123]

This conviction had been formed in Tillich's mind during his university years under the influence of Kähler and as the result of debates with Schafft and other friends. He gave expression to it again and again in his books, essays, and lectures, for it constituted his basic certitude, spiritually and intellectually.

Another lecture bears the title "Mysticism and Guilt Consciousness." One is led to expect a summary of Tillich's theological dissertation, which was published under the same title and contained an analysis of Schelling's philosophy of religion. But in this lecture Tillich limited himself to a consideration of various types of mysticism (nature mysticism, cultural, social, aesthetic, and intellectual mysticism, and, finally, religious mysticism) and the principles that contradict them. Thus nature mysticism, the experience of unity with nature, is seen as contradicted by ugliness, pain, and death; and cultural mysticism, i.e., the sense of unity with one's cultural-technological achievements (Tillich mentions the construction and operation of intricate and complicated machines like ocean liners and railroad stations) as disturbed by the pangs of conscience that are aroused by the cost of such enterprises in men and materials. Finally, religious mysticism, the experience of unity with God the "absolute spirit," is first seen as the acme of bliss and then as marred by the limitation and finiteness of all human experience. This entire discussion is infused with Schelling's spirit and that of Plotinus.

The mood that then permeated Tillich's thought is well expressed by him in the following reference to Henrick Steffens:[124]

Steffens's account of how with greatest intensity and tears in his eyes he read without interruption Schelling's "Transcendental Idealism" from beginning to end and how he recovered his own innermost self in this dialectical history of self-consciousness, must be seen as a typical experience [Erlebnis] of intellectual mysticism. All true passion of thought arises from this insatiable drive of the spirit to return to itself in becoming unified in mystical identity with itself and all its forms.[125]

The source and inspiration of Tillich's entire thought was the nature mysticism he had first experienced under the immediate influence of Schelling's philosophy of nature and under the impact of his own enthusiastic experience of nature in all the variety of its moods.

Not to reflect about nature, refusing to let it become a mere object of natural science in order that it be used for the enhancement of human life and the increase of its productivity, but to view it as the immediate expression of the spirit itself and thus to regain oneself in it—this is the aim of nature mysticism. And this unity can be intended so deeply that suffering, perishableness, and death are felt as one's own suffering . . .[126]

Thus the practitioner of mysticism is driven from the extension (Breite) of the many to ever-greater heights and finally to the very summit of the one, to religious mysticism. Then he is turned away from this vision until once again he carries the many to the height of eternal unity, and then he says: I have fled from the world and the disquietude of its variety to the eternal One who is called God and now I see God in all the wealth that fills the world. And when my gaze weakens, I turn back and I see God face to face. . . . Let us affirm theoretically and practically this experience in which we become one with eternal unity and truth itself.[127]

In this description of mysticism, positive and negative elements are related to one another. Tillich spoke with great warmth and appreciation of mysticism (in his early years more so than later), but nevertheless he found it necessary to declare that it represented an impossibility. "It is impossible," he said, "to experience the absolute unity with God,"[128] not only because God ever transcends any perception of him, but primarily because "we are not what we should be."[129] Moreover, this contradiction is characteristic not only of man, but also of nature, and indeed, of the world. Nature mysticism, however deep and ecstatic it may be, cannot overcome the limitation that marks all nature, namely the fact that it produces and manifests unity and destruction at the same time. This inner conflict of nature repels the human spirit from it or at least prevents it from being drawn to it to the point of unity.[130] Thus separation from God is experienced in unity with him. That which ought not to be and the contradiction that fills the world *[der Weltwiderspruch]* are felt to be an abyss from which despair arises and all desperate efforts to avoid despair mystically and aesthetically can only deepen it. Hence Tillich concludes, "Kierkegaard was right when he, the aesthete and mystic, gave expression to his innermost experience by speaking of it as the despair which is the sickness unto death. For despair is nothing else than the irreconcilably disruptive opposition between that which is and that which ought to be."[131] This is guilt consciousness; it disrupts all mysticism, all mystical unity.

Anyone acquainted with Tillich's thinking can see that the subject of this lecture is the basic ambiguity with which he struggled in his own thinking from the very beginning of his career. On the one hand, he was attracted to the confident spirit emanating from German Idealism. On the other hand, his mind was filled with the realization that there is something wrong with the world, that ultimately men are in the wrong before God. Thus he could speak with deep appreciation of mysticism and its search for unity and harmony, but at the same time acknowledge that the world is full of conflict and suffering, disunity, and separation.

Against the background of such ideas, the last lecture on "Redemption" assumes special significance, for it shows to what extent Tillich was under the influence of Schelling and how he gave expression to Schelling's synthesis of philosophy and theology, of metaphysical speculation and biblical revelation. Like Schelling, he saw in Christ incarnate divinity taking upon itself the suffering of the world in order to heal it from all conflicts and dispersions. He saw the disruption of the world overcome in the disclosure of the One in the Many, in the manifestation of the absolute in the relativities of nature and history. God is both the Redeemer in whom all seekers find peace, liberating them from all imperfection; and the savior who draws them into communion with himself, healing all their pains and diseases. Unity with God as it was envisaged in Plotinus is here identified with the personal communion with the living God which the Apostle Paul affirmed on the basis of his own experience.

On reading Tillich's lecture on "Redemption" one senses also the nearness of his thought to that of Schleiermacher and Augustine. His interpretation of salvation as redemption [Erlösung] is noteworthy. The figure of Christ is viewed primarily as healer, again in accordance with the teachings of the Apostle Paul. A few passages of the lecture will illustrate this:

A truly religious person will regard it as godless if he deals with the things of everyday life without seeing the absolute in them, indeed, if he enjoys [geniesst] them without enjoying God in time, if he thinks, wills, and acts autonomously [aus sich selbst] instead of from and for God. He knows that all this conflicts with his absolute dependence [Gebundenheit] on God. Out of this conflict he yearns for redemption . . .[132]

Like Schelling, Tillich occasionally describes the conflict in which human beings find themselves involved as a conflict between the relative and the absolute; indeed, throughout his life his thinking was determined by this opposition; it is interesting therefore to note that in this early lecture (he was twenty-six years old when he delivered it) he found it important to state, echoing Schelling, that "the existence of the relative as such does not constitute a conflict with the absolute, but the fact that the relative is and aspires to be something for itself apart from the absolute, represents the conflict in its religious form."[133]

The concluding passage of this lecture is an eloquent summary of Christology. Tillich adopted it from Schelling in order to include it in his own interpretation of redemption:

The immediate religious consciousness has become one with the speculative idea, namely the conception of the redeemer and his work. . . . The religious consciousness views redemption as the suffering of an individual who is God and man . . . a religious conception that is alive can not be maintained in the sphere of abstractedness; it needs something concrete and living and finds it in that personality whose nature *[Wesen]* and work are nothing else than the perfect expression of the completed idea of redemption: the absolute unity of a single individual with the absolute where the individual is presented as highest moral perfection and at the same time as annulled in a criminal's death. And since we see in this human image, which is depicted for us in the New Testament, the features of the God who redeems us, we call this man the redeemer, for through his lifework he has given mankind an image of God which bestows on us the certainty of redemption. We call him redeemer because in his actions and his being God has revealed himself as redeemer—we do not concern ourselves about what we do not know about him, even if this includes his name, but about that which we do know about him, namely, that his communion with God is the guarantee *[Grund]* of ours. God has redeemed us through him.[134]

The lecture ends with a moving, finely balanced statement of faith that affirms what has been the basis of Christian theological thought throughout the generations and which is remarkably relevant to the present state of Christian thought, especially in Protestantism. It is of particular significance for the ongoing discussion between Barth and Tillich and their followers. It is a statement Tillich* could have formulated at the end of his career. He says:

There is something in us that is greater than we, something that judges us *[was sich kritisch verhält gegen uns]* and takes hold of us with immediate power liberating us from ourselves. This is why the religious person says: Not by myself but through God I am who I am. On the other hand, it is of course correct to say that we can be redeemed only through that

---

*Paul Tillich was born in 1886 and died in 1965.

which is within us, that which is the innermost core of our being. We cannot be redeemed by something that is alien to us [etwas uns Fremdes], but only be transformed and destroyed.[135]

NOTES*

1. Paul Tillich, *On the Boundary* (New York: Charles Scribner's Sons, 1966), p. 58.
2. Ibid., p. 59.
3. Ibid., p. 75.
4. He should have qualified the comprehensiveness of this ecclesiastical self-characterization. For in terms of denominational classification, he never was exclusively a Lutheran. He was born and educated as a member of the "Evangelical Church of the Old Prussian Union," a church which though originally Lutheran had undergone a modification of its Lutheran heritage through the interference of the rulers of Brandenburg and Prussia in ecclesiastical affairs.

   In 1613 the Elector of Brandenburg, John Sigismund, changed from a Lutheran to a Calvinist affiliation. According to the terms of the Peace of Augsburg, which had brought the conflicts of the German Reformation to a conclusion (1555), he expected his subjects to follow his example; but they protested so violently that he found himself compelled to guarantee to them the preservation of their Lutheran faith and order. More than two hundred years later, on 27 September 1817, the Prussian King Frederick Wilhelm III decreed the union of the Lutheran and Reformed (Calvinist) churches in Prussia; but the consensus which he had hoped would result in an actual and not merely legal union did not materialize. In 1834 he was forced to issue another order, according to which the union between the two traditions was redefined in such a way that it did not require the abandonment of former creeds or confessions but would stimulate a spirit of denominational moderation and restraint. Thus the "Evangelical Church of the Prussian Union" came into being. During the nineteenth century, it underwent a development which continued to link it spiritually, through the use of the Augsburg Confession and Luther's catechism, with Lutheranism; but organizationally it was set apart from the Lutheran churches. As a result, the German Protestant churches of Lutheran descent are to this day divided into Lutheran and Evangelical bodies which are confederated in the "Evangelical Church in Germany," but find themselves unable to agree on forms of worship or creed.
5. Tillich, *On the Boundary*, p. 75.
6. Paul Tillich, *My Search for Absolutes* (New York: Simon & Schuster, 1967), pp. 25, 26. Cf. *Gesammelte*, ed. Renate Albrecht (Stuttgart: Evangelisches Verlagswerk, 1971), XII:16.
7. *On the Boundary*, p. 77. The first American version as translated from Tillich's original German reads (Paul Tillich, *The Interpretation of History* [New

---

*Translations into English are by the author unless otherwise indicated. Materials noted as being in a "private collection" are held by the author/editor unless stated otherwise. A few abbreviations by initials have seemed convenient for the Notes, in view of frequent reference: G.A. (German Archive), GW *(Gesammelte Werke)*, and H.A. (Harvard Archive).

York: Charles Scribner's Sons, 1936], p. 56): "However mutable human nature may be, it is impossible to stretch this mutability to the moral realm." The German version, as it appears in a volume of selections from Tillich's writings, published in 1962 under the title *Auf der Grenze* (Stuttgart: Evangelisches Verlagswerk), p. 54, reads: "*So ungeheuer wandlungsfähig die menschliche Natur sein mag, so unmöglich ist es, diese wandlungsfähigkeit auf das Moralische auszudehnen.*"

It is no longer possible to determine how Tillich originally phrased this sentence or whether he had a hand in the translation of the first English version into German, or whether he approved the translation.

8. Paul Tillich, *Systematic Theology*, I (Chicago: The University of Chicago Press, 1951), pp. 50–51, n. 13.

9. In his late teens, he read *Hamlet* in the classical German translation of A. W. Schlegel and L. Tieck and identified himself to such a degree with the melancholy Dane that years later he could recite from memory long passages of the drama. He imagined himself as being identical with Hamlet, almost perilously so, he later acknowledged (Tillich, *On the Boundary*, p. 27). Even in his old age he remembered the impression the existentialist elements in *Hamlet* had made upon him. Cf. Sidney and Beatrice Rome, ed., *Philosophical Interrogations* (New York: 1964), p. 362. He said: "I reached an extraordinary degree of identification with the symbol Hamlet which was more real to me than empirical reality."

10. Tillich, *On the Boundary*, p. 46 f.

11. This and all subsequent quotations are taken from Tillich's correspondence with his father. Private collection.

12. At another time, Tillich said: "Kähler's course is grandiose. But I do not want to register for Lütgert's introduction because I prefer to sleep between eight and nine. Moreover, listening for three hours in the forenoon would be too strenuous for me."

13. As a letter writer Tillich had several odd habits which he retained throughout his life. The most common one was that he failed to date his writings. Most of the time he also did not indicate where he was writing from. The correspondence with his father with which we are dealing here took place in June 1906, as we can learn from the father's letters.

14. *Problemverschlingung.*

15. The distinction between "historical" *(geschichtlich)* and "historic" *(historisch)* was made by Kähler in his famous essay "Der Sogenannte Historische Jesus und der Geschichtliche Biblische Christus" (1902), New Edition by E. Wolf (München: Kaiser, 1956); English translation by Carl E. Braaten (Philadelphia: Fortress Press, 1964), in which he argued that the "historical Jesus" as described by modern historians who read the Gospels as biographical sources must be regarded as a dubious construction whereas "the picture of Jesus as the Christ" as presented on the basis of the biblical witness throughout the history of the Christian church is the trustworthy "historic" revealer of divine truth.

16. This refers to debates in the Wingolf about the meaning and validity of the "Christian principle" which supposedly held the group together.

17. John 8:32. "You shall know the truth, and the truth will set you free."

18. These letters are in H.A.

19. Cf. Tillich, *On the Boundary*, pp. 36 ff. and Tillich, "Autobiographical Reflections," in C. W. Kegley and R. W. Brettall, eds., *The Theology of Paul Tillich* (New York: Macmillan Co., 1952), p. 8.

20. Ibid. Authors' editorial change.
21. Cf. Paul Tillich, *The Dynamics of Faith* (New York: Harper & Row, 1957), p. 10. "There is no faith without a content toward which it is directed. . . . And there is no way of having the content of faith except in the act of faith." Cf. also Tillich's discussion of the "theological circle" in *Systematic Theology*, I:10 f., and 15.
22. Tillich, *On the Boundary*, p. 31 f. Cf. also *GW* XII:23.
23. The letter is undated. H.A.
24. Paul Tillich, *Perspectives on 19th and 20th Century Protestant Theology* (New York: Harper & Row, 1967), p. 154.
25. Ibid.
26. "Autob. Ref.," p. 11 f; *GW* XII:66. Cf. also Tillich, *Systematic Theology*, III:228. "This is in line with Augustine's statement that in the situation of doubt the truth from which one feels separated is present insofar as in every doubt formal affirmation of truth as truth is presupposed."
27. Tillich, *Systematic Theology*, III:pp. 174–76.
28. Tillich, *On the Boundary*, p. 90. *GW* XII:p. 53.
29. In his biography of Martin Buber *(Martin Buber. Sein Werk und Seine Zeit. Ein Beitrag Zur Geistegeschichte Mittel-Europas 1880–1930*, (Köln: J. Melzer, 1961) p. 356.) Hans Kohn speaks of "a longing for community" which he says was characteristic of many people in the period following World War I. He states that Buber was profoundly aware of this and that he therefore endeavored to promote personal fellowship *(Bünde)* of communication and education. Kohn also notes that E. Troeltsch commented on this trend. Cf. E. Troeltsch, *Der Historismus und Seine Überwindung* (Berlin: Panverlag, 1924), p. 57 f. Tillich's own well-considered judgment of the youth movement is to be found in Paul Tillich, *The Religious Situation* (New York: Meridian Books, 1956), pp. 131–35. Cf. Paul Tillich, *Die Religiöse Lage der Gegenwart* (Berlin: Ullstein, 1926), pp. 83–7.
30. Cf. the article "Jugendbewegung" in Kurt Galling, ed. *Die Religion in Geschichte und Gegenwart* (3d edition, Tübingen: Mohr, 1959), II:col. 1015.
31. Later, under the inflience of Hermann Schafft, he interested himself in the movement. Cf. his article "Jugendbewegung und Religion," written in 1924 *(GW* XIII:130–34) in which he speaks as a friendly outsider, seeing the youth movement as a protest against the unproductive lifestyle of the bourgeoisie.
32. Cf. Herrmann Schmalenbach, "Die Soziologische Struktur des Bundes," in *Die Oskuren* II (1922), as quoted by Alexander Rüstow, *Ortsbestimmung der Gegenwart* (Zurich: Rentz, 1957), III:239.
33. Paul Tillich, "Das Ende der Protestantischen Ara I" (1937); *GW* VII:158. Cf. also Paul Tillich, *The Protestant Era* (Chicago: The University of Chicago Press, 1948), p. 222.
34. Paul Tillich, *Travel Diary 1936* (New York: Harper & Row, 1970), p. 42.
35. Tillich to Alfred Fritz, January 1940. H.A.
36. Cf. Tillich's own characterization of Schafft in Werner Kindt, ed., *Hermann Schafft. Ein Lebenswerk.* (Kassel: Stauda Verlag, 1960), pp. 11–16. On 8 August 1919 Schafft asked, in a letter which was probably a greeting to Tillich on his birthday: "Are you still the humble Paul you were in 1906, the same Paul who experienced the doctrine of justification? *("Bist Du noch der alte demütige Paul von 1906, der die Rechtfertigung erlebte?")* H.A. cf. also Tillich, *On the Boundary*, p. 48.

37. The first German translations of Kierkegaard's religious and theological writings began to appear during the first decade of this century (the translator was A. Bärthold). The first volumes of his Collected Works in German translation (by Christoph Schrempf and Joh. Gottsched) were published in 1909. In *On the Boundary,* Tillich remarked that he came under Kierkegaard's influence during 1905–06. He was perhaps mistaken about this date. In his Chicago lectures on "Perspectives in 19th and 20th Century Protestant Theology," p. 164, he said: "I recall with pride how as students of theology in Halle we came in contact with Kierkegaard's thought through translations made by an isolated individual in Württemberg." Tillich studied in Halle during 1905–07. He mentions the same date in a letter written on 22 April 1950 to a certain Mr. Morris, who had asked him when he first become acquainted with Kierkegaard. Tillich replied as follows: "My first encounter with S. Kierkegaard was in my student time in the years 1906–7; the second through Karl Barth in the early twenties, and the third through Martin Heidegger at the end of the twenties. Even since my student time, the concepts of anxiety, despair, leap, infinite passion, and many other things have been elements of my thought . . ."

The isolated individual of whom Tillich speaks in this letter was probably the Swabian minister Christopher Schrempf, who had got into difficulties with the church authorities on account of several acts of insubordination, but particularly because of his refusal to recite the Apostles Creed in official church services. Finally dismissed from his pastorate, he turned to a study of Kierkegaard, whom he considered his spiritual ally. He began to publish the first German translation of Kierkegaard's *Collected Works,* Volume I of which appeared in 1909. This edition cannot have been available to Tillich and his friends during 1905–07. It seems that one of the first of Kierkegaard's books Tillich read was the treatise *The Sickness Unto Death.* What he says abuot Kierkegaard's significance for his own thinking leads one to this conclusion. A German translation of this work published by A. Bärthold was available; a second edition appeared in 1905.

It is not impossible that Tillich was introduced to Kierkegaard by his friend Emanuel Hirsch, with whom he corresponded in a lively intellectual exchange. Hirsch was a doctoral student of Karl Holl, whose ideas and preferences he adopted, often deepening them by his own reading of primary sources. He became a lifelong Kierkegaardian. Indeed, he was one of the world's most thorough Kierkegaard scholars. It is quite probable that Hirsch was directed to Kierkegaard by the interpretation Holl used to give of him in his course at the University of Berlin on "The History of Protestant Theology." When I took this course during 1921–22, I was struck by Holl's personal interest in and passion for Kierkegaard. I daresay that Hirsch heard the same lecture a decade or so earlier. Holl, a native Swabian, had studied at the University of Tübingen as a member of the Protestant theological seminary *(Stift)* there. One of his tutors had been the same Christoph Schrempf who, stimulated by his own conflict with his home church, had turned to Kierkegaard as a like-minded ally and then decided to publish a German translation which would make Kierkegaard widely known.

38. Werner Kindt, ed., *Hermann Schafft,* p. 14.

39. Tillich contributed an occasional article; he lectured often in the *Neuwerk Kreis.* At the very beginning of his German professorial career Karl Barth paid a visit to Schlüchtern in order to become acquainted with the leaders of

the *Neuwerk Kreis* (December 1921). Tillich's friend Schafft was among them. He made a deep impression on Barth, who wrote about him to E. Thurneysen: "I met a man who is not easy to get acquainted with: Hermann Schafft, a minister from Kassel: another of those Germans, always tense, full of insights and moods, all tongue, and able to turn in any direction." *("Ich lernte einen steilen Mann kennen: den Kasseler Pfarrer Schafft, auch wieder so ein Deutscher im Sprung, voll Einsichten und Schrullen, ganz Zunge, mit Möglichkeiten nach allen Seiten.")* (Karl Barth, *Gesamt-Ausgabe*, V: *Briefe*, II: Karl Barth-ed. Thurneysen, p. 33. Cf. Eberhard Busch, *Karl Barth. His Life From Letters and Autobiographical Texts* (Philadelphia: Fortress Press, 1976), p. 145.

   Cf. also G. Dehn's characterization of Schafft in *Die Alte Zeit-Die Vorigen Jahre* (München: Kaiser, 1962), p. 238 f.

40. He was much concerned for the renewal of the liturgy of the church and for the proper observance of the turning points in human life. This is why he joined the Movement of Berneuchen, which endeavored to make worship relevant to the modern day. Tillich also participated in this undertaking, at least for a time.

41. This was the highest "earned degree" in theology, the equivalent of the Ph.D. degree (now no longer given).

42. Cf. Tillich, *Perspectives*, p. 153.

43. The students referred to them as *Expauken*. Cf. Tillich, P. "Hermann Schafft", *Hermann Schafft, Ein Lebenswerk* (Kassel: Stauda, 1960). p. 12.

44. Here Tillich errs: the occasion for the feast was Kähler's seventieth birthday.

45 Lütgert too was a Wingolfite.

46. In his *Geschichte der Protestantischen Dogmatik im 19. Jahrhundert,* edited by his grandson Ernest Kähler (München: Kaiser, 1962), p. 276, Kähler quotes this same sentence, attributing it to J. A. Bengel, the Swabian Biblicist. It must have been one of his favorite sayings, for it is mentioned in other writings of his.

47. In his *Apologetik,* #13, Kähler writes, "Christ cannot be separated from his history.... In the meaning *(Gehalt)* of this history there presents itself ... something which is more than a historically changing content *(Inhalt).* A permanent meaning presents itself which is universally valid although it is not unconditionally effective ... the bearer of this meaning is the personal God and he is present in the living *(geschichtliche)* Christ of history."

48. Ibid., par. 180.

49. Ibid., par. 172.

50. Ibid.

51. Cf. H. R. Landon, ed., *Reinhold Niebuhr. A Prophetic Voice in Our Times* (Greenwich, Conn.: Seabury Press, 1962), p. 34. Tillich frequently used the term *Wesenswidrigkeit* as a definition of sin in his early German writings, especially in the essay "Das Dämonische," *GW* VI:53 f.; cf. also the English translation in Tillich, *The Interpretation of History,* p. 93, where the term is translated "contrariness to essential nature." This definition of sin is preserved in Tillich's American writings, even though the earlier word is no longer employed. Cf. *Systematic Theology,* II:45: "Man as he exists is not what he essentially is and ought to be. He is estranged (!) from his true being."

52. M. Kähler, *Der sogennante historische Jesus und der geschichtliche biblische Christus,* ed. E. Wolf (München: Kaiser, 1956), p. 9 f., 103.

53. Tillich, *Systematic Theology,* I:34; III:62.

54. Tillich, Ibid., I:35.

55. Cf. Tillich, *Perspectives*, p. 213f. Also Tillich's "Foreword" to Carl E. Braaten's translation of Kähler's book on the so-called historical Jesus, etc., p. xif.

56. Tillich's interpretation of justification was a synthesis of several traditional doctrinal themes, and he meant to stay in line with Luther's teaching. He wished to see the term "justification" replaced by the word "acceptance" in the sense "that we are accepted by God although unacceptable according to the criteria of law (or our essential being) and that we are asked to accept this acceptance" [Tillich, *Systematic Theology*, III:224 f.]. Tillich felt that he had restated Luther's doctrine of justification in terms of this profound "psychology of acceptance," and he held it to be confirmed by the "best insights of contemporary depth psychology" [Ibid., p. 227]. He permitted himself an exaggeration of dubious significance when, in one of his last lectures, he stated the meaning of justification in the following words: " . . . there is a power of acceptance in the depth of life. It is the power by which life accepts us in spite of the violation of life we may have committed by making a wrong decision" [Paul Tillich, *My Search for Absolutes*, (New York: Simon & Schuster, 1967), p. 111].

57. In 1917 Tillich wrote to his friend E. Hirsch: "The right to believe must not be made dependent upon a work, including the intellectual work of affirming the idea of God." E. Hirsch and P. Tillich, *Briefwechsel 1917–1918* (Berlin: Verlag Die Spur, 1973), p. 10. Tillich adhered to this view throughout his life. Cf. Tillich, *Systematic Theology*, III:224.

58. Paul Tillich, *Rechtfertigung und Zweifel* (1924) in *GW* VIII:89.

59. Cf. his statement as reported in Anna Kähler, ed., *Theologe und Christ. Erinnerungen und Bekenntnisse von Martin Kähler* (Berlin: Furche Verlag, 1926), p. 269. Cf. also Tillich, *The Courage to Be* (New Haven: Yale University Press, 1952), p. 176: "No actual negation can be without an implicit affirmation. . . . The negative lives from the positive it negates."

60. Tillich, *Systematic Theology*, III:228.

61. Tillich, *Biblical Religion and the Search for Ultimate Reality* (Chicago: The University of Chicago Press, 1955), p. 61. The whole section from which this section is quoted illustrates how Tillich was able to shift from philosophy (ontology) to theology and conversely.

62. Tillich, *The Protestant Era*, p. xivf. Cf. also *GW* VII:14 f.; also Tillich, *Systematic Theology*, III:238 ff.

63. Tillich, *The Protestant Era*, p. xiv, xv. A paraphrase.

64. Ibid.

65. Ibid.

66. Kähler liked the saying of R. Rothe: "The picture of Jesus in the gospels cannot have been invented, for it is larger than our heart." Cf. Anna Kähler, ed., *Theologe und Christ*, p. 92. In a sermon on "spiritual presence" Tillich uses the phrase "God is greater than our hearts." Tillich, *The Eternal Now* (New York: Charles Scribner's Sons, 1963), p. 82. In the background of this statement is the saying of I John 3:20: "If our heart condemns us, God is greater than our heart" [RSV]. Or, as the NEB says with greater precision: "Even if our conscience condemns us, God is greater than our conscience." Luther quotes this verse in his *Lectures on Romans* in connection with his exposition of Romans 2:15, and then goes on to remark: "As our defender he (God) is greater than our accuser and infinitely so. God is our defender, the heart our accuser." It is interesting to note that in a discussion of conscience in his lecture "The Transmoral Conscience," *The Protestant Era*, pp. 145 ff., Tillich quotes extensively from Luther (without documenting his

exposition) and then paraphrases the passage before us as follows: "While God is the accuser in the *Anfechtung* and our heart tries to excuse itself, in 'justification' our heart accuses us and God defends us against ourselves."

67. M. Kähler, *Wissenschaft der Christlichen Lehre*, #596. *"Das Dogma bedarf einer geschichtlichen Auslegung und zugleich einer zeitgemässen Umprägung."* In his *Geschichte der Protestantischen Dogmatik*, p. 146, he criticized Adolf Harnack's interpretation of dogma. He said that Harnack, not content with having dissolved the dogma, affirmed that it (the dogma) represented a "Hellenic deformation and encapsulation of Christianity."

68. M. Kähler, *Der sogenannte historische Jesus*, p. 104.

69. Ibid.

70. M. Kähler, *Geschichte der Protestantischen Dogmatik*, p. 104.

71. Cf. Luther's *Hauspostille* in Martin Luther's *Werke. Kritische Ausgabe* (Weimar: Böhlau), 52 passim.

72. Kähler, *Der sogenannte historische Jesus*, pp. 55, 68. Hans-Georg Link, in his work *Geschichte Jesu und Bild Christi (Die Entwicklung der Christologie Kählers in Auseinandersetzung mit der Leben-Jesu-Theologie in der Ritschl Schule)* (Neukirchen-Vluyn: Neukirchen Verlag, 1976), offers a full, critical analysis of Kähler's Christology. He pays attention to Kähler's concept *Bild Christi* (picture of Christ), but his discussion is not as thorough as it could have been. (cf. p. 249 ff.)

73. Tillich, *Systematic Theology*, II:114 ff.; III:144 ff.

74. Cf. Paul Tillich, *Morality and Beyond* (New York: Harper & Row, 1963), p. 64.

75. Tillich, "Das Neue Sein als Zentralbegriff Einer Christlichen Theologie," *GW* VIII:231.

76. Ibid., 232.

77. Tillich, *Systematic Theology*, II:116.

78. Cf. Klaus-Dieter Nörenberg, *Analogia Imaginis. Der Symbolbegriff in der Theologie Paul Tillichs* (Gütersloh: Mohn, 1966), p. 139.

79. Cf. Tillich's memorial article on Schafft, as mentioned in note 36. Cf. also E. Troeltsch, "Rückblick auf ein halbes Jahrhundert der Theologischen Wissenschaft," in *Gesammelte Schriften* (Tübingen: Mohr, 1913), II:213.

80. A copy of the paper can be found in the German Archive.

81. Theses 6 and 20.

82. Theses 47.

83. Thesis 116.

84. Thesis 117. This sentence echoes words of Kähler, who wrote *(Der sogenannte historische Jesus*, p. 49 f.): "Faith in Jesus Christ does not depend either on the Christological dogma or on an allegedly reliable picture of Christ produced by means of historical research.... Indeed, speaking simply in the name of faith in Christ, it is the task of the theologian to keep a papacy of scholarship *(den gelehrten Papst)* in bounds."

85. Paul Tillich, *The Dynamics of Faith* (New York: Harper & Row, 1957), p. 87 f. As in some other instances, the author has changed sentence structure.

86. In 1966 the editors of the *Journal of Religion* published a special issue (Vol.46, no.1, Part II), *In Memoriam Paul Tillich*, which contains a thoughtful, critical article by D. Moody Smith on "The Historical Jesus in P. Tillich's Christology" (pp. 131–47), and a rejoinder by Tillich himself (pp. 191–94). Tillich makes this interesting statement (p. 192): "If I am asked: 'Does Christian faith guarantee that the synoptic picture of this man (Jesus) is guaranteed as historically correct, including his name?', I would say, 'No.' If

I am asked 'Does Christian faith guarantee that this picture is an expression of the bearer of the Spirit who, through this picture, creates and recreates human beings spiritually?' I would say, 'Yes.'"

87. Tillich, *Systematic Theology*, II:97.
88. Ibid., 99.
89. Ibid., 117.
90. In 1911, Medicus accepted a call to the chair of philosophy at the Swiss Institute of Technology in Zürich. He spent the rest of his life there; he retired in 1946 and died in 1956. He continued to cultivate his interest in Fichte and Idealist philosophy. He and Tillich stayed in touch with one another as good friends. Medicus adopted several of Tillich's ideas, particularly those which were developed in dependence upon Schelling. He also took an active interest in the philosophy of religion and Tillich's theology of culture. (See his books *Das Mythologische in der Religion* [1944], and *Menschlichkeit* [1951], English translation by Fritz Marti under the title *On Being Human* [New York: F. Ungar, 1973].)
91. Cf. Wolf-Dieter Marsch, ed., *Werk und Wirkung Paul Tillichs* (Stuttgart: Evangelisches Verlagswerk, 1967), p. 62 f. When Haendler reminded Tillich of this fourteen years later, Tillich remarked: *"Ja, damals habe ich eine kräftige Lanze für Gunkel gebrochen."*
92. Tillich mentions it in his doctoral dissertation on Schelling's *Construction of the History of Religion*, published in 1910 and now translated by Victor Nuovo (Lewisburg, Pa.: Bucknell University Press, 1974), p. 166. Troeltsch's writing was entitled "Protestantisches Christentum und Kirche in der Neuzeit." It was part of a collaborative work on the history of the Christian religion, published as part I, section IV:1 of the encyclopedic collection *Die Kultur der Gegenwart* (Berlin: Teubner, 1906); 2d ed. 1909, pp. 431–793.
93. Cf. his moving memorial article "Zum Tode von Ernst Troeltsch" (1923), GW XII:175–78, Tillich writes: "I have never taken any of his lecture courses but I have felt the power of his work for twenty years. Though I have been in personal touch with him only rarely, I am conscious of what I have received from him."

Tillich mentions two of Troeltsch's writings: *The Social Teaching of the Christian Churches* (about which he says: "The effects of this book upon me were extraordinary. I shall never forget the impression it made upon me when I first read it.") and then his long essay on *The Absoluteness of Christianity and the History of Religion*, published in 1902 and in several later editions, the last one of which appeared in 1969 as no. 138 of *Siebenstern Taschenbücher*, ed. Trutz Rendtorff; English translation by David Reid (Richmond, Virginia: John Knox Press, 1971). In this work Troeltsch argued that one cannot defend the absoluteness of Christianity either by the traditional absolutistic and exclusivistic methods or by interpreting it comparatively with other religions in terms of the history of religion, but *only* by a full and unqualified expression of its moral and religious spirit.

One of Troeltsch's most outspoken critics, Theodor Kaftan, a distinguished, conservative churchman and theologian, called him a "neoplatonic Christian." It is worth remarking that Tillich did not take note of this in view of the fact that his own thinking was sometimes characterized in the same way.

Throughout his life Troeltsch was a voracious reader. Few important publications escaped him, especially if they contributed to the analysis and criticism of the mood or spirit of the times, a task in which Troeltsch was continually engaged. So he also came upon Tillich's suggestive article on the *Kairos* in the cultural journal *Die Tat* (August 1922). In his own last great book, *Der Historismus und seine Probleme* (Tübingen: Mohr, 1923), p. 698, he gave expression to the conviction he had held throughout his life. "As far as life on this earth is concerned," he wrote, "every moment confronts us anew with the task of shaping future history on the basis of the one that is past." Then he added this footnote: "A similar idea is expressed by Paul Tillich in a recent issue of 'Die Tat'. He gives it the name *Kairos* which is a term commonly used in the George Schule." Troeltsch was referring to the followers of the poet Stephan George who desired to form a new cultural and intellectual élite in order to overcome the crisis of civilization. Troeltsch remarked also that Tillich was advocating religious socialism as a postulate of the *Kairos*.

94. Friedrich Büchsel who, three years older than Tillich, had graduated from Halle (1907) with a thesis he had prepared under Medicus' partial supervision, became a professor of New Testament exegesis in the University of Rostock in 1918 as Tillich, then an Army Chaplain, noted not without a little envy.

95. During his first year at Halle, probably in 1906, Tillich and Büchsel privately studied Schleiermacher's *Glaubenslehre*. At the same time, Tillich and Schafft collaborated in reading F. H. R. Frank's *History and Criticism of Recent Theology* (1894) and R. Seeberg's *History of the German Church in the 19th Century* (1903). This shows how thorough and conscientious Tillich was as a student.

96. Cf. Wilhelm and Marion Pauck, *Paul Tillich: His Life & Thought*, vol. I: Life, (New York: Harper & Row, 1976), p. 34f. In other connections (cf. vol. I:281) we have suggested that it was Tillich's habit to discuss an important decision with his friends, carefully weighing the reasons for or against its adoption. He then gave the impression that the matter to be settled was wide open, whereas he personally had already arrived at a resolution. Thus Tillich, even in his student days, was determined to become a university teacher. But for years he gave to himself as well as to others the impression that he had not yet made a final decision. An important confirmation of this is to be found in a letter he wrote to A. von Harnack in 1912. (It is preserved in the *Deutsche Staatsbibliothek* in East Berlin in Carton 43 of the Harnack *Nachlass*. A copy has been made available to us through the courtesy of Professor Gary Lease of the University of California at Santa Cruz, California, who found it by chance in connection with research he was doing at the library. The letter reads as follows:

"Your Excellency will allow me herewith to express once more my thanks for the conversation with you at the beginning of this month [December 1912]. It was of extraordinary value to me. A thorough consideration of the points of view I then obtained concerning my career and my work in Apologetics has now led me to conclude that I should discontinue my lecturing activity in the coming winter and devote myself exclusively or at least mainly to scholarly work. I have not yet been able to decide where I shall attempt a habilitation . . . in any case, I ask your Excellency to disregard my wish to be introduced to a group of your Excellency's acquaintances and I apologize for any trouble I may have caused in this connection. It was not possible for me to reach an earlier decision. Most respectfully and faithfully yours, P. T."

The style of this letter reflects the esteem in which Tillich held Harnack. He never agreed with him on theological matters; for example, the Hellenization of the Gospel of Christ was not brought about by an intellectualization of the Christian faith, as Harnack believed, but by its immersion in Hellenistic piety and religious philosophy, as Tillich thought. Yet he respected him as one of the foremost scholars of his time and as a man of extraordinary achievements. In a memorial address, which he wrote on the occasion of Harnack's death in 1930 but which he apparently never delivered, he praised him "as one of the most illustrious representatives of his era in whom all motive powers of a spiritual and religious kind were united" (*GW* XII:165).

As far as we know, Tillich later never mentioned his call on Harnack. Apparently, he discussed with him plans and possibilities concerning the academic career toward which he aspired. What Harnack said to him led him, so it seems, to abandon plans for further *Vernunft-Abende* and to concentrate instead on the acquisition of learning and scholarship (cf. *GW* XIII:544 ff). But Tillich remembered until the end of his life something else that Harnack said to him, presumably in the same conversation. In his course at the University of Chicago in the spring of 1963 on Modern Protestant Theology, he stated that Harnack "himself once told me that in the year 1900 the main railway station in the city of Leipzig, one of the largest in central Europe, was blocked by freight cars in which his book *What is Christianity?* was being sent all over the world" (Tillich, *Perspectives*, p. 222; cf. also *GW* VIII:15). We should note here that Harnack's book quickly ran through several editions: in 1903, three years after its first publication, 50,000 had been printed; in 1925, Harnack wrote in a last Foreword that 70,000 copies had been sold and he did not count the size of the editions of the almost twenty translations into languages other than German.

The requirements a candidate for the degree of Lic. Theol. had to fulfill were the following: (1) He had to write a dissertation on an important subject, preferably one that had not been treated before, and therefore demanded original research. (2) On the recommendation of the candidate's advisor, the entire theological faculty had to find the dissertation acceptable. In an oral examination, lasting for several hours, the candidate had to demonstrate his general mastery of the basic methods and accomplishments of theological scholarship. (3) Finally, the candidate was required to formulate a series of theses, dealing with debatable issues of modern theological scholarship and to defend them in public debate against members of the faculty and young scholars who had recently acquired higher degrees.

Generally, it was the candidate's privilege to designate with the dean's consent two or three opponents for the debate.

Paul Tillich fulfilled all these requirements. He wrote an acceptable dissertation; and he successfully argued for the acceptance of the propositions he had formulated for the academic debate. (The opponents he had designated were his friends Friedrich Büchsel, Lic. Theol., and Richard Wegener, Ph.D.)

The disputation dealt with the following theses or propositions:

(1) The concept *(Begriff)* of religion must be derived from the concept of God, and not conversely.
(2) The idea *(Idee)* of truth rather than the idea of morality must form the basis of the doctrine of God.
(3) The concept of the living God is conditioned upon the doctrine of the "nature in God."

(4) "Natural" and "supernatural" are related to one another neither like nature and non-nature *(Nicht-Natur)*, nor like nature and spirit, but rather like relativity and absoluteness.

(5) Any deduction of sin invalidates the concept of sin.

(6) The unity of ethics and aesthetics is proved by their relation to truth. Moral and aesthetic actions are related to one another like active and contemplative affirmations of truth.

(7) The eschatalogical materials in the writings of the prophets are older than the prophetic period in Israel's religion.

(8) Nowhere in the New Testament are baptism and the Lord's Supper of merely symbolical significance but throughout, they are of sacramental importance.

(9) The present-day intellectual and religious revival of German Idealism can be historically explained by the fact that the so-called collapse of Idealism was caused not by a conquest from within but by an external abandonment.

(10) The church can fulfill its responsibility toward the educated classes only if it neither undertakes a defense of church doctrines nor attempts to regulate the borderlines between faith and knowledge. It must instead show plainly the living dialectical relationship between the prevailing cultural life and Christianity.

Reading these statements in the light of Tillich's fully ripened thought, we are immediately made aware of the fact that the problems and issues which marked his mature thinking were already preoccupying him at a time when he had just concluded his academic studies. He demonstrated that he possessed a broad theological knowledge and he showed that he was well acquainted with the philosophy of the German Idealists, especially that of Schelling. A detailed discussion of these matters can be found in the article of Hermann Brandt on *Konstanz und Wandel in der Theologie Paul Tillichs im Licht der wiedergefundenen Thesen zu seiner Lizentiaten-Dissertation*, "Zeitschrift für Theologie und Kirche 75" (Tübingen: Mohr, 1978), p. 360–74).

Here we direct special attention to the first thesis: "The concept of religion must be derived from the concept God, not conversely." This statement assumes special significance if it is read in conjunction with the revealing statement which Tillich included in his "Autobiographical Reflections", an introduction to the symposium *The Theology of Paul Tillich*, ed. Charles W. Kegley and Robert W. Bretall (New York: Macmillan Company, 1952), p. 6. He speaks there of the deep impression the observance of the Christian Year made upon his imagination in the small Lutheran towns of Schönfliess and Königsberg in the territory of Brandenburg, where his father was the minister. "It is the experience of the 'holy' which was given to me at that time as an indestructable good *(ein unverlierbares Element)* and as the foundation of all my religious and theological work. When I first read Rudolf Otto's *Idea of the Holy*, I understood it immediately in the light of these early experiences *(Erlebnisse)* and took it into my thinking as a constitutive element. It determined my method in the philosophy of religion, wherein I started with the experience of the holy and advanced to the idea of God and not the converse way. Equally important, existentially as well as theologically, were the mystical, sacramental, and aesthetic implications of the idea of the holy, whereby the ethical and logical elements of religion were derived from the presence of the divine, and not conversely. (This made Schleiermacher congenial to me, as he was to Otto. . .)."

In the light of this illuminating statement, we must judge that the straight-forward affirmation made in the first thesis does not agree with, indeed, goes counter to, the conviction Tillich held throughout his life. It is clear that the sense of the presence of God, the awareness of the Spiritual Pres-ence, and the experience of the holy had priority in Tillich's thinking. On the basis of this understanding he could say that the concept of God must be derived from the concept of religion. He held this view until the end of his life. In his last lecture, delivered a few days before his death, he said: The universal basis of religion "is the experience of the Holy within the finite." *(Korrelationen* (Stuttgart: Evangelisches Verlagswerk, 1975), p. 149. See also Paul Tillich, *The Future of Religions,* (New York: Harper & Row, 1965), p. 86.

In order to understand this definition correctly, one must not fail to keep in mind what Otto and also Tillich, following Otto, took the Holy to be namely the *mysterium tremendum ac fascinosum* which in terms of what man can know is the "wholly other" *(das ganz Andere).*

97. Cf. *GW* IV:137.
98. Tillich, *Perspectives,* p. 142.
99. *GW* IV:133; cf. also D. MacKenzie Brown, ed., *Ultimate Concern: Tillich in Dialogue* (New York: Harper & Row, 1965), p. 13.
100. Schelling quotes this sentence from Isaac Newton's *Principia (Werke,* x:261). Tillich comments on it in his thesis on *Mysticism and Consciousness of Guilt* (Lewisburg: Bucknell Univ. Press, 1974) translated by V. Nuovo, p. 98 f.
101. Paul Tillich to Emanuel Hirsch, 20 February 1918, as quoted in Hans-Wal-ter Schuette, ed., *E. Hirsch and P. Tillich-Briefwechsel 1917–18* (Berlin: Die Spur, 1973), p. 21. Schelling's philosophy passed through several phases of development. In contrast to other interpreters, Tillich was persuaded that there were only two such phases, the first of which was represented by the "Philosophy of Identity" and the second by the "Positive Philosophy," the major tenets of which Schelling had first formulated in his essay *The Nature of Human Freedom* (1809). Modern scholars tend to take the same position as Tillich. Cf. Horst Fuhrmanns, *Schellings Philosophie der Weltalter. Schelling Philosophie in den Jahren 1806–1821* (Düsseldorf: L. Schwann, 1954), p. 75 ff.
102. Paul Tillich, "Absolutes in Human Knowledge," *My Search for Absolutes,* p. 67.
103. Cf. Tillich's review article "Christianity and Idealism" (1927), *GW* XII:234 f.
104. Tillich, *On the Boundary,* pp. 82 f. Cf. Tillich's answer to some of his philo-sophical critics in *The Theology of Paul Tillich,* p. 333. "Theology ... presup-poses that meaning is rooted in reality itself and that the world can be recognized because its structures and laws have the essential character of being intelligible. ... No reduction ... can argue away the correlation be-tween subjective and objective reason, between the functions of the mind and the structure of reality."
105. Cf. Tillich, *GW* I:first page of "Preface."
106. Cf. Tillich, "Existential Philosophy: Its Historical Meaning," *Theology of Cul-ture* (New York: Oxford University Press, 1959), pp. 76–111; *The Courage to Be,* pp. 116–54; "Schelling und die Anfänge des Existentialistischen Pro-testes," *GW* IV:133–44.
107. It is now in H.A.
108. Schelling died on 20 August 1854 and Tillich (who was born on 20 August 1886)) first matriculated in the University of Berlin in the fall of 1904.
109. *GW,* IV:133.
110. Daniel J. O'Hanlon, *The Influence of Schelling on the Thought of Paul Tillich,* Thesis (Pontifical Gregorian University, Rome: 1957), p. 5; 192 f. O'Hanlon

asserts that Tillich's lecture in 1954 at Stuttgart "is of interest principally as a check to show that Tillich's understanding of Schelling has undergone no substantial changes since the two writings of his youth."

111. Both writings have been translated by Victor Nuovo and published by Bucknell University Press, 1974. The German text of the theological dissertation was published in *GW*, I:13–108.

112. It is set forth mainly in the treatise *On the Nature of Human Freedom* (1809), translated by James Gutman (Chicago: Open Court, 1936), which Tillich used as the key to his interpretation of Schelling; and also in the *Lectures on Philosophy of Mythology and Revelation,* chiefly the *Introductions* to these lectures; and finally in related materials as published in Schelling's *Sämtliche Werke,* ed. by his son K. F. A. Schelling, vols. XI–XIV (Stuttgart: Rhein, 1856–1861).

113. Cf. the notes of R. Wegener in Tillich, *GW,* XIII:544.

114. Cf. note 96.

115. Tillich, *GW,* XIII:59 ff. It should be noted that the discussion mentioned last did not deal with the topic "Religion and Culture," as originally announced, but with "Religon and Art." Tillich was the speaker. The manuscripts of his lectures have been preserved and are now part of a private collection of Tillich papers. The largest group met in the home of a Mrs. Schweitzer in Berlin's most fashionable district, near the Tiergarten. Its members (among whom there were some Jews and Roman Catholics) belonged to the educated classes. The group which convened in Lichterfelde was dominated by intellectuals, among whom there was a number of Monists and Theosophists. The meetings held in Charlottenburg in the home of Privy Councillor Leese, the father of one of Tillich's close friends, were attended mainly by lawyers and officers. The fourth circle, which also met in Charlottenburg, namely in the manse of a Pastor Burckhardt, was described by Tillich "as in many respects the most Christian one of all."

116. Ibid.

117. *GW,* XIII:34–8.

118. D. M. Brown, ed., *Ultimate Concern,* p. 191. Italics added.

119. Tillich, *Systematic Theology,* III:195.

120. Tillich, *Systematic Theology,* I:6.

121. Tillich, *GW,* XIII:34 f.

122. The topic was much too large and complicated for treatment in a comparatively small book, and the style in which it was written was extremely abstract. Tillich's friend E. Hirsch, who became professor of church history in Göttingen in 1921, had assumed the editorship of the famous *Theologische Literaturzeitung.* In this capacity he solicited reviews of Tillich's work from competent experts; but everyone he approached refused to undertake the task because it was regarded as too difficult. Finally, Hirsch himself, feeling that Tillich's work should not be disregarded by serious scholarship, wrote the review. Cf. *Theologische Literarzeitung,* 51 (1926), pp. 97–103.

123. Manuscript of the Lecture "Mut zur Wahrheit," pp. 19–24. H.A., Private Collection.

124. Henrick Steffens (1773–1845) was a Danish naturalist and philosopher who was in touch with most German philosophers and poets of his own time; as a young man he was an ardent Romantic who cultivated a friendship with Schelling. His autobiography *Was Ich Erlebte* (10 volumes, 1840–44) is a remarkable portrait gallery of himself and his contemporaries.

125. Manuscript on "Mysticism and Guilt Consciousness," p. 11 f. H.A., Private Collection.

126. Ibid., p. 5.
127. Ibid., p. 13.
128. Ibid., p. 27.
129. Ibid., p. 21.
130. Ibid., p. 27.
131. Ibid., p. 27 f. Tillich's further definition of guilt consciousness is noteworthy. He writes, "He who by thought and deed says no to that in himself which should not be, has a consciousness of guilt ... even though he may not be concerned to show contrition or sorrow; he may even object to such grieving because he feels that it may paralyze the will." ["Wer mit Gedanken und Willen Nein sagt zu dem was nicht sein soll in ihm, der hat Schuldbewusstsein ... auch wenn ihm Reue und Schmerz fernliegen, oder als willenslähmend von ihm bekämpft werden."] ... "Now what is said here is not meant to arouse a bad conscience but rather and primarily to achieve clear insight and understanding (Einsicht) from which a firm will to action can come forth."

In a footnote added to a lecture on "Idealist Philosophy and Christianity" (Gütersloh: Bertelsmann, 1926), p. 95, E. Hirsch remarks on Hegel's close coordination of creation and the fall and then goes on to point out that in Schelling's later writings creation and fall are put into very close connection, and this indicates to him that Schelling was entirely dominated by the mystical idea of guilt. By this Hirsch must have meant that Schelling failed to recognize that guilt and repentance together with contrition and sorrow constitute the weight of personal responsibility or irresponsibility in any act or occurrence in which a person may be involved. In other words, he suggests that the mystical idea of guilt lacks an awareness of personal contrition and repentance. He then intimates that Tillich's study of Schelling, namely his thesis on mysticism and guilt consciousness, is faulty because it does not contain a criticism of the mystical idea of guilt and therefore lacks a criterion for the proper assessment of Schelling's Positive Philosophy. This subtle observation is probably quite correct also in respect of Tillich's later writings.
132. Manuscript on "Redemption" (Erlösung), p. 14. H.A., Private Collection.
133. Ibid., p. 29.
134. Ibid., p. 27 f.
135. Ibid., p. 28 f.

A Chronology of the Life of Wilhelm Pauck*

1901, January 31	Born, Laasphe (Kreis Wittgenstein), Germany
1901, March 26	Baptized
1902	Family moves to Burgsteinfurt
1906–07	First year in school
1907	Family moves to Berlin
1908–10	Attends private school, Berlin
1912–20	Attends Paulsen Realgymnasium, Berlin-Steglitz, is *primus omnium* throughout
1915	Father leaves for military service, World War I; Mother critically ill
1916, September 24	Confirmed, *Markuskirche*, Berlin
1919, April 9	Younger brother Hans dies, Berlin
1920	Graduates valedictorian; receives prize from Kaiser Wilhelm II; speaks on "the golden time of youth," moving audience to tears
1920–25	Studies at universities of Berlin, Göttingen, and again at Berlin
1923–24	First, second, and third chargé of Wingolf Fellowship

---

*For additional biographical and bibliographical information, cf. "Wilhelm Pauck: A Biographical Essay," by Marion Hausner Pauck, and "Bibliography of the Published Writings of Wilhelm Pauck," in J. J. Pelikan, ed., *Interpreters of Luther* (Philadelphia: Fortress Press, 1968). Cf. also David W. Lotz, ed., *In Memory of Wilhelm Pauck (1901–1981)*, Union Papers 2, November 1982, published by Union Theological Seminary, New York, containing Memorial Notices, Liturgical Pieces, Essays, and Addresses. Numerous book review articles and essays have appeared in the following journals: *Christendom, Christianity and Society, Church History, Journal of Modern History, Journal of Religion, Review of Religion, The Chicago Theological Seminary Register, The Christian Century, Theologische Literaturzeitung, and Union Theological Seminary Review*.

1925, July 25	Passes examination for Licentiate of Theology
1925, August 31	Receives degree of Licentiate of Theology, University of Berlin, *magna cum laude*
1925	Rejects offer of *Privatdozent*, University of Königsberg
	Accepts scholarship from Theological Faculty, the University of Berlin, and the Federal Council of German Churches as first post-World War I German exchange student, Chicago Theological Seminary, Chicago
1925, September 24	Arrives in New York; first American speech, "The Importance of The University of Chicago," to immigration officials
1925–26	Graduate exchange student, Chicago Theological Seminary; studies Jonathan Edwards
1926	Becomes Instructor in Church History, Chicago Theological Seminary
1928, April 15	Ordained minister in the Hyde Park Congregational Church, Chicago
1928, May 1	Marries Olga Dietz Gümbel, Chicago
1928	Publishes *Martin Butzer, Das Reich Gottes auf Erden (Martin Bucer: The Kingdom of God on Earth)*
1931	Publishes *Karl Barth, Prophet of a New Christianity?*
	Becomes Professor of Church History, Chicago Theological Seminary
	Founding member Theological Discussion Group; later permanent chairman, nicknamed "Papa Pauck"
1933, November 10	Receives D. Theol., University of Giessen, *honoris causa*, on Martin Luther's 450th birthday
1934, Fall Quarter	First lecture tour, speaks at 80 colleges in the United States, under auspices of the Spiritual Emphasis Committee of the YMCA
1934	Publishes *The Church Against the World* (with H. R. Niebuhr and F. Miller)
1935, September 25	Mother, Maria Hofmann Pauck dies, Potsdam

1936	President, American Society of Church History; Presidential Address, "The Nature of Protestantism"
1937, November 3	Becomes American citizen
1937	Visiting Professor, Union Theological Seminary, New York
1938	Visiting Professor, University of Geneva, Switzerland
1939–53	Professor of Historical Theology, Chicago Theological Seminary and the Divinity School of The University of Chicago
1940	President, American Theological Society, Midwest branch
1941, April 4	Father, Wilhelm Heinrich Paul Pauck, dies, Paris, France
1942–53	Chairman, Theological Field, The University of Chicago
	Chairman, Ecumenical Study Group, Chicago
1943–53	Editor, with James H. Nichols, of "Church History"
	Member, Board of Editors, The University of Chicago Press
1944	Visiting Professor, Pomona College, California
1945–53	Professor of History, The University of Chicago
1946	President, American Theological Society
	Visiting Professor, Maywood Lutheran Seminary, Illinois
	Visiting Professor, Garrett Biblical Institute, Evanston, Illinois
1947	Visiting Professor, Union Theological Seminary, New York
1948	Theological Consultant to the Amsterdam Assembly of the World Council of Churches
1948–49	Exchange Professor at the University of Frankfurt and the University of Marburg, Germany; receives Goethe plaque from the city of Frankfurt

1949	Chairman, Committee of Professorial Exchange between Frankfurt and Chicago
1950	Publishes *The Heritage of the Reformation*
1951	Speaker Annual Trustee Dinner, The University of Chicago
1952	Visiting Professor Graduate School of Ecumenical Studies, Chateau de Bossey, Geneva, Switzerland
1953	Resigns from The University of Chicago
1953–60	Professor of Church History, Union Theological Seminary, New York
1954	Founding member, Renaissance Society of America
1958	Visiting Professor, Princeton University, Princeton, New Jersey
1959	Visiting Professor, University of Southern California, Los Angeles, California
	Elected member of the American Academy of Arts and Sciences
1960	Publishes *Luther's Lectures on Romans*
1960–67	Charles A. Briggs Graduate Professor of Church History, Union Theological Seminary, New York
1961	Delivers Introductory Address on "Luther and Melanchthon," second Luther Research Congress, Münster, Germany
	Publishes revised, enlarged edition of *The Heritage of the Reformation*
	Visiting Professor, Yale University Divinity School, New Haven, Connecticut
1962–63	President, American Theological Society (for the second time)
1963, January 15	Wife Olga dies, New York
1964, November 21	Marries Marion Katherine Hausner, New York
1964–65	Elected member of The Century Association
1964, June 7	Receives Litt. D., Upsala College, New Jersey, *honoris causa*

1967, May 18	Retires from Union Theological Seminary, New York, as Charles A. Briggs Graduate Professor Emeritus
1967, June 28	Receives D.D., Gustavus Adolphus College, Minnesota, *honoris causa*
1967–72	Distinguished Professor of Church History, Vanderbilt University Divinity School, Nashville, Tennessee
1967, November 9	Receives D.D., Thiel College, Pennsylvania, *honoris causa*
1968, April 27	Receives *Interpreters of Luther*, ed. J. J. Pelikan, *Festschrift* in his honor, at dinner following meeting of The American Society of Church History, Vanderbilt University
1968	Publishes *Harnack and Troeltsch: Two Historical Theologians*
1968, July 3	Receives D.D., University of Edinburgh, Scotland, *honoris causa*
1969	Publishes *Melanchthon and Bucer*
1970	Visiting Professor, Duke University Divinity School
1971, January 31	Celebrates 70th birthday, Munich, Germany
1972, May 14	Retires from Vanderbilt University Divinity School; receives key to the city of Nashville; is commissioned Colonel of the State of Tennessee
1972–76	Visiting Professor of Religious Studies and History, Stanford University, Stanford, California
1975, September 24	Celebrates 50th anniversary of arrival in the United States
1976, February 20	Final retirement, Stanford University, 50th anniversary of teaching career celebrated at Stanford University
1976, Summer	Visiting Professor *Historische Kommission zu Berlin*, Berlin, Germany
1976, September 1	Publishes *Paul Tillich: His Life and Thought, vol., I: His Life* (with Marion Pauck)
1977, January 22	His younger brother, Paul, dies

1977, April 25	Union Theological Seminary, New York celebrates his life and career, "Autobiographical Reminiscences"
1979, March 31	Last public lecture, New Harmony, Indiana, "To Be or Not To Be: Paul Tillich on the Meaning of Life"
1980, February 20	Last class lecture, Stanford University, "Faith and Reason: Luther and Calvin"
1980, December 29	Special session in honor of 80th birthday, American Church History Society, Washington, D.C., "The State and Future of Historical Theology"
1981, January 31	Celebrates 80th birthday, Palo Alto, California
1981, September 3	Dies, Hoover Pavillion, Stanford University, Stanford, California
1981, September 7	Memorial service, Stanford University Lutheran Chapel, Stanford
1981, September 11	Memorial minute and prayer, Vanderbilt University Divinity School, Nashville, Opening Services
1981, November 6	Memorial service, Union Theological Seminary, New York
1982, February 12	Memorial lectures, Chicago Divinity School, Chicago
1983, July 29	Final interment, Alta Mesa Memorial Park, Palo Alto, California

Credits

Grateful acknowledgment is made to the editors of the several journals and to the publishers of the several books for their permission to reprint these writings, now chapters in this book.

"Wilhelm Pauck: A Tribute". First published in *Interpreters of Luther*, edited by J. J. Pelikan. Philadelphia: Fortress Press, 1968.

"Luther's Faith". First published in *Religion in Life*, vol. XVI (1946–47): pp. 3–11, written in commemoration of Luther's death on February 18, 1946. Also published in Wilhelm Pauck, *The Heritage of the Reformation*. Boston: Beacon Press and the Free Press, 1950. Paperback edition, New York: Oxford University Press, 1968.

"Luther and Butzer". First published in *The Journal of Religion*, vol. IX (1929): pp. 85–98. Also published in *The Heritage of the Reformation*.

"Calvin and Butzer". First published in *The Journal of Religion*, vol. IX (1929): pp.237–256. Also published in *The Heritage of the Reformation*.

"Luther and Melanchthon". First published in *Luther and Melanchthon*, edited by Vilmos Vajta. Philadelphia: Muhlenberg Press, 1961. The chapter represents the lead address given at the Second International Congress for Luther Research in August 1960, at the Westphalian Wilhelms-Universität, in Münster (Westphalen), West Germany.

"Schleiermacher's Conceptions of History and Church History". First published in *Schleiermacher as Contemporary*, edited by Robert W. Funk. New York: Herder & Herder, 1970. The address was delivered in the chapel at Vanderbilt University Divinity School, in conjunction with a theological consultation on the topic "Schleiermacher as Contemporary" in 1968.

"Adolf von Harnack". First published in *Harnack and Troeltsch: Two Historical Theologians* by W. Pauck. New York: Oxford University Press, 1968.

"Ernst Troeltsch". First published in *Harnack and Troeltsch: Two Historical Theologians* by W. Pauck. New York: Oxford University Press, 1968.

"Karl Holl". First published as an Introduction to *The Cultural Significance of the Reformation* by Karl Holl (translated by Karl and Barbara Herz and John H. Lichtblau). New York: Meridian Books, 1959.

"A Brief Criticism of Barth's Dogmatics". First published in the *Union Seminary Quarterly Review*, vol. XII, No. 4 (May 1957): pp. 107–110. Cf., also *The Heritage of the Reformation*, 1961.

"Paul Tillich: Heir of the Nineteenth Century". Hitherto unpublished. Sections thereof delivered in an address to the American Academy of Religion in October 1975. We thank Hannah Tillich and Robert Kimball, Paul Tillich's literary executors, for granting permission to quote from Tillich's unpublished papers. Translations of German into English are by the author, unless otherwise indicated.

Index